Hitting Home

Hitting Home

The Great Depression in Town and Country

Revised Edition, Edited with an Introduction by Bernard Sternsher

Elephant Paperbacks
Ivan R. Dee, Inc.
Publisher
Chicago

 For information, address: Ivan R. Dee, Inc., 1332 North Halsted Street, Chicago 60622. Manufactured in the United States of America.

Grateful acknowledgment is made to the authors and publishers noted herein for permission to reprint copyrighted materials.

Library of Congress Cataloging-in-Publication Data
Hitting home.
Bibliography: p.
1. United States—Economic conditions—1918–1945. 2. United States—Social conditions—1918–1932. 3. United States—Social conditions—1933–1945. I. Sternsher, Bernard, 1925– .
HC106.3.H54 1989 330.973'091 89-11998
ISBN 0-929587-13-8

PREFACE TO THE 1989 EDITION

Over the years my inquiries into the 1930s have evolved from the national scene and its macroeconomic aspects, to developments at state and local levels throughout the United States, to individuals' experiences. Thus my book *Rexford Tugwell and the New Deal* (New Brunswick, N.J.: Rutgers University Press, 1964) discussed the life and career of one of the most influential of Roosevelt's advisers; and my *The New Deal: Doctrines and Democracy* (Boston: Allyn and Bacon, 1966) considered the issues of laissez faire, antitrustism, concentration and control, Keynesianism, socialism, and neomercantilism.

When *Hitting Home* was first published in 1970, my introduction referred to studies of the emotional impact of unemployment in suggesting the importance of individuals' experiences, feelings, and attitudes in the history of the depression. I expanded on this subject at length in "Victims of the Great Depression: Self-Blame/Non-Self-Blame, Radicalism, and Pre-1929 Experiences" (in *Social Science History*, 1 [Winter 1977], 137–77), offering conclusions which, with the help of William R. Phillips, I have recently tested by examining first-person history—an inquiry which can be found as the new concluding essay in this revised edition. An article comparing Burlington, Vermont, in the 1930s and 1960s has been dropped from this edition.

I have also included herein a new bibliography of *general* studies of states and cities in the pre-1933 or pre–New Deal phase of the depression (although some of these also treat the New Deal era). I say "general" because a more specialized and categorized bibliography would run to many pages. Since 1949 I have kept a card file of article titles culled from listings in the American Historical Association's *Recently Published Articles* and the *Journal of American History*, and I have collected many titles that do not appear in *The Great Depression: A Historical Bibliography* (Santa Barbara, Calif.:

ABC-CLIO, 1984) and *New Day/New Deal: A Bibliography of the Great American Depression, 1929–1941* (New York: Greenwood, 1988). I am grateful to the interlibrary loan office of the Jerome Library of Bowling Green State University for obtaining a number of articles and to the library administration for purchasing a number of doctoral dissertations.

In the suggestions for further reading I have included studies of governors, mayors, and political bosses because these writings introduce the human (leadership) element into responses to the Great Depression. The governorships of Cross of Connecticut, La Follette of Wisconsin, Murray of Oklahoma, Pinchot of Pennsylvania, Olson of Minnesota, and Rolph of California also extended into the New Deal period. A number of 1930s governors, about whom books have been written, did not hold office until the New Deal era: James M. Curley of Massachusetts, Theodore F. Green of Rhode Island, Alfred M. Landon of Kansas, Herbert H. Lehman of New York, Paul V. McNutt of Indiana, Frank Murphy of Michigan, W. Lee O'Daniel of Texas, C. Ben Ross of Idaho, and Eugene Talmadge of Georgia.

The literature on the pre–New Deal phase of the Great Depression includes books about five mayors: James M. Curley of Boston (elected mayor in 1917, 1920, 1930, and 1947, and governor in 1935); Anton J. Cermak of Chicago (mayor from 1931 to 1933); Frank Hague of Jersey City (mayor from 1917 to 1947); James J. Walker of New York (mayor from 1925 to 1932); and Frank Murphy of Detroit (mayor from 1931 to 1933, and governor from 1937 to 1938). Three well-known mayors of the 1930s about whom books have been written did not hold office until the New Deal era: Edward J. Kelly of Chicago, Fiorello LaGuardia of New York, and Maury Maverick of San Antonio.

Also available are books about political bosses Edward J. Flynn of the Bronx, Tom Pendergast of Kansas City, and Ed Crump of Memphis, and about political machines in Albany, Chicago, and Pittsburgh. There are no scholarly studies of Curley and Jimmy Walker. Richard J. Connors's volume on Hague, Alex Gottfried's on Cermak, and Sidney Fine's, J. Woodford Howard, Jr.'s, and Richard D. Lunt's on Murphy are solid works. Fine's volume is the history of a city in the early 1930s as well as a biography, and is listed in the bibliography under "Cities" as well as under "Mayors."

I am grateful to Professor Michael H. Ebner of Lake Forest College for his encouragement and to Ivan R. Dee for his sponsorship of this reprint. I hope it will prompt instructors to assign reading in local history, whether chosen from my bibliography or theirs. I have pursued state and local history myself ("Depression and New Deal in Ohio: Lorena A. Hickok's Reports to Harry Hopkins, 1934–1936," *Ohio History*, 86 [Autumn 1977], 258–77; "Scioto Marsh Onion Workers Strike, Hardin County, Ohio, 1934," *Northwest Ohio Quarterly*, 58 [Spring/Summer 1986], 39–92; "The Harding and Bricker Revolutions: Party Systems and Voter Behavior in Northwest Ohio, 1860–1982," *ibid.*, 59 [Summer 1987], 91–118), and I have compiled an exhaustive bibliography (not limited to selected categories) of literature on Ohio in the 1930s—writings to which students at Bowling Green State University have responded enthusiastically.

None of this is meant to imply that local history is a substitute for national history. Elsewhere I have referred approvingly to Frances Fitzgerald's contention in *America Revised* that if American history were written from the point of view of every ethnocultural group, the texts would tell us that "Americans have no common history." This would also be true if the history of the 1930s were written from the point of view of every locality. Nearly all Americans—including the 50 percent who did not suffer actual economic deprivation or loss as well as the 50 percent who did—felt the impact of the Great Depression. Still, this national experience must be reconciled with and illuminated by the history of states and localities which went through the national crisis, and which affected—and were affected by—national policies in different ways.

ACKNOWLEDGMENTS

History colleagues at Bowling Green State University to whom I am indebted are Gary R. Hess, for his interest and criticism; Michael A. Moore, for familiarizing me with the "Yankee City" series; and especially James Q. Graham, Jr., for giving me the benefit of some of his vast knowledge of the literature on crowd behavior, violence, and revolution. I should like to express my gratitude to Arthur G. Neal and Joseph B. Perry, Jr., of the Department of Sociology at Bowling Green, for directing me to relevant writings in their discipline. I also wish to thank two students in directed-readings courses: Miss Robin Reid, who summarized several studies of the psychological impact of unemployment, and Mrs. Susan Brown, who did a comparative analysis of the Lynds's *Middletown* and *Middletown in Transition.* Emily Grimm and Angela Poulos of the University library staff were very helpful in identifying materials and acquiring items through inter-library loan.

CONTENTS

Hitting Home

Introduction

I. RE-CREATING THE GREAT DEPRESSION

Every generation, seeking in the past a relevance to its present concerns, writes its own history. So it produces, either intentionally or unconsciously, distorted history. It is impossible for historians successfully to carry out the task Leopold von Ranke assigned them of scientifically re-creating the past *as it was* (not to mention the task of discovering the "meaning" of the past). I have not kept count of how often historians cite these limitations of their practice when speaking of various historical phenomena, but I have the general impression that historians of the Great Depression are unusually concerned about the difficulty of telling their story "like it was." Perhaps this is because most historians who have written about the depression, at least until now, have their *own* memories of it—something which cannot be said of historians, say, of the Age of Jackson. Yet it seems to me that even historians of more recent events in American life (with the possible exception of the interpreters of McCarthyism) also show less concern about communicating with today's youth than their colleagues who treat the Great Depression. The chroniclers of collapse, frequently and with some emotion, implore their readers to try to "feel" what life was like after the Great Crash.

The historian who seeks to know the Great Depression from those who remember it faces formidable obstacles. As in the case of every other historical development, each individual had his own unique experience, and the inquirer will unearth a bewildering variety of accounts.[1] Commenting on the years after 1932, Leslie Fiedler claims that the version of the thirties (one of many) that sees the decade as "a period in which we moved from defeat, and if not to victory at least toward victory; a period in which we conquered fear, in which we laid down the basis for future prosperity . . ." has nothing to do with *his* thirties, the thirties of the Radical Left who "greeted Roosevelt . . . with condescension and mild contempt" and went down to defeat with a number of lost causes.[2]

The first obstacle faced by the interrogator of eyewitnesses is the unwillingness of many of them to talk at all. Some, it is true—especially strikers and organizers—are quick to express a romantic nostalgia for their time of struggle; but many people among the 50 per cent of Americans who remember the Great Depression do not like to talk about it. "People like to talk about the 'good old days.' They don't like to recall the bad days." [3] This preference often vitiates the reliability of those who are willing to recall hard times. "Time . . . has an anesthesia for memories of the unpleasant." This may be nature's way of maintaining the emotional stability of the human race, but it does not make for accurate history—"we remember only what we want to remember." [4] Accordingly, Alfred Kazin writes, "while a great many people understandably lost their heads, no one can now admit it." [5]

Besides the healing effects of time, another psychological factor played a part in people's actual experience of the Great Depression and contributes to the tricks of their memories: the matter of causation or responsibility. More precisely, what or whom one blamed for his ill fortune conditioned his response to the Great Depression. If one blamed himself or Providence, his attitudes and conduct were likely to be different from those of people who held "man," or some men, or one man—Herbert Hoover—responsible for economic collapse. People moreover often changed their minds about this during the course of the depression and in subsequent years. Those who lost their heads but cannot now admit it, those who believe they thought then as they think now, provide us with inexact recollections.

Even these brief remarks suggest the variety of individual attitudes toward causation or responsibility in the depression. Midwestern farmers, for example, overlooked their own contribution—in the form of excessive land speculation in the early 1920's—to their sad condition at the end of the decade.[6] The article in this book on Ann Arbor reveals that middle-class debtors of that city were ashamed of their failure to pay bills, while working-class debtors in default were less ashamed or free of shame. This difference undoubtedly reflected, at least in some cases, a difference in views on the larger question of personal responsibility for one's situation. The novelist Sherwood Anderson reported "picking up hitchhikers on the highway who apologized for being down and out. They accepted the whole responsibility themselves. The only exception he could find was the coal miners," [7] who are the subject of the article on Harlan County, Kentucky. By 1932, looting for food was a commonplace across the nation; many, though not all, of the looters presumably felt neither personal responsibility for the plight which moved them to this action nor guilt over the action itself. But when Joseph Drusin of Indiana Township, Pennsylvania, in November 1930 stole a loaf of bread from his neighbor for his starving children and was caught, he hung himself.[8] His theft and its dénouement may have derived from feelings of responsibility and guilt about his circumstances. Well-being could also produce guilt feelings and affect retrospective comments: people who profited from the depression usually will not admit it.

If the historian, seeking sources not subject to the deception of memory, turns to contemporary accounts, again he encounters bewildering variety. It is difficult, Harvey Swados concludes, to determine from such commentaries what America was like:

> In a vast country, contradictory impressions were inevitable in the observations of journalists, novelists, and storytellers of vastly different backgrounds and predilections; contradictory viewpoints were often expressed by the same writer.[9]

Returning to the present, we find that estimates of the impact of the depression are frequently determined not by faulty memory but by political considerations. Frank Freidel writes: "Critics have not only denied that anything constructive could have come from the New Deal but they have even succeeded in creating the impression in the prosperous years since 1945 that the depression really did not amount to much. How bad it was is worth remembering.

. . ." [10] As Freidel implies, postwar prosperity has blurred the impact of the Great Depression, with the result that the New Deal may appear not only radical and crackpot but unnecessary. Especially among the young who have no memories of the depression, affluence is a barrier to understanding what it was like to live in hard times. Arthur M. Schlesinger, Jr., confesses:

> I don't know what is to be done to persuade people that the Great Depression took place. So far as I can tell, more and more Americans are coming to believe that it never really occurred. . . . The whole thought of widespread economic collapse a generation ago in a nation as spectacularly opulent as ours is now, has for many—perhaps for most of us—no more reality any longer than a bad dream. Worse, the actualities of depression—bread lines, soup kitchens, Hoovervilles, etc.—have become clichés rejected by the sophisticated as corny and the unsophisticated as communistic.[11]

Referring to the "fat decades since," Saul Maloff complains: "Now that despair breeds amid surfeit, it is next to impossible to convey that other, 'realler' despair to the contemporary young." For myself, I can say—though not with precise chronological accuracy—that I was over twenty-one before I could begin to understand why well-to-do people sought the help of psychiatrists. My father's law practice shrank considerably, but we did not suffer physical want. My family's problem was to adjust to a partial decline in economic condition—a problem of the middle class. I did not, however, at least consciously, think in psychological terms. How could people have problems, I wondered, if they did not have "real" (money) problems? There weren't any other kinds. Swados, recalling how he answered the door when hungry men knocked to ask his mother for food, asks, "If I had no idea, really, of what life was like for the men at the door, how can those who have grown up hearing not even the knock but only the brassy klaxon, the horn of plenty?" [12]

II. ACTIVE PROTEST: MOTIVES AND CONDUCT

Although Marx's analysis of capitalism, class conflict, and revolution had to do with highly industrialized nations, the major social revolutions of the twentieth century—such as those in Mexico, Russia, China, and Cuba—have occurred in predominantly agricultural countries. In the highly industrialized United States, moreover, in the depths of the depression, "The American proletariat . . . showed a truly remarkable unwillingness to stage any kind of revolution." [13] The most formidable active protest of the period 1929–1933 was mounted by conservative Midwestern farmers.

Apparently applicable to the American farm revolt are some common generalizations about the French Revolution, one of which is that "extreme suffering or poverty seems to induce apathy rather than rebellion, for people in these circumstances are too busy simply surviving to give much thought to government." [14] This axiom holds for the Midwestern farmers in a general way, but in detail there are significant differences between the French and American situations. John L. Shover, who has done pioneering work in considering the farm rebellion within the larger issues of mass behavior, points out that the farm strike which began in Iowa in the summer of 1932 and spread to Nebraska was carried on by "farmers who had a high level of expectation. . . ." Farm protest, Shover explains, "was most intense in areas of western Iowa, eastern Nebraska, and southern Minnesota where land values were high and gross income per farm well above the state average. Collaterally, protest was almost absent in extremely depressed areas where land value was low and tenancy was high." [15] In the selection on the Farmers' Holiday Association strike in the Sioux City area, Shover notes that "the farm strike centered in some of the most prosperous counties in the livestock and dairy belts." So far, so good. Just as the initiative for the French Revolution lay with the bourgeoisie, not the destitute, so the American farm rebellion arose among the better-off livestock and dairy producers.

In the selection on the Holiday Association strike, Shover also asserts: "The farm strike was a response of individuals whose level of expectation had been conditioned by better times, and some immediate crisis, in this instance foreclosure or drouth, threatened to deprive them of property or accustomed income." This statement suggests the limitations of the French-American analogy. In 1789 the French middle class, especially the upper middle class, had been enjoying increased economic strength and, given the trend of the economy, could expect to continue to enjoy it: "The revolution was born, not out of misery, but out of strength and hope." [16] The Midwestern farmers, on the other hand, had suffered a severe economic decline in the early 1920's and a further decline from 1929 to 1932. "Men who had lost their farms," as well as heavily mortgaged owners, "made up the bulk of the picket lines [around Sioux City] and the mobs who blocked foreclosures." If the expectations of both the dispossessed and the owners were rooted in their past, if not their recent, experience, there was no reason in 1932 for them to assume that economic recovery would soon fulfill their high expectations. In short, the bourgeoisie's expectations were associated with rising economic fortune; the farmers' expectations must be viewed in the context of a deep depression.[17]

None of this is meant to imply that the Midwestern farmers were devoid of hope that they could recapture a decent economic status. If the despairing pauper class did not provide the initiative for the French Revolution, the farm rebellion, as Shover notes in his article, "was not a movement from the social depths." The farmers by no means suffered utter despair; nor had their depressed condition, though prolonged, obtained for even twenty years. In acting on their hope, the American farmers, unlike the French bourgeoisie, did not set in motion a series of events that resulted in a genuine revolution "in which a social or economic group is superseded in control of the state by another group under circumstances of violence." [18] Their objectives—higher farm prices and the halting of foreclosures—were limited.

In his analysis of an activist farm group, Shover is careful to concede the limitations of his generalizations from a single incident, and he calls for similar inquiries to provide a basis for comparison. In a commentary on Shover's article on the Sioux City strike, A. William Hoglund raises a methodological question that often arises in connection with characterizations of activists and reformers: the need for a control group. Hoglund wants a more detailed description of the strikers' economic condition with respect to such factors as mortgage debt and market experience, and comparison of their economic condition with that of strikers in other states and of nonstrikers in the Sioux City area. (Shover calculates for two counties that only about one-fifth of the farm families were represented on the picket line.) Hoglund agrees with Shover that low prices frustrated farmers and moved them to strike, but, as to frustration, "the same could be said of most nonstrikers. . . ." If the economic condition of strikers and nonstrikers was similar, "was there anything unique in the individual striker's experience or outlook that moved him to strike?" [19]

Hoglund's findings in his own study of Wisconsin milk producers' strikes in 1932 and 1933 make the tasks of analysis and generalization even more difficult. He discovered that the members of the activist Wisconsin Co-operative Milk Pool "came largely from the poorest dairy farmers of eastern Wisconsin." This fact does not agree with Shover's findings for the Sioux City area, where the farmers who were most well-to-do, presently or previously, led the strike. It does not, however, alter the factor of economic condition, good or bad, as a rough or general constant, since not all the poor dairy farmers of eastern Wisconsin struck. Nor does it weaken the proposition that "extreme suffering or poverty seems to induce apathy rather than rebellion," since the poor dairy farmers of eastern Wisconsin were not paupers. Hoglund's comments on Shover's Sioux City study indicate that where economic condition, as between strikers and nonstrikers, was a rough constant, other variables came into play. Hoglund rules out one such possible variable in Wisconsin, concluding that "the milk pool was formed essentially from economic factors rather than ethnic factors." [20]

In the article on the Iowa "Cow War," Frank D. DiLeva refers to a possibly significant variable when he mentions the "type of personality that appeared as active members of the revolt" and remarks that the active leaders were "straightforward and uncompromising" men. Shover, in an article on the Farm Holiday movement in Nebraska, writes of a "spontaneous movement of strongly individualistic men. . . ." In another article, describing the Communists' penetration of the farmers' protest movement in Newman Grove, Nebraska, Shover maintains that "No economic or social variables segregated the Newman Grove vicinity from other comparable areas in eastern Nebraska or western Iowa. . . . The main point of difference was . . . a respected elderly farmer, Andrew Dahlsten, a Socialist and free-thinker. . . ." [21]

With some reservations, because of the work that remains to be done, I accept Shover's contention that the farm rebellion was "not a movement from the social depths." The absence of activism among laborers also seems to support the generalization that severe suffering and poverty induce apathy rather than rebellion. To be sure, one can easily compile a long list of incidents of active protest by workers—most of them staged by the unemployed, some of them arranged by Communists. Here is just a sampling:

Chicago	February 1930	Unemployed march on city hall
Cleveland	February 1930	Unemployed march on city hall
Los Angeles	February 1930	Unemployed march on city hall
Philadelphia	February 1930	Unemployed march on city hall
Various cities	March 6, 1930	International Unemployment Day
New York	March 1930	Raid on Bowery Hotel bread truck
Oklahoma City	January 1931	Looting of food
Minneapolis	February 1931	Looting of food
Minneapolis	March 1931	Gateway Riot
Henryetta, Okla.	July 1931	March on stores
Chicago	August 1931	Eviction riot
Washington, D.C.	December 1931	National Hunger March
Washington, D.C.	January 1932	Cox's Army
Dearborn, Mich.	March 1932	Ford Hunger March
Washington, D.C.	June–July 1932	Bonus Army
Minneapolis	July 1932	Hunger March
High Point, N.C.	July 1932	Hosiery workers' strike

"Melancholia and defeat," observes labor historian Irving Bernstein, "were . . . the hallmarks of the most notable venture of the jobless during the Great Depression—the Bonus Army." [22] The point is that all of these incidents and many others like them taken together did not amount to an attempted revolution or even formidable active protest. The unemployed were poor material for a revolution, and the significant activism among employed workers came after New Deal legislation and the rise of the unions.

In *The Crowd in History,* George Rudé writes:

> Yet, bad, even abysmal, economic conditions were not an automatic "trigger" to disturbance. In England, strikes and trade-union activity tended to occur not at the moment of deepest trade depression and unemployment, but rather on the upswing of a boom: as in 1792, 1818, 1824, and 1844–46. . . .[23]

Rudé makes the same point about France in the 1790's. Significant activism on the part of militant workers in the United States came with partial recovery. Note in the article on Ann Arbor how workers on relief and the Ann Arbor Trades Council engaged in vigorous protest *after* the unemployed received work relief. Also note in the article on Harlem that the explosion came in 1935, *after* it was apparent that the bottom was not going to fall out of the economy. Feelings of deprivation among the blacks were undoubtedly intensified by their knowledge of gains enjoyed outside as well as inside Harlem. The same theme dominates the actions of the most poverty-stricken farmers: the Southern Tenant Farmers Union was not formed until 1934, and important sharecroppers' demonstrations did not occur until well into the thirties.[24]

Turning from the motives of the active protesters to their conduct, we find that recent studies of crowd behavior undermine some traditional generalizations. A common assumption is that "the mobs . . . furnish excellent materials for leaders intent on causing a genuine revolution or in arrogating power for themselves." In other words, the crowd itself lacks the capacity for conceiving and executing a protest action. In this view, the march of the women on Versailles during the French Revolution had to be initiated and directed by outsiders: "Most of these women were of the dregs of the city and could scarcely have undertaken such a march on their own volition. This looks like a case of clever organization on the part of well-disguised leaders." [25] In an essay on the American Revolution, Jesse Lemisch raises serious questions about such an assumption of the crowd's incapacity:

> A merchant speculated the next day that the Tea Party was conducted so efficiently that there must have been "People of sense and more discernment than the vulgar among the Actors." . . . But certainly there is nothing beyond the most uneducated man's capacity in the events of that December night in 1773: that the mob showed up with lanterns and hatchets, attached block and tackle to the chests, raised them from the holds, and emptied the tea in the harbor seems more nearly to suggest the skills of the lower class than to be evidence of an operation so clever as to be explicable only by upper-class manipulation.[26]

There is no reason to assume that the Tea Party was given by

Harvard men. As the reader will learn here, Jake W. Lenker of Cedar County, Iowa, and his neighbors were capable of launching the "Cow War" without outsiders' direction, and the picketing around Sioux City was a spontaneous development quite apart from the stated policies of the Farmers' Holiday Association leaders.

We must not underestimate the crowd's capacities; nor should we overestimate its lack of restraint and resort to violence, especially indiscriminate violence. Rudé observes:

> . . . these Cleehill colliers of 1766 . . . "entered the town [of Ludlow] in a very orderly manner, proceeded to the house, pulled it down, and then returned without offering any other violence to any person whatever." In fact, the study of the pre-industrial crowd suggests that it rioted for precise objects and rarely engaged in indiscriminate attacks on either property or persons.[27]

Concerning the Stamp Act riots, Lemisch declares: "Again and again when the mob's leaders lost control, the mob went on to attack the logical political enemy, not to plunder." [28] Although the picketing by Midwestern farmers was "a spontaneous movement lacking effective organized leadership," [29] it was not marked by indiscriminate violence and plundering. Another example of what I prefer to call "pre-targeted" behavior occurred during the hosiery workers' strike in North Carolina in the summer of 1932: "The men said they had wrecked a motor in the Diamond Hosiery mill 'to teach the big fellows that we hain't going to stand for no more bad treatment.' " [30] The article on the Black Shirts of Atlanta notes that one of their few acts of violence was their beating up a young lawyer who had signed a petition condemning the "fascist" organization. Finally, in a now familiar behavioral pattern, the Negroes of Harlem, in the outburst of 1935, looted stores owned by *white* merchants.

This is not to deny the fact of violence in the protests of the early thirties; but most of it falls within the scope of Rudé's conclusions about crowd behavior in England and France in an earlier time:

> The crowd was by no means irrational in the wider meaning of the term. It might be diverted or provoked by panic, as it might be stirred by Utopian pipe dreams or millennial fantasies; but its pur-

> poses were generally rational enough and often led it, as we have seen, not only to choose the targets but the means appropriate to the occasion.[31]

Crowd violence, moreover, must be considered in the light of the conduct of those who were not active—four-fifths of the farmers in the case of the Iowa picketing incident—and in comparison with the violence used by the authorities. Rudé concludes: "From this balance sheet of violence and reprisal it would appear, then, that it was authority rather than the crowd that was conspicuous for its violence to life and limb." [32] We shall return to the matter of government response to protest in the next section of this introduction.

Like Rudé, Shover, in his study of the Farmers' Holiday Association strike, considers the matters of irrationality, rationality, ends, and means. The means of the farmers' movement, he says, were "ill-defined" and its ends "vague." Some Holiday Association leaders stressed legislation as the way to attain the farmers' objectives; others advocated the strike. Shover distinguishes between the strike movement that proceeded in accordance with the official Holiday Association policy of simply withholding farm products from the market, and a spontaneous movement that involved picketing and resulted in some violence. Finally, he remarks, "The farm strike was a spontaneous effort pursuing immediate and sometimes irrational goals, different from those of the leaders."

The designation of ends and means as irrational or rational depends, of course, on one's criteria or frame of reference. The means which the leaders advocated—peaceful withholding—was more rational than the means which some of the rank-and-file adopted—picketing—if we assume that nonviolence is more rational than violence. Both peaceful withholding and picketing were irrational in that neither could affect farm prices, for the chronic surplus of agricultural products could be significantly reduced only by *national* policy. The leaders' concept of cost-of-production as a single measure that would by itself create "an endless chain of prosperity and happiness in this country" was irrational or, as Shover affirms, a "panacea."

Cost-of-production, however, was an end as well as a means. It *was* rational in that its attainment would meet the farmers' needs.

Nor was this idea a pipe dream in terms of the theoretical possibility of achieving it. Its achievement, to be sure, would have required a drastic reordering of the whole economy, with wage and price and many other kinds of centralized controls. The virtual impossibility of obtaining the enactment of such a program is what made a rational—that is, theoretically feasible—approach to achieving cost-of-production a fantasy. Ironically, as Shover indicates in an article on "The Battle for the AAA" in 1933, it took a firm stand by the Roosevelt administration to prevent the enactment of the impractical or "panacea" version of cost-of-production.[33] That enactment of the rational was impossible and enactment of the irrational was possible was fantasy compounded.

III. THE RESPONSE TO ACTIVE PROTEST

The response to active protest by government and individuals reflected the spectrum of human attitudes and behavior. Generally speaking, the principal responses were repression and concern—and, somewhere between these, unconcern.

A recurring feature of repression was the use of the "Red" tag. Sometimes it was justified, as in Madison County, Nebraska, where Communists led the farm rebellion; sometimes it was not, as is evident in the article on Harlan County—at least with regard to the initial stage of the miners' protest. Nor was it justified in Atlanta, where anti-unionists made every effort to associate American Federation of Labor activities with Communists, and where the Black Shirts mixed their white-supremacy economic doctrine with allusions to the horrors of communism and the Red menace. Critics of a dairy farmers' strike in Wisconsin attributed it to the "Red Preaching [and] radical ideas . . . turned out of the La Follette theory factory at Madison." [34] Often this tactic was effective. Shover asserts that "the 'red' charges by the rival Holiday Association [against the Communist farm organization] bore considerable weight in Madison County," and one of the radical leaders there commented, "The red scare is something awful in this state." [35]

Another salient aspect of repression was the appeal to law and order. Critics accused the Wisconsin dairy strikers of causing "anarchy, violence, bloodshed, and mob rule," one newspaper warning that " 'the forces of law and order' alone could cope with what seemed to be a 'general riot and insurrection.' . . ." The police, the national guard, and the army were the forces of law and order, and they were usually prepared to act with vigor, sometimes with brutality. The police used "brutal tactics" in breaking up an unemployed workers' demonstration in New York in early March 1930. They broke up some of the demonstrations on International Unemployment Day, March 6, 1930, "with considerable violence." The article on Atlanta describes the police use of double standards, pretexts, and loose interpretations of laws and ordinances in arresting demonstrators, while the article on Harlan County reveals law-enforcement officers resorting to arrests, beatings, and even murder in repressing unionism and radicalism.[36]

Vested interests were also a source of repression. In Wisconsin the collapse of the milk pool was partly due to "the strong opposition of public and private groups who feared that new farm organizations endangered existing ones." The mine operators of Harlan County who systematically fired union organizers and union sympathizers are an obvious example of a repressive vested interest. The article on the Indians in Oklahoma relates how the Indian Bureau stifled internal attempts to expose its shortcomings and relied on influential friends to resist Indian demands for positions as field agents. In some instances there were ties between such vested interests and law-enforcement officials. In Dearborn, Michigan, where police fired on the Ford Hunger Marchers on March 7, 1932, the mayor was a distant cousin of Henry Ford and owned a Ford agency, while the chief of police was a former Ford detective. In Harlan County, when the police took two journalists to the state line to beat them, the automobile escort included many representatives of the "respectable element" of Pineville. In Atlanta, pursuing a permissive policy toward the Black Shirts, the police had the "tacit approval of the city's power structure," and they provided an escort for a Black Shirt parade with the full approval of the mayor.[37]

It has been said, with reference to the French Revolution, that "governments are not overthrown, they commit suicide. . . . Against a government which is strong and alert (and avoids defeat in war), the chances of a successful uprising are slight." [38] During the depression, government in the United States was strong and alert, enjoying the firm support of the law-enforcement agencies. The regime rested on strength because, as Rudé notes in regard to

France and England in the eighteenth and nineteenth centuries, "as long as the army remained substantially loyal, any serious threat to the government or the established order was negligible or nonexistent." The crucial role of the army's defection to the people in both the French and Russian revolutions is well known. According to Rudé, however, historians "beg the further and more important question of why the army refuses to obey or why the government loses control of its means of defense. Essentially, this is a social and political rather than a military question." [39] Thus one should be careful not to overemphasize evidence of ties between vested interests and law-enforcement agencies. The performance of the police during the depression was not the result of their being tools, lackies, or dupes of vested interests or the government. They *believed* in the "system" or the "American Way of Life" as they saw it. Above all, the regime was in no real danger because most of the people, too, even in the grip of the worst depression in the country's history, held the same belief.

Of course there were instances in which government officials acted with restraint, even sympathy, toward protesters. Governor Dan Turner of Iowa, for example, stressed the need for law and order and called out troops in the "Cow War." But during the Sioux City strike, though he "ventured no active support . . . , he spurned requests that the national guard be dispatched to the troubled areas." [40] In northeastern Pennsylvania, attitudes toward the bootlegging of coal, on which anthracite towns depended for survival, demonstrated that law and order had little appeal when there was a community-wide stake in illegality:

> . . . local courts were disinclined to sentence bootleggers; wardens released them from jail. . . . Public opinion, rather than considering the men thieves, esteemed them as heroes for facing the hazards of their trade. Storekeepers depended upon bootlegging; the newspapers winked; the police shrugged; parish priests in a predominantly Catholic community argued that the Eighth Commandment had no bearing; Governor Pinchot's sympathies were with the miners.[41]

Repression sometimes went too far and became counter-productive, evoking sympathy for the protesters even from those who disapproved of protest and favored or tolerated vigorous repression. When the Communists acquired martyrs as the result of police action—and frequently they were disappointed when they did not—they used them to attract sympathy, outside as well as inside the movement (there were only six thousand party members in 1930, twelve thousand in 1932). The article on Harlan County describes the funeral in New York of Harry Simms, a young National Miners Union organizer whom a Kentucky deputy sheriff shot to death; an estimated ten thousand persons attended what amounted to a mass demonstration. The law-enforcement action that was most unpopular on a nationwide basis was the dispersing of the Bonus Army: "The public reaction to the use of armed force against jobless veterans, regardless of the merits of their bonus claim, was shock and dismay." [42]

Excessive repression indicates that law and order, as an abstraction, has limitations (a concentration-camp prisoner who escapes—is he violating law and order?), that ultimately it must rest on justice and widespread well-being. At the same time, protest can be counter-productive by assuming a form that makes the public's concern for law and order the overriding factor; thus protest becomes a source of repression and delays the winning of its aims. Note in the article on Atlanta the declaration by Emory University personnel that a "policy of repression will exaggerate the importance of false ideas, and is likely to open the flood gates for future repression of progressive social movements."

Unconcern with the protesters was closer to repression than to concern. It represented indifference toward those conditions which some found intolerable and toward repression itself. This unconcern also reflected persistent strains in American thought. The influence of "Puritanism" and the "Protestant Ethic" was evident in the attitude toward public relief which held that aid to the poor made them lazy and destroyed their morale. The article on Philadelphia tells us that the City Fathers clung to "the orthodox belief that there was something sinful about public relief. . . ." Stark "Conservative Social Darwinism" was expressed in a note Governor Henry Horner of Illinois received from a fellow member of a Chicago social club: "While it is probably true that we cannot allow everyone to starve (although I personally disagree with this philosophy and the philosophy of the city social worker), we should tighten relief all along the line, and if relief is to be given it must be on a bare subsistence allowance." The article on the Oklahoma

Indians cites the widely held view that the tribesmen were ignorant alcoholics undeserving of aid, which would merely further pauperize them.

Unconcern was sometimes displayed by one economic group toward another in the same industry. In the Milwaukee area the milk producers who delivered milk for fluid use in the city markets were hostile to striking milk-pool members, whose milk went largely into manufacturing, because "they [the producers for fluid use] were the 'kings' among dairy farmers and did not want to lose their comparatively better position." Shover concludes that "The program of the Holiday Association was little concerned with the plight of the nearly fifty percent of American farmers who were tenants. . . ."[43]

If repression and unconcern were negative responses to protest, there were also some positive results, though tangible gains were limited. The campaign of Midwestern farmers against foreclosures through the use of "penny auctions" and "Sears, Roebuck sales"—the former referring to real estate, the latter to chattel foreclosures—met with some success. By March 1933 nine states had provided a two-year moratorium on forced sales, and six of the largest insurance companies had suspended foreclosures indefinitely. In Nebraska, after three thousand farmers marched through Lincoln on February 17, 1933, a mortgage-moratorium bill became law in three weeks. This high point of Communist activity in the farm belt obviously hastened the passage of legislation.[44]

Unlike their influence on legislation, the impact of the farmers' protest on the agricultural economy was negligible. Blockading a single market, as noted above, could not reduce the overall supply significantly:

> When receipts of grain and livestock dwindled to zero at the Sioux City market, there was an increase at neighboring markets. Indeed, prices for farm products dropped to a year's low while the farm strike was in progress. Even had the farm strike been temporarily successful, the withheld produce released like an open flood-gate on the market at its conclusion would have broken the bottom out of the farm price structure.[45]

And no strike could last very long because the farmer could not protest indefinitely without income. In Wisconsin, state officials adopted milk-price controls for the Milwaukee area in late 1932, and the legislature extended them to other areas in a law enacted in April 1933. These controls, however, did not apply to sellers of milk for nonfluid uses—the members of the milk pool who conducted the Wisconsin strikes of February, May, and October 1933.[46]

The most important positive result of farmers' and others' protests was the concern they evoked through the publicizing of the protesters' plight. Despite the devastating impact of the Great Depression, this publicity was badly needed. "Walking through an American city," Frederick Lewis Allen writes, "you might find few signs of the depression visible. . . . The major phenomena of the depression were mostly negative and did not assail the eye." " 'No one has starved' said the complacent and comfortable. But the fact is that people did starve." Respondents in a National Economic League Poll of January 1930 ranked unemployment eighteenth as a national problem; two years later, amid far worse conditions, they ranked unemployment tenth. The article on the Oklahoma Indians notes the effectiveness of "Indian Bureau propaganda which repeatedly asserted that the tribesmen were being civilized, educated, and protected." That the governors' conferences of 1931 and 1932 engaged in hardly any serious discussion of the depression indicates the need for publicizing the plight of the poor in order to generate pressure on public officials.[47]

Observers of the farm rebellion in fact consider publicity to be the main achievement of the farmers' protest. In the article on the Farmers' Holiday Association strike, Shover says: "The spontaneous movement in northwest Iowa publicized the farmers' plight. . . . Elected public officials in the Middle West and national candidates could no longer ignore such dramatic evidence of rural discontent." In his study of the Farm Holiday movement in Nebraska, Shover states that the strike "for a brief moment focused national attention on the desperate condition of the midwestern farmers." Concerning the dairy farmers' strikes in Wisconsin, Hoglund concludes that "the milk pool was given some credit at least for dramatizing the farmers' plight and their need for government help. . . . Striking farmers made the nation more farm-minded than before."[48]

The main achievement of the Harlan County miners was the publicity given to their plight by the "Dreiser Commission" of writers—Sherwood Anderson, John Dos Passos, Waldo Frank, Josephine Herbst, and Lincoln Steffens, among others—who published their findings in a pamphlet in 1932. According to the article on Harlan County, this commission gave the Communist National Miners Union "a new lease on life." Irving Bernstein points to the publicity-generating effect of demonstrations by the unemployed:

> These Communist demonstrations in early 1930 failed to produce the revolution in America. They did, however, have two important results that the party could hardly have anticipated or enjoyed. Bleeding heads converted unemployment from a little-noticed to a page-one problem in every important city in the United States. No one could any longer afford to ignore it. Non-Communist forces seeking relief and employment were strengthened.[49]

Bernstein's reference to page-one coverage suggests the role of the press during the depression, a vast subject into which even a cursory inquiry indicates a mixed picture. The article on Ann Arbor notes that when the city relief workers went on strike in early 1933, "The newspapers, which had generally ignored both the depression and labor in the city, gave excellent coverage to the workers for the first time. . . ." Compare the indiscriminate hanging of the "Red" label by the *Harlan Daily Enterprise* and the *Mt. Sterling Gazette* with the stand of the *Knoxville News-Sentinel,* which called for evidence to support charges of radicalism. Also compare the coverage, or lack of coverage, of the Black Shirts by the *Atlanta Constitution* and the *Georgian* with the early, forthright condemnation voiced by the *Macon Telegraph*. What the newspapers did not print was undoubtedly as important as what they did print. We shall never know how many incidents involving self-help on the part of the desperate unemployed "are lost to history; the press in many communities refused to publish the news in fear of stimulating similar action." [50]

If protest produced publicity, publicity evoked concern—the other side of the coin of response to active protest. During the Great Depression, an economist states, "Almost everyone felt some discomfort, but, for at least 50 per cent of Americans, these were *not* years of great deprivation." [51] Actual physical want most acutely afflicted "the masses of industrial workers, especially the unskilled, and millions of small farmers and tenants." [52] Others were concerned, however, partly out of altruism as both a personal and a traditional response to crisis, and partly out of enlightened self-interest. If Conservative Social Darwinism was a persistent strain in American thought, the nation also had "a long tradition of neighborliness and of charity and philanthropy." [53] Thus landlords in Ann Arbor were unwilling to evict the unemployed, and case-workers marveled at "the humanity of the poor towards the poor" in Philadelphia, where Mayor Harry Mackey declared that the unemployed were out of work "through no fault of their own," and businessmen assumed "greater social responsibility than ever before."

We may, perhaps for lack of a better term, call enlightened self-interest the "Who's next?" phenomenon. It is mentioned frequently in the literature on the Great Depression:

> . . . the sense of imminent catastrophe, not among those to whom it had already happened, but among those who might be next.[54]
>
> . . . even if they were not hungry and hopeless themselves, the depression generation had burned into them the dulled and shamed glances of men who were. . . .[55]
>
> . . . the strained faces of those millions of Americans who still had jobs but didn't know how long they would continue to have them.[56]
>
> Despair and demoralizing fear spread through the ranks of America's middle classes—fear of losing one's job, of being dispossessed of one's home, of the humiliation of asking for relief.[57]

Most Americans wanted a more effective response to the crisis than the Hoover administration provided. This desire for action from Washington, evident in the election of 1932, serves as a reminder that publicizing the plight of the unfortunate was essential to generating concern that would be expressed at the polls. The electorate called for national action which was essential to solving many of the country's problems. The articles on Ann Arbor and Philadelphia demonstrate that adequate relief was beyond the capacity of both city and state; the crisis caused Philadelphia's "most traditionally oriented citizens . . . to advocate direct federal relief." In Harlan County, mine operators preferred to undertake "new operations in the southern coal fields where there was no unionization." Only national legislation such as the Wagner Act could promote the unionization that would eliminate the wage discrepancies between the union and nonunion mines. Senator Wagner explained why unemployment was a national problem: "The reasons . . . are inherent in our economic organization. State boundaries are not economic barriers. . . . The stability of industry . . . must be national. . . ." California and New York were among the seven states with the greatest unemployment; the article on Arizona quotes the State Superintendent of Banks: "It was necessary to extend Arizona's banking holiday due to the holidays in California and New York." Hoglund remarks that about three-fourths of Wisconsin's dairy products were sold outside the state, which meant that "more action was expected from government officials in Washington than in Madison." Governor Charles W. Bryan of Nebraska "insisted that the farm problem was national in scope and could not be assuaged by local picketing and farmers' strikes." "The truth was," James T. Patterson asserts, ". . . that national solutions had to be devised to cure the complex and centralized economy of 1933."[58]

IV. THE LIMITS OF THE INITIAL RESPONSE TO THE GREAT DEPRESSION

The limits of active protest and of the remedial response to it together marked the boundaries of the initial response (1929–1933) to the Great Depression. The active protesters comprised only a small minority of the adult population. Their demands were nonrevolutionary and rather easily defused.

Many people who feared imminent revolution perceived this threat as a product of communism, both as a doctrine and as an organized movement. Actually, the Communists' successes were limited and temporary, their failures far more significant. In 1932 Theodore Dreiser, an avowed Communist, conceded that "the workers do not regard communism as their cause." Irving Bernstein states: "Despite momentary successes . . . the Communist program among the unemployed was a failure. . . . The real aim—organization of the jobless for revolution—did not come to pass." Regarding employed workers, Harvey Swados maintains that, "Despite its hard work in organizing the CIO, and although it captured the leadership of some unions, the Communist party never succeeded in sinking roots in the American working class. . . ."[59]

Shover has described and analyzed in great detail the futile efforts of the Communists to gain permanent advantage from the Midwestern farm rebellion by winning support among the farmers for the proletarian revolution. Although "some few farmers momentarily embraced extremist remedies," he writes, ". . . the rank and file of the participants in the Farm Holiday were concerned only with immediate goals such as raising prices in thirty days or stopping a forced sale today." The Communists who gained significant influence in the Nebraska Farm Holiday movement "fared well enough when they met the farmers on their own terms and shaped pragmatic programs based upon immediate economic needs . . . ," but when they "showed the face of the party," the farmers rejected them. Thus the Communists found themselves in a dilemma. Having initially rejected the "right-wing opportunism" of the Peasants International—which held that radical activity among the farmers was pointless until long-run processes of consolidation reduced most farmers to the status of wage workers—and having, after a time, put aside "moderate opportunism"—winning mass rural support by advancing the farmers' immediate grievances—the Communists followed the instructions of the sectarian leadership in New York: "Communists had not joined in rural protest simply to achieve price and property gains for stricken farmers . . . [but] to advance the party in the process. . . ." When the Nebraska group tried "to guide and educate individualistic farmers," however, they met with "resistance, hostility, and recrimination. . . ." "It is clear," Shover concludes, "that the Communists rode the crest of the rural rebellion. The party's successes came when the protest was at its peak." [60]

Negroes, as victims of segregation and discrimination, should have responded to Marxist appeals—according to Marxist doctrine. Yet, as R. C. Miller, a disillusioned black defector from the Communist party, testified (as recorded in the article on Atlanta), the Negro did not put much faith in the party's "social equality" doctrine. The black man simply wanted better working conditions. The Communists' quest for support among black workers and farmers came to almost nothing, and in fact the conflict between the American Communist party and the National Association for the Advancement of Colored People was heated.[61]

During the depression, Marxism had less appeal to workers than to intellectuals, especially writers, many of whom "moved . . . to an identification with a political movement that was never accepted by the people at large." [62] In August 1932 George Soule observed: "If you want to hear discussions of the future revolution in the United States, do not go to the bread lines and the milltowns but to Park Avenue and Wall Street, or to the gatherings of young literarv men." [63] Marxist intellectuals and writers, not all of whom joined the Communist party, were, however, armchair revolutionaries. A Military Intelligence Report, submitted by the National Guard to the Governor of Illinois in early 1933, had this to say about the Champaign-Urbana area: "There is considerable radical activity in this vicinity, but it is practically confined to the 'intelligentsia' group. There has always been a radical element around the university. These activities have been quite well confined to the 'debate' stage and no direct action on the part of this element is anticipated." [64] James P. Cannon, long-time leader of the American Trotskyites, declares that "at least 99 out of every 100 intellectuals . . . who approach the revolutionary labor movement turn out to be more of a problem than an asset" because they cannot effect a "transfer of class allegiance unconditionally and without any reservations." [65] In short, the active protesters among workers, farmers, and Negroes were bad material for revolution, while the literary exponents of revolution were bad material for a violent overthrow of the system.

Often those who feared revolution not only condemned protesters as Reds or dupes of Reds but also used a general kind of *ad hominem* argument. They charged that protesters were emotionally unstable self-seekers, or purveyors of crackpot ideas. Critics of the Wisconsin milk pool "questioned the character of the kind of people in it, especially its leadership": they were greedy, irresponsible in stirring up farmers "for the fun of doing so," hoodlums, exponents of "dubious and risky . . . half-digested schemes. . . ." [66] These allegations represented half of the psychological-environmental controversy that accompanied protest action. The psychological argument was simply that the trouble lay with the protesters' own emotional problems; these "cripples," who would have had something to complain about in any case, found a catharsis in the protest movement. The environmental argument was the protesters' reply, which was, in effect, "The trouble is not in us—it is in the defects of society." The responses to remedial measures by workers, farmers, and Negroes shed some light on this debate as it developed during the depression.

The workers, unemployed or employed, sought not a panacea but immediate amelioration of their condition. Commenting on the Bonus Expeditionary Force, Bernstein notes that President Hoover "viewed it as a potential insurrection; in fact, it was a manifestation of transient joblessness. The answer . . . was not the bayonet but the ham sandwich." Fiorello H. La Guardia, who in the 1920's had been the only spokesman in Congress for the urban immigrant masses, recognized that the unemployed had short-term goals—relief and jobs—and insisted that the way to defeat communism was to restore full employment. In a protest incident staged by employed workers—the hosiery workers' strike in North Carolina in the summer of 1932—Governor O. Max Gardner claimed that the Communists had nothing to do with it, chaired a tripartite board that restored a wage cut, and saw the strikes peter out.[67] With the rise of the unions after the enactment of New Deal enabling legislation, labor, it is true, stepped up its protest action. The aim of this militant movement, however, was not to overthrow the capitalistic system but to secure for the workers a bigger slice of the pie. And this commitment to the system was evident even though unemployment had been reduced by only 50 per cent!

The farmers, too, sought not a panacea but immediate amelioration of their condition. Essential to the Communist party's "agrarian offensive," Shover asserts, "was the assumption that the farm crisis was a permanent and worsening state of affairs [but] . . . they seriously misgauged the ameliorative potential of the system they attacked," and they overestimated how much amelioration it would take to quiet down the countryside: "Rural discontent . . . did not survive even the promise of better times." [68]

> Once the crop-reduction program of the Agricultural Adjustment Act presented a viable alternative to radical action, even though that alternative was anathema to the leaders and accepted with misgivings by most farmers, neither the persuasion of the leaders nor the ideology they professed could rouse the intensity of the earlier movement.[69]

Milo Reno and Fred Kriege, Holiday Association leaders, detested the domestic-allotment plan and bitterly denounced Roosevelt and the whole New Deal, but the vast majority of farmers participated in the program: "The promise of amelioration had undercut the

Farm Holiday movement." In 1936 William Lemke, the only presidential candidate whose platform in any way resembled the policies advocated by Holiday Association leaders, received 2 per cent of the vote in Nebraska.[70] As the author of the article on the "Cow War" maintains, dealing with the farm rebellion was "not a matter of suppressing a group of radicals but aiding a group of citizens in a time of need."

The article on the Negroes of Harlem notes that the *Evening Journal* attributed the riot of 1935 to "Communistic agitators circulating lying pamphlets." The *Sun* replied: "Actually, Communists are more likely to have been passengers on the ebullience of a volatile population than authors of its effervescence." A Negro YMCA official stated: "It is true that there were Communists in the picture. But what gave them their opportunity?" Black leaders asserted that "the disorder had deep social, economic, and political roots." In fact, militant Negro protest in the 1930's was unusual, and black citizens, concerned more with economic aid than civil rights, overwhelmingly shifted their allegiance from the party of Abraham Lincoln to the party of Franklin D. Roosevelt.[71]

These responses of workers, farmers, and Negroes to remedial measures indicate that the most fruitful analysis of protest focused on the defects of society, not on "outside agitators." Remedial measures, partially effective at best, did not silence the doctrinaire, self-seeking, foolish, or pathological protesters, but they eventually deprived the agitators and demagogues of their audience. They did not rid society of problems—they "solved a few problems, ameliorated a few more, obscured many, and created new ones."[72] They *did* minimize alienation from society by demonstrating that the government would respond to legitimate grievances.

It may appear that these generalizations are undermined by the case of the Negroes, among whom mass militancy emerged during World War II and who mounted a revolution in the postwar period. On the contrary, the case of the blacks shows that the partial amelioration of their grievances in the 1930's, which related to survival, did not resolve their basic long-standing grievances with "deep social, economic, and political roots." This became manifest in the election of 1948, when the Negroes' emphasis on New Deal economic benefits gave way to a primary concern with the civil rights planks of the Truman program.[73]

What of the majority who suffered the Great Depression passively? Louis Adamic wrote in December 1931: "I have a definite feeling that millions of them, now that they are unemployed, are licked." [74] The *New Yorker,* in June 1932, found that America suffered from melancholia and hypochondria: "People are in a sad, but not a rebellious mood." [75] A historian states that "the predominant mood after the third winter of depression was less one of revolt than of apathy. . . . People were sullen rather than bitter, despairing rather than violent. Instead of fuming with resentment and rushing to the barricades, they sat at home, rocked dispiritedly in their rocking chairs, and blamed 'conditions.' " [76] Another historian comments, "Unemployment and the distress resulting from it were bound to lead to unrest. The wonder of it now, looking back, is that there was so little of it and that most of it was mild." [77] Still another historian declares, "Fear of violent revolt was rather widespread during the depths of the depression, but for all of the bitterness and the talk of revolution in America during the early thirties, the remarkable thing was the relative lack of violence and the extraordinary patience of the people during such an ordeal." [78]

Why the use of the words "wonder" and "remarkable"? Writing of Radical Republican constitutions in the Southern states after the Civil War, Donald Sheehan remarks on some historians characterizing the passage of these documents as "strange" or "miraculous":

> Either the author means that the readers will be surprised but he is not, in which event it would appear that something has been kept from the readers; or the author means that he himself is surprised, which is tantamount to an unintended confession of an incomplete understanding.[79]

The fact is that historians have never attempted a systematic explanation of the lassitude that gripped many Americans after the Great Crash. We cannot pretend to fill this historiographical gap in a few pages, but we can suggest some relevant factors: historical, intellectual, nationalistic, psychological, and political—all interrelated.

The historical factor that contributed to the failure of so many Americans to protest actively is implicit in the term "Great Depression." Although the depressions of the 1870's and 1890's cannot be lightly dismissed, by definition the severest—deepest, widest, and longest—economic slump in the nation's history had no precedent. People did not expect what had never happened before to happen now. "As 1930 opened, scarcely anyone believed the nation had already entered a long depression. . . . Even if the stock market collapse heralded a depression, surely, most people thought, it could not last long. Was not the United States a rich nation?" [80] The author of the article on Philadelphia comments, "Although severe unemployment created a grave emergency, most people doubted that the Depression would continue for a long time or that it would prove extensive or devastating." This inability to anticipate the unprecedented undoubtedly contributed to the optimism of many at the outset of the depression. The article on Ann Arbor refers to the optimism of the middle, though not the lower, class. James T. Patterson mentions the "remarkable . . . optimism of most state governors between 1929 and early 1932." [81] A historian comments:

> At first Americans were determinedly optimistic, and even when the depression increased its inexorable toll they continued to be hopeful. They early began to apply what Dixon Wecter called the "solvent of American humor." Trained in the cult of the stiff upper lip, they hated to admit that something terrible had happened to "the land of the free." People in Cincinnati wore buttons reading: "I'm sold on America. I won't talk depression." Billboards appeared with the words: "Wasn't the Depression Terrible?" In 1930 Elmer Davis coined a memorable phrase when he spoke of the Second Year of the Abolition of Poverty in America. . . . The cheerful desperation of 1931 was revealed in a popular song entitled "Life Is Just a Bowl of Cherries." [82]

To ridicule such optimism by leading figures in government, business, and education, as Edward Angly does in his frequently quoted compilation, *Oh Yeah?*,[83] may be inappropriate, for a great deal of early optimism was surely genuine. As the depression dragged on, of course, optimism became more and more unfashionable. It could only be expressed with sincerity by ignoring the facts.

The intellectual factor that contributed to Americans' failure to protest actively was partly a matter of inability to anticipate the unprecedented. If one expected nothing really new to happen, he saw no need to revise or discard old concepts. Even when something new did happen, the inertial force of long-held ideas often resulted in adamant adherence to familiar notions.

Much has been written about this phenomenon of "intellectual lag," which is a psychological matter to the extent that those who cling to conventional thoughts do so out of an emotional commitment to them. Gardiner C. Means describes well its general source:

> . . . I want to liken social theory to a straight line and social reality to a curve. The social reality is constantly changing. . . . This is the curve of social reality. But a social theory . . . because it cannot change beyond the limits of its own basic assumptions, has to travel in a straight line.
>
> A good social theory . . . is one which closely fits the reality of a given time. We can say that it is a line tangent to the curve of reality . . . and while a social theory is tangent to reality it can be an effective guide to social policy. . . .
>
> But then as the social reality changes, the line of theory gets further and further from the curve of reality.[84]

Some will cling to a theory twenty-five or fifty or a hundred or more years after it has been overtaken by events. Even among those who change their views when confronted with new facts, as most Americans did during the New Deal era with respect to the role of government in the economy, a lag persists. Regarding fiscal policy, for example, under the New Deal "government investment was *meant* as a helping hand for business. It was *interpreted* by business as a threatening gesture." By the 1960's big business, if not small business, had changed its views on public spending. Such changes in attitudes are often partly concealed by words—that is, many people profess one thing and practice another, playing the dual role of ideological conservative and operational liberal.[85]

The principal exemplar of intellectual lag during the depression was Herbert Hoover, who, Rexford Tugwell observes, exhibited "immersion in an ideology immune to events." In the fall of 1931 Hoover sponsored an aid-at-the-top program of government intervention in the economy, but he remained opposed to direct federal relief and clung to the sacred business tenets of the balanced budget and the gold standard. By 1932 a number of business leaders advanced proposals for some kind of economic planning, but "the ordeal of depression caused some businessmen to hold on grimly to traditional laissez-faire assumptions." To them the New Deal was anathema.[86]

Many farm spokesmen offered traditional ideas while insisting on having their cake and eating it too. The Farm Holiday solution for the plight of the tenant farmers was their restoration to propertied status: Milo Reno stated, "I can hardly agree with you that the farmers must understand that they are only laborers and not businessmen and capitalists." The ideology of Reno and Fred Kriege "was deeply rooted in traditional thinking. In an age of commercial agriculture the leaders of the movement conjured up the Jeffersonian dream of the independent, virtuous yeoman beset by powerful and immoral enemies." The Holiday Association view required, as it were, that everyone else be regulated in the farmers' interest, that prices be guaranteed under a recovery plan that would "in no way limit the farmer's right to determine what he produced and how much. . . . They spurned solutions which in any way compromised the traditional individualism and self-government of those chosen of God who labored in the earth." [87]

Union leaders, too, clung to traditional concepts. American Federation of Labor officials, holding to Gompers' doctrinaire voluntarism and displaying bureaucratic wariness of any change that might affect their control of the organization, only belatedly addressed themselves to the question of unemployment insurance. A striking example of the potency of orthodoxy occurred in Reading, Pennsylvania, where the Socialist city government drew vehement criticism from the unemployed for a program that one commentator labeled "Unemployment Relief in Hands of 'Capitalists.' " [88]

The article on Philadelphia stresses that city's "strong adherence to the theory of local responsibility." As late as the spring of 1932, after local relief payments had been suspended for eleven days, a member of the Community Council asserted, "Taking the community as a whole there seems to be no united sentiment in favor of federal relief"—a situation which changed shortly afterward. The article on Orange County relates how the *Santa Ana Register* "reflected the dichotomy in local thinking when, in the same issue, it called for federal relief of unemployed . . . and yet strongly recommended substantial reductions in government expenditures at all levels. . . ." In the campaign of 1932, letters to the newspapers of Orange County stressed budget-balancing and retrenchment as cures for the sick economy.

A nationalistic factor with paradoxical qualities also contributed to inaction. The depression, "although challenging many traditional American assumptions, nevertheless elicited responses that combined to give a new character and energy to a resurgent American nationalism"—this is the theme of Charles C. Alexander's *Nationalism in American Thought, 1930–1945.*[89] One might have expected amid the throes of collapse widespread rejection of the whole American experience, but many citizens rallied around the nation as they never had before. The writers who in the 1920's had fled a relatively prosperous America in the 1930's returned to an afflicted country with the conviction that they could make something out of it after all. Many of them advocated Marxism, but many other social critics, including some of a radical stripe, espoused a non-Marxist nationalism. They challenged nineteenth-century liberalism and laissez-faire capitalism, offering various alternatives, and they questioned the American faith in the inevitability of progress. At the same time, they rediscovered and affirmed the virtues of the American people and the American past. They derived reassurance in the stormy present from the historic strength, energy, vitality, idealism, and collective wisdom of "the people," the cultural richness of their life, the merits of their democracy, and the worth of their traditional values. The basic theme implicit in Alexander's book is, "There is nothing wrong with the American Way and the American people, but they have been betrayed by a selfish, irresponsible elite." If progress was not inevitable, it was attainable through change that was essentially nonradical in its ends and means—restoration of America to "the people."

The psychological factor contributing to inaction—the emotional impact of unemployment—is an extremely complicated affair. Despite a number of studies, much research was never done, and it is obviously no longer possible to observe directly the unemployed during the thirties. The same kind of inquiry conducted with today's workers is helpful, but the impact of selective, structural, or recession unemployment is not the same as that of the depression joblessness. Those who investigated the workers' response during the depression generally agreed that unemployment reduced emotional stability and morale, especially among transients. They were not so sure about workers' self-sufficiency, submissiveness, and introversion or unsociability. The measurement of impact on such personality traits as feelings of superiority and self-confidence was made more difficult by the question of causation or responsibility—whether the unemployed person believed his loss of a job was his own fault.

Some research was done on the interests of the unemployed, such as reading and movie attendance, their various personal habits, "total personality," general attitudes of life, ego and aspiration levels, class-consciousness, and moral, religious, and political attitudes. Summarizing numerous inquiries, two students of the psychological effects of unemployment found that different attitudes fell into three broad categories:

> (1) *The unbroken.* The unresigned, aggressive individuals who are far from content with their present situation, who will not give up and sometimes go so far as to try to change the social order. (2) *The broken.* The resigned, apathetic individuals who have lost all hope, are indifferent, even "lying flat on their backs." These are by no means the revolutionaries. (3) *The distressed.* The anxious, bitter, hopeless individuals who do not know which way to turn and who alternate between fits of gloominess and outbursts of rage. These are too disorganized a group to become revolutionaries; they more frequently go into flights from reality.

Individual differences in attitude resulted from differences in predisposing factors: past economic and social status, age, sex, type of personality, extent of the impact of the depression on the individual, length of unemployment, and a combination of these factors. Long unemployment caused significant changes in attitude—an individual's attitude often reflected his stage of unemployment.[90]

Within the three broad categories of the unbroken, the broken, and the distressed, there were various gradations with different relative weights. One study of 147 relief clients revealed this distribution of attitudes:

1. Expressed confidence in the present order 6%
2. Admitted depression was very trying but thought it would pass 10%
3. Needed help to get back on their feet, and were trying to help themselves 23%
4. Asked for what they could get without protest or thanks, their courage spent 14%
5. Critics of the social order, felt that they were entitled

to a job 27%
6. Had abandoned hope 8%
7. Ready to fight against the present order 12%

For our present purposes, categories (5) and (7), designating potential sources of active protesters, call for further consideration. The crucial point that emerges from various studies of attitudes is the gap between thought and practice. The unemployed may have criticized the government and wanted change, but "there was no revolutionary attitude produced by unemployment . . . the unemployed are not revolutionaries." The conclusion that "although there is a definite change in expressed attitudes . . . there does not seem to be a change toward more radical behavior" undoubtedly applied even to those in category (7): there is a great difference between voicing a desire to fight and actually fighting. A study of those with incomes below $1,000 found them poor material for recruitment to the Communist cause because such a commitment required "active support which this group, because of its apathy, is not prepared to give." Similarly, class-consciousness arose from "insight into the social situation" and economic distress that produced demoralization *short of* apathy.[91] To sum up, in broad terms, the unemployed who were active devoted their energy to looking for a job or surviving without one; the others were apathetic.

The matter of causation or responsibility does not provide a complete framework for explaining the various factors contributing to inaction, but it is present in connection with each of them. The historical factor, which operated at the outset of the depression and involved the optimistic assumption that what had not happened before would not happen now, did not include an attribution of responsibility for severe, prolonged collapse since it did not allow for such an eventuality. The nationalistic factor, on the other hand, resting on the proposition that the American Way and "the people" had been betrayed, did provide grounds for identifying the perpetrators of treachery. The psychological impact of unemployment obviously depended on whether the jobless individual thought he or other persons or causal agents were responsible for his receiving a pink slip. The intellectual "lag" can be better understood than it has been by considering it in the light of causation or responsibility.

It is conceivable that a person who believes a light bulb will not break when dropped on a sidewalk from a height of a hundred feet will cling to this belief after seeing a hundred bulbs destroyed in this manner, but most witnesses of such a demonstration, holding such a belief, would give it up when it came to wagering on the fate of the 101st bulb. Yet, as is evident in the article on Orange County, people will approve of departures from an orthodox ideology in an emergency—only to embrace the ideology more zealously than ever when the emergency has passed, and to demand the virtually total eradication of emergency measures. Insisting on a return to the policies of the pre-depression "good old days," they do not see in the pre-emergency situation the sources of the emergency itself.

Since the measures initiated to deal with the emergency are never wholly eliminated, neither does the old ideology, the object of renewed, fervent allegiance, accurately describe the post-emergency situation. In Orange County an additional factor has entered the picture since the depression. Those citizens who work in the aerospace industry are not loafers like, as *they* see it, recipients of welfare assistance; but in terms of their ideology, defense spending—questions of foreign and defense policy aside—serves the same economic function as did the New Deal relief agencies. Basil Rauch asserts, "Defense and space exploration contracts and the enlarged armed forces serve—and overserve—the functions of New Deal agencies which were intended to be temporary, such as PWA and WPA." [92] Although the Orange Countians employed in defense plants may attribute their well-being to the validity of their ideology and their own superior virtues, they are direct beneficiaries of what is now commonly called "military Keynesianism." Thus in one sense intellectual lag is essentially an intellectual matter: old ideas hang on because of the inadequacy or absence of causal analysis.

We shall never know how long the unemployed would have remained passive if the government's response to the depression had continued to be grossly inadequate. We do know that

> 1932 was bringing signs of new resentment. For the first time a bitterness was beginning to rise against the rich and respectable. It took its start perhaps in the battle against federal relief. . . . Even more important was the impression that the rich were trying to contract

> out of what was, after all, a national crisis. . . . [Especially] irritating was the ingenuity with which some avoided the payment of taxes.[93]

A historian of relief in Minneapolis writes that "1932 was the year of discontent. . . . Left-wing agitators were everywhere." [94] Yet deprived Americans and the concerned who were better off still felt they could find constructive means to combat the depression, and nonviolent ways to bring about the utilization of those means. We shall never know what they would have done if they had not felt this way. In any event, "as the sense of crisis deepened, there remained one hope. 1932 was a presidential election year." [95]

In this situation the historical and the political were mutually reinforcing. Because the American people were what they were—reluctant, as Jefferson said in the Declaration of Independence, to abolish the forms to which they were accustomed "for light and transient causes"—they had given the two-party system a chance to work. Because the two-party system had "worked"—that is, granting its shortcomings—the American people were what they were. Except for a significant segment of intellectuals, "They anxiously looked around for a 'liberal' leader among the ranks of politicians of the two major political parties under whose banner they could continue to struggle for reform and progress." [96] Perhaps this point is made most vividly in the article on the Oklahoma Indians, many of whom, in their pitiful plight, "convinced that the source of their problems was politics, . . . decided that political action was the only way to solve them." Thus 1932, the "Year of Crisis," saw another testing of democracy:

> Perhaps the old machinery of American politics could be used, as it had been at times of crisis in the past, to solve the people's problems. Perhaps the political parties would offer new programs, new leaders, who could find peaceful solutions to the problems posed by the depression. Many felt that 1932 was democracy's last chance to justify itself. If it failed . . . if the existence of personal liberty could not be reconciled with the need for economic security, there was little doubt that personal liberty would suffer. And if democracy lost in America, what chance would it have in the rest of the world? [97]

Many historians and political scientists have judged the policies of the man who was elected in November 1932 to be a vindication of democracy, a demonstration that alternatives were available other than "political democracy and economic chaos" or "economic direction and political tyranny," that, contrary to the feelings of many in the 1930's, the free state was not "spent as a means of organizing human action." [98]

The residents of the Hoovervilles were still on the scene a decade later, bearing what Caroline Bird has designated *The Invisible Scar* of the most traumatic economic event in our history, but they were back, or ready to go back, to work. The author of an article on the unemployed published in a journal of psychiatry concludes, "We came to the end of this study [of 1940] impressed that a group from the beginning underprivileged, faced with an acute and extreme crisis, could make so adequate an adjustment, calling on all their human reserves and resources." The American people hung on grimly, like the bombed-out British, through the hopeless early years of the depression, and their response—their opting for a New Deal, and the New Deal itself—"if not always equal to the challenge, at least showed that the country was not materially or spiritually bankrupt, and not susceptible to the totalitarian virus." This immunity was no small matter, if one recalls the Nazi regime: "Whatever the social costs of the system there can be no doubt that it was extremely successful in terms of recovery from the depression." [99] Americans, with slower recovery, suffered terribly. It is impossible to quantify human suffering, but we can rejoice that the American people rejected a Nazi-like solution, which produced, along with rapid recovery, an unimaginable infamy. They shunned the barricades and the *putsch* and seized power through the ballot box.

Some survivors of the depression express both pride in the strength that democracy displayed in the thirties and doubt that it will perform so effectively in the face of a comparable future crisis.[100] If present and future generations dispel this doubt—should the occasion arise—they may engage in self-congratulation which will in effect pay tribute to those Americans who endured the Great Depression.

V. THE VALUES OF LOCAL HISTORY

Local history offers unique perspectives, but it is too little used. Its neglect is quite apparent in the case of the Great Depression.[101] In general, historians have focused on the Hoover administration, emphasizing the formulation of policy and its effects from the standpoint of men in Washington looking outward across the nation, or of men across the nation fixing their sight on the national capital. Economic historians also have stressed developments at the national level, providing necessary but cold aggregate statistics: from mid-1929 to early 1932 the gross national product declined 40 per cent, industrial production 50 per cent, residential construction 75 per cent, industrial and commercial construction 70 per cent; unemployment, as a percentage of the labor force, quadrupled, and by 1932 the unemployed (not counting several million on short work-weeks) numbered 13 million or more.

A vast body of contemporary materials, largely produced by psychologists and sociologists, deals with the impact of the depression on human beings, but historians have barely begun to use this information in writing local history. Much of the literature describing individuals and families is particularly valuable.[102] Some of it draws together observations from throughout the nation; some reports on individuals and families in particular localities, but even the studies in this category do not amount to local history.[103] Most of them lack that dimension of time that necessarily characterizes historical inquiries, or are only partially descriptive. An investigation dealing almost exclusively with the unemployed in a given locale, for example, does not tell us about other residents in other situations, or about the relationships between various groups in the same place. Local history involves a more comprehensive consideration of a unit with its own special place on the continuum of socio-political-economic entities: the individual, the family, the neighborhood, the locality, the state (the subject of two of the articles in this book), and the nation.

I have selected historical articles primarily for two reasons: their authors have a wider perspective than contemporary observers, both with respect to the availability of relevant data and the analytical perspective afforded by the passage of time; and they have, unlike excerpts from books, a unity that derives from their being entities in themselves. Of the dozen items reprinted here, including the final selection by an anthropologist, all except the one on Harlem are historical articles. Six of the eleven articles have appeared in the period 1968–1970; three others were published in the years 1965–1967. Clearly, the dearth of local historical studies has only recently begun to be remedied. Let us hope the effort grows, for we need history from the bottom up as well as from the top down.[104]

A recent historiographical development, analysis of the "community-society continuum," has a special relevance for local history. Samuel P. Hays, a leading exponent of this approach, comments that historians

> . . . have erroneously assumed a uniform perspective in local and national political history, emphasizing that national history is either local and state history writ large or that local and state history is national history writ small. But political life at one level is of an entirely different order from that at another. They are linked not by logical similarity but by human interaction.

Hays maintains that a "community-society dimension" provides a framework "which will account for different levels of political behavior and the interaction between them." [105] Robert Wiebe considers the community-society dimension—in its various ramifications besides the political—in his brilliant national history *The Search for Order* (1967). Two sociologists have in effect illustrated the approach in tracing the evolution of Benson, Minnesota, from an autonomous small town with merely local interests to a locality caught between local and translocal interests.[106] No doubt more studies of this kind will appear.

The virtues of local history commonly noted by its advocates are: the illumination of national trends—the illustration of the national generalization with the local specific; the simultaneous fostering of skepticism about national generalizations—the identification of variations on the national theme; and the demonstration of the importance of the individual's role in history.[107] Certainly the reader of this book is not likely to forget the larger dimensions of the nation's history during the early years of depression. At the same time, he will read studies in microhistory that suggest the diversity of the American scene. Just as studies of the unemployed show great variety in the impact of adversity on idle workers and their marital and family relations, so do the studies reprinted here indicate variety.

A comparison of the problems of relief in Ann Arbor, Philadelphia, Harlem, Oklahoma, Tucson, and Orange County, for example, reveals important differences as well as similarities. Clearly, too, the prosperity of the twenties (which was not all that has often been claimed for it[108]) was enjoyed less in some places than in others. For the workers of Philadelphia, the Negroes of Harlem, the farmers of Cedar County and Sioux City and Custer County, the miners of Harlan County, and the Indians of Oklahoma, the depression began sometime before the Great Crash. The active protest of Midwestern farmers and the Harlan County miners was exceptional. Most Americans sat around waiting for something to happen. Just as Boccaccio found that upright clerics made for less colorful copy than those who strayed from the path of rectitude, so do historians of the early thirties devote less attention to inaction than to action. But inaction was the dominant theme in Americans' initial response to the Great Depression.

That local history demonstrates the importance of the individual's role in history is evident in this anthology. Surely, the fact that Herbert Hoover was President of the United States was significant for the history of the nation's communities. Surely, too, Mayor Edward Staebler of Ann Arbor, Horatio Gates Lloyd and Mayor Harry Mackey of Philadelphia, Holt J. Gewinner of Atlanta, W. T. Anderson of Macon, Georgia, Jake W. Lenker of Wilton Junction, Iowa, and Walter R. Bimson of Phoenix made a difference in the history of their communities.

My primary concern is with the period from the Great Crash to the inauguration of Franklin D. Roosevelt. Emphatically, I do not mean to imply that Roosevelt and the New Deal brought the depression to an end. Gross National Product for 1929, then the all-time high, was not regained until eight years later—in 1937, just before the recession of 1937–1938. Unemployment for 1932, the all-time high, was not reduced by as much as half until five years later, in 1937. Roosevelt's admirers translate partial success into total victory; his detractors convert partial failure into total defeat. It is better to have some recovery than no recovery or continued decline. Full recovery, needless to say, is preferable, but it was not in the cards in the thirties given the state of economic knowledge.

More important than economic figures in distinguishing the Hoover from the Roosevelt era are emotional factors—what a Phoenix real estate man, speaking of developments during Roosevelt's first two weeks in office, called "the psychology of better times." Not long ago, an effort on my part to compare Hoover's and Roosevelt's policies in cold, doctrinal terms moved a friend to write me that he regretted my contribution to the apotheosizing of Herbert Hoover. That was not my aim. I was concerned only with the classification of policies, and I relegated the difference in the effectiveness of the two Presidents' policies to a footnote.[109] Hoover was never what his opponents in 1932 said he was, but by no stretch of the imagination was he one of the great statesmen of the twentieth century, as overcorrectors and "neo-Hooverites" would have us believe. His response to the Great Depression was inadequate. If Roosevelt's was also inadequate, it was less so. In this distinction lay the difference between a nation's despair and a nation's hope.[110]

NOTES

1. For substantiation of this point, see Studs Terkel, *Hard Times: An Oral History of the Great Depression* (New York: Pantheon, 1970).

2. Leslie A. Fiedler, "The Two Memories: Reflections on Writers and Writing in the Thirties," in Morton J. Frisch and Martin Diamond, eds., *The Thirties: A Reconsideration in the Light of the American Political Tradition* (DeKalb: Northern Illinois University Press, 1968), pp. 52–53, 58.

3. Milton Meltzer, *Brother, Can You Spare a Dime?: The Great Depression, 1929–1933* (New York: Knopf, 1969), p. 3.

4. Burton Crane, *The Practical Economist* (New York: Collier Books, 1962), p. 68.

5. Alfred Kazin, "The Historian as Reporter: Edmund Wilson and the 1930's," *Reporter,* March 20, 1958, p. 43.

6. John L. Shover, "The Farm Holiday Movement in Nebraska," *Nebraska History,* XLIII (March 1962), 56, 77.

7. Irving Bernstein, *The Lean Years: A History of the American Worker, 1920–1933* (Baltimore: Penguin Books, 1966), pp. 435–436.

8. *Ibid.*, p. 422.

9. Harvey Swados, ed., *The American Writer and the Great Depression* (Indianapolis: Bobbs-Merrill, 1966), p. xii.

10. Frank Freidel, *The New Deal in Historical Perspective,* 2nd ed. (Washington, D.C.: American Historical Association, Service Center for Teachers of History, 1965), p. 1.

11. Arthur M. Schlesinger, Jr., review of *The American Earthquake* by Edmund Wilson, in *New York Times Book Review,* February 9, 1958, p. 3.

12. Saul Maloff, "The Mythic Thirties," *Texas Quarterly,* XI (Winter 1968), 111. Swados, *The American Writer and the Great Depression,* p. xi.

13. M. S. Venkataramani, "Some Aspects of Life and Politics in the United States of America in 1932," *International Review of Social History,* III, Part 3 (1958), 365.

14. Carl G. Gustavson, *A Preface to History* (New York: McGraw-Hill, 1955), p. 100.

15. Shover, "The Farm Holiday Movement in Nebraska," p. 55. John L.

Shover, "The Communist Party and the Midwest Farm Crisis of 1933," *Journal of American History,* LI (September 1964), 248–249n.

16. Gustavson, *A Preface to History,* p. 101.

17. When historians and social scientists use the term "expectations" in studies of social movements, they refer to expectations based on past experience and now internalized, rather than to expectations in the ordinary sense of what can reasonably be expected under present circumstances. If the former exceed the latter, the result may be efforts to change present circumstances. Recently, "expectations" has largely been replaced by the sociologists' concept of "relative deprivation": a perceived discrepancy between what people believe they are rightly entitled to and what they actually manage to attain.

18. Gustavson, *A Preface to History,* p. 99.

19. A. William Hoglund, "A Comment on the Farm Strikes of 1932 and 1962," *Agricultural History,* XXXIX (October 1965), 213–216.

20. A. William Hoglund, "Wisconsin Dairy Farmers on Strike," *Agricultural History,* XXXV (January 1961), 26, 27.

21. Shover, "The Farm Holiday Movement in Nebraska," p. 77. Shover, "The Communist Party and the Midwest Farm Crisis of 1933," p. 253.

22. Bernstein, *The Lean Years,* p. 436.

23. George Rudé, *The Crowd in History: A Study of Popular Disturbances in France and England, 1730–1848* (New York: John Wiley, 1964), p. 218.

24. Jerold S. Auerbach, "Southern Tenant Farmers: Socialist Critics of the New Deal," *Labor History,* VII (Winter 1966), 6. Louis Cantor, *A Prologue to the Protest Movement: The Missouri Sharecropper Roadside Demonstration of 1939* (Durham, N.C.: Duke University Press, 1969), is an excellent study.

25. Gustavson, *A Preface to History,* pp. 100, 106.

26. Jesse Lemisch, "The American Revolution from the Bottom Up," in Barton J. Bernstein, ed., *Towards a New Past: Dissenting Essays in American History* (New York: Vintage Books, 1969), p. 25.

27. Rudé, *The Crowd in History,* pp. 253–254.

28. Lemisch, "The American Revolution from the Bottom Up," p. 20.

29. Shover, "The Farm Holiday Movement in Nebraska," p. 54.

30. Bernstein, *The Lean Years,* p. 421.

31. Rudé, *The Crowd in History,* p. 254.

32. *Ibid.,* p. 256.

33. John L. Shover, "Populism in the Nineteen-Thirties: The Battle for the AAA," *Agricultural History,* XXXIX (January 1965), 17–24.

34. Hoglund, "Wisconsin Dairy Farmers on Strike," p. 31.

35. Shover, "The Communist Party and the Midwest Farm Crisis of 1933," p. 260.

36. Hoglund, "Wisconsin Dairy Farmers on Strike," p. 31. Bernstein, *The Lean Years,* p. 427. Fon W. Boardman, Jr., *The Thirties: America and the Great Depression* (New York: Henry Z. Walck, 1967), p. 35.

37. Hoglund, "Wisconsin Dairy Farmers on Strike," p. 30. Bernstein, *The Lean Years,* p. 433.

38. Gustavson, *A Preface to History,* p. 103.

39. Rudé, *The Crowd in History,* pp. 264, 266.

40. Shover, "The Farm Holiday Movement in Nebraska," p. 61.

41. Bernstein, *The Lean Years,* p. 425.

42. *Ibid.,* pp. 431, 434, 454. See also Donald J. Lisio, "A Blunder Becomes Catastrophe: Hoover, the Legion, and the Bonus Army," *Wisconsin Magazine of History,* LI (Autumn 1967), 37–50.

43. Thomas B. Littlewood, *Horner of Illinois* (Evanston, Ill.: Northwestern

University Press, 1969), p. 110. Hoglund, "Wisconsin Dairy Farmers on Strike," p. 26. Shover, "The Communist Party and the Midwest Farm Crisis of 1933," p. 249n.

44. *Ibid.*, pp. 258, 265. Shover, "The Farm Holiday Movement in Nebraska," p. 69.

45. *Ibid.*, p. 60.

46. *Ibid.* Hoglund, "Wisconsin Dairy Farmers on Strike," p. 33.

47. Frederick Lewis Allen, *Since Yesterday: The Nineteen Thirties in America* (New York: Bantam Books, 1961), pp. 46, 47. Jack Salzman and Barry Wallenstein, eds., *Years of Protest: A Collection of Writings of the 1930's* (New York: Pegasus, 1967), p. 13. Boardman, *The Thirties,* p. 25. James T. Patterson, *The New Deal and the States: Federalism in Transition* (Princeton: Princeton University Press, 1969), pp. 45–46.

48. Shover, "The Farm Holiday Movement in Nebraska," p. 64. Hoglund, "Wisconsin Dairy Farmers on Strike," pp. 32, 34.

49. Bernstein, *The Lean Years,* p. 427.

50. *Ibid.*, p. 422.

51. Eugene Smolensky, *Adjustments to Depression and War, 1930–1945* (Atlanta: Scott, Foresman, 1964), p. 7.

52. Dewey W. Grantham, Jr., "Recent American History and the Great Depression," *Texas Quarterly,* VI (Winter 1963), 22.

53. Boardman, *The Thirties,* p. 32.

54. Maloff, "The Mythic Thirties," p. 111.

55. Swados, *The American Writer and the Great Depression,* p. xi.

56. Daniel Aaron and Robert Bendiner, eds., *The Strenuous Decade: A Social and Intellectual Record of the Nineteen-Thirties* (New York: Anchor Books, 1970), p. 31.

57. Grantham, "Recent American History and the Great Depression," p. 22.

58. Quoted in Bernstein, *The Lean Years,* p. 501. Hoglund, "Wisconsin Dairy Farmers on Strike," p. 33. Shover, "The Farm Holiday Movement in Nebraska," p. 61. Patterson, *The New Deal and the States,* p. 49.

59. Quoted in Bernstein, *The Lean Years,* p. 435. *Ibid.*, p. 434. Swados, *The American Writer and the Great Depression,* p. xviii.

60. Shover, "The Farm Holiday Movement in Nebraska," p. 54. Shover, "The Communist Party and the Midwest Farm Crisis of 1933," pp. 261–265.

61. Wilson Record, *The Negro and the Communist Party* (Chapel Hill: University of North Carolina Press, 1951); and Record, *Race and Radicalism: The NAACP and the Communist Party in Conflict* (Ithaca: Cornell University Press, 1964).

62. Swados, *The American Writer and the Great Depression,* pp. xvii–xviii.

63. Quoted in Grantham, "Recent American History and the Great Depression," p. 24.

64. Littlewood, *Horner of Illinois,* p. 92.

65. James P. Cannon, *The Struggle for a Proletarian Party* (New York: Pioneer Publishers, 1943), p. 19.

66. Hoglund, "Wisconsin Dairy Farmers on Strike," p. 31.

67. Bernstein, *The Lean Years,* pp. 422, 427, 434, 456.

68. Shover, "The Communist Party and the Midwest Farm Crisis of 1933," pp. 265–266.

69. Shover, "The Farm Holiday Movement in Nebraska," p. 54. For a study of a Missouri farm leader who supported FDR in 1932 and then deplored the domestic-allotment plan, see Richard O. Davies, "The Politics of Desperation:

William A. Hirth and the Presidential Election of 1932," *Agricultural History,* XXXVIII (October 1964), 226–234.

70. Shover, "The Farm Holiday Movement in Nebraska," p. 77.

71. For a list of studies of Negro voting behavior in the 1930's, see "Politics and the Negro," in Bernard Sternsher, ed., *The Negro in Depression and War: Prelude to Revolution, 1930–1945* (Chicago: Quadrangle Books, 1969), pp. 328–329; see also *ibid.,* pp. 224–263, for selections on politics. A recent article is Rita Werner Gordon, "The Change in the Political Alignment of Chicago's Negroes During the New Deal," *Journal of American History,* LVI (December 1969), 584–603.

72. Paul K. Conkin, *The New Deal* (New York: Crowell, 1967), p. 106.

73. Richard M. Dalfiume, "The 'Forgotten Years' of the Negro Revolution," *Journal of American History,* LV (June 1968), 90–106. Ernest M. Collins, "Cincinnati Negroes and Presidential Politics," *Journal of Negro History,* XLI (April 1956), 134.

74. Quoted in Bernstein, *The Lean Years,* p. 435.

75. Quoted in *ibid.*

76. Arthur M. Schlesinger, Jr., *The Crisis of the Old Order* (Boston: Houghton Mifflin, 1957), p. 252..

77. Boardman, *The Thirties,* p. 34.

78. Grantham, "Recent American History and the Great Depression," p. 24.

79. Donald Sheehan, "Radical Reconstruction," in Sheehan and Harold C. Syrett, eds., *Essays in American Historiography* (New York: Columbia University Press, 1960), p. 43.

80. Boardman, *The Thirties,* p. 24.

81. Patterson, *The New Deal and the States,* p. 30.

82. Grantham, "Recent American History and the Great Depression," p. 20.

83. Edward Angly, ed., *Oh Yeah?* (New York: Viking, 1932).

84. Gardiner C. Means, *The Corporate Revolution in America* (New York: Collier Books, 1964), p. 26.

85. Stuart Chase, "American Values: A Generation of Change," *Public Opinion Quarterly,* XXIX (Fall 1965), 362–367. Robert L. Heilbroner, *The Worldly Philosophers* (New York: Simon and Schuster, 1953), p. 267. See also, C. Joseph Pusateri, "A Study in Misunderstanding: Franklin D. Roosevelt and the Business Community," *Social Studies,* LX (October 1969), 204–211. John H. Bunzel, "The General Ideology of American Small Business," *Political Science Quarterly,* LXX (March 1955), 87–102. Lloyd A. Free and Hadley Cantril, *The Political Beliefs of Americans: A Study of Public Opinion* (New Brunswick, N.J.: Rutgers University Press, 1967). See also R. Joseph Monsen, Jr., and Mark W. Cannon, *The Makers of Public Policy* (New York: McGraw-Hill, 1965), pp. 24–63, on the distinction between "small business" ideology and "managerial" ideology.

86. Rexford G. Tugwell, "The Protagonists: Roosevelt and Hoover," *Antioch Review,* XIII (Winter 1953–1954), 421. Grantham, "Recent American History and the Great Depression," pp. 21, 25.

87. Shover, "The Communist Party and the Midwest Farm Crisis of 1933," p. 249n. Shover, "The Farm Holiday Movement in Nebraska," pp. 72, 77–78.

88. Daniel Nelson, *Unemployment Insurance: The American Experience, 1915–1935* (Madison: University of Wisconsin Press, 1969), *passim.* Henry G. Hodges, "Four Years of Socialism in Reading, Pennsylvania," *National Municipal Review,* XXX (May 1931), 288.

89. David D. Van Tassel, Editor's Preface, in Charles C. Alexander, *Na-*

tionalism in American Thought, 1930–1945 (Chicago: Rand, McNally, 1969), p. viii. See also Alfred Kazin, *On Native Grounds* (New York: Vintage Books, 1956), pp. 378–406.

90. Philip Eisenberg and Paul F. Lazarsfeld, "The Psychological Effects of Unemployment," *Psychological Bulletin,* XXXV (June 1938), 359–369, 372, 374–379.

91. *Ibid.,* 369–370, 373.

92. Basil Rauch, *The History of the New Deal, 1933–1938* (New York: Capricorn Books, 1963), pp. x–xi.

93. Schlesinger, *The Crisis of the Old Order,* pp. 252–253.

94. Raymond L. Koch, "Politics and Relief in Minneapolis During the 1930's," *Minnesota History,* XLI (Winter 1968), 157.

95. Robert Goldston, *The Great Depression: The United States in the Thirties* (Indianapolis: Bobbs-Merrill, 1968), p. 66.

96. Venkataramani, "Some Aspects of Life and Politics in the United States of America in 1932," p. 366.

97. Goldston, *The Great Depression,* p. 66.

98. Arthur M. Schlesinger, Jr., *The Politics of Upheaval* (Boston: Houghton Mifflin, 1960), pp. 645–646. See also Heinz Eulau, "Neither Ideology nor Utopia: The New Deal in Retrospect," *Antioch Review,* XIX (Winter 1959–1960), 523–537.

99. Sol Wiener Ginsburg, "What Unemployment Does to People," *American Journal of Psychiatry,* XC (November 1942), 446. Aaron and Bendiner, *The Strenuous Decade,* p. xi. Derek H. Aldcroft, "The Development of the Planned Economy Before 1939," *Journal of Contemporary History,* IV (October 1969), issue entitled "The Great Depression," 134.

100. Terkel, *Hard Times, passim.*

101. Clifford L. Lord, *Teaching History with Community Resources,* Localized History Series (New York: Bureau of Publications, Teachers College, Columbia University, 1964), pp. vi, 17–18, discusses the neglect of local history in general.

102. Eisenberg and Lazarsfeld, "The Psychological Effects of Unemployment," is valuable in itself and has a bibliography of 112 relevant items, pp. 385–390.

103. See below, "Suggested Reading," for items in this category.

104. See, for example, Lemisch, "The American Revolution from the Bottom Up."

105. Samuel P. Hays, "Political Parties and the Community-Society Continuum," in William Nisbet Chambers and Walter Dean Burnham, eds., *The American Party Systems: Stages of Political Development* (New York: Oxford University Press, 1967), p. 153.

106. Don Martindale and R. Galen Hanson, *Small Town and the Nation: The Conflict of Local and Translocal Forces* (Westport, Conn.: Greenwood, 1969).

107. Lord, *Teaching History with Community Resources,* pp. 8–17.

108. Robert L. Heilbroner, in *The Future as History* (New York: Grove Press, 1961), p. 121, points out that "in 1929 *no* system of distribution would have yielded entirely satisfactory results. . . . Had the nation's disposable income been divided equally among all thirty-six million households, the result would have been an income of $2,300 per household—about halfway between a living standard of bare necessities and one of minimal comfort."

109. Bernard Sternsher, ed., *The New Deal: Doctrines and Democracy* (Boston: Allyn and Bacon, 1966), p. 173n.

110. Gene Smith, *The Shattered Dream* (New York: Morrow, 1970).

Town I

Ann Arbor: Depression City

David M. Katzman

This selection and the next, on Philadelphia, are case studies of a nationwide phenomenon: the exhaustion of local resources—first private, then public—which served as a practical demonstration of the failure of President Hoover's theory of local responsibility for relief. Ann Arbor, unlike Philadelphia, "was able to delay the collapse of private and municipal services to the indigent and unemployed until the federal government, under the New Deal, provided relief." The funds of private agencies were rapidly expended, and the city assumed more and more responsibility, directly providing relief work beginning in May 1931 and becoming the major relief agency in 1932. In early May 1933 the city's relief program began to collapse. Reconstruction Finance Corporation funds prevented a complete cessation of these activities before Federal Emergency Relief Administration aid became available in July. (Another Michigan city is the subject of William H. Chafe, "Flint and the Great Depression," Michigan History, *LIII [Fall 1969], 225–239, which is largely devoted to post-1932 developments.)*

The 1930's, a decade of despair and depression, contrasted sharply with the prosperity of the roaring twenties. Apple vendors pushed aside flappers on the center stage. Economic tragedy and despair

[Reprinted from *Michigan History,* L (December 1966), 306–317.]

replaced the Horatio Alger myth in American life; success and security were things of the past.

At first the federal government, paralyzed by an outdated philosophy that rejected governmental intervention in the economy, did little. Private philanthropy was quickly bankrupted by the skyrocketing needs of the unemployed, and municipalities were unable to meet the people's needs as tax revenues dropped and debt limits were reached. At a time when the need was greatest, most American cities were forced to cut back sharply their relief activities.

Ann Arbor was able to delay the collapse of private and municipal services to the indigent and unemployed until the federal government, under the New Deal, provided relief. The city, under the leadership of an energetic and humanitarian mayor, Edward Staebler, early accepted responsibility for providing for those who were unable to provide for themselves.

Ann Arbor, the seat of the University of Michigan, had a population of 29,944 persons in 1930, predominantly native born of German stock. Less than 4 per cent of the community was Negro. The University of Michigan was the major industry in the city, employing over 20 per cent of the labor force, although an almost equal number were employed in the city's eleven factories. In addition, the city's 12,200-person working force, ballooned by a large population of unmarried women serving the clerical needs of the university, was actively engaged in servicing the agricultural community of which the city of Ann Arbor was the hub.[1]

During the 1920's occasional unemployment was frequent. Although the university provided full-year employment for many, a large number of workers were employed at university construction projects and were sometimes unemployed during the winter. The industries in the city were sensitive to subtle changes in demand, and when orders temporarily decreased, so also did the number of workdays.

The town was not indifferent to this problem. On April 16, 1928, Mayor Edward Staebler appointed a committee to study unemployment in Ann Arbor and told the Common Council that "Ann Arbor has just passed one of the worst periods of unemployment in its history—more serious, it has seemed, than even in the depression years following 1921." The mayor concluded that many workers were unemployed and "have been able to secure only haphazard employment." He asked the committee to determine whether Ann Arbor had a permanent surplus of workers, to study whether fluctuations in employment were predictable, and to suggest remedies.[2]

Studying 1,659 workers employed during May 1928 in the construction and manufacturing industries in the city, as well as the buildings and grounds department of the university, the committee concluded that during the year May 1, 1927, to April 30, 1928, 3 per cent of the workers had been unemployed six months or more, 26 per cent from one to six months, and 4 per cent one month or less. In addition, the committee found that construction workers suffered 79 per cent of their unemployment from October to March. The report closed with a positive attitude: 67 per cent of the workers suffered no unemployment. But the committee's emphasis on the 67 per cent masked the significance of the minority total; 33 per cent of the men had been unemployed at some time during the year.[3]

Mayor Staebler accepted the findings of the panel and sought to eliminate seasonal unemployment by stimulating winter construction. The record of building permits filed during the fall and winter in the following years reveals that the mayor's program was unsuccessful. Above all, the 1920's showed that while the leaders of the community could make their own economic lives secure, the majority of the community could not. Even during the 1920's the protection of the general welfare of the community was beyond the city's grasp.[4]

The depression hit Ann Arbor hard, and the sharp business fluctuations left in their wake a steadily increasing roll of permanently unemployed workers. The fall of 1929 and the following winter foreshadowed the years to come. When the Detroit-Interurban ended service in September, a few Ann Arbor men were thrown out of work. Eight weeks later United Reproducers, a manufacturer of radio sets, withdrew its offices from Ann Arbor, fired twenty-five office employees, and temporarily laid off two hundred factory workers. Although a large number of the factory employees worked a few weeks in December, they were unemployed again in January, and the company continued to provide occasional employment until the following year, when the corporation went into receivership. The Michigan Artificial Ice Products Company went into receivership in 1929 and withdrew from Ann Arbor in 1930.[5]

During December 1929 almost all industry came to a halt, and the dollar value of construction permits issued shrank sharply. Although Hoover Steel Ball Company worked twenty-four hours a day in September, its entire factory work force of over five hundred men was laid off in January 1930. The large amount of unemployment in December was reflected in the Family Welfare Bureau's increased activities; by February, the bureau was short of funds. The city government was cognizant of the widespread unemployment and, following Detroit's lead, waived the late penalty for unpaid taxes. The president of the council said the action was necessary "to relieve the financial depression felt by many of the citizens." [6]

Many city businesses and retail stores were unable to meet their bills. At 328 South Main Street, the two retail tenants, Wahl's Cleaners and one of the seven local branches of Kroger's, were respectively four and two months behind in rent by January 1930. The Heart Lake Development Corporation, a real estate firm, was in arrears; less than $800 of $8000 due every month was being received. Westgate Furniture Shops were forced to neglect some of their bills, and the owner of the largest drugstore chain in the city had to ask for an extension on accounts payable.[7]

The nonskilled and semiskilled workers suffered the most. Their inability to find work and to pay their bills produced much frustration. When bills piled up they were ignored, and little explanation was offered to creditors. Only when pressed by collection agencies and when subject to pressure did debtors reply. These replies were free of the shame and optimism of the middle class. The workers' wives offered simple explanations: "my husband is unemployed"; or, "you don't seem to realize times are hard and work is scarce." [8]

The middle class—white-collar workers, retailers, local businessmen—could not ignore bills. They seemed to feel that every creditor unpaid was entitled to an explanation and an assurance that the bill would be paid next month. The wife of a drugstore proprietor wrote: "this is the first time I have been so long overdue in thirty years of buying in your store," and the wife of a credit collector promised to sell some property to pay her bill. A stenographer gave Mack & Co. a detailed account of her health and the difficulties she had encountered in selling her automobile. These people and their neighbors were ashamed. Unable to settle their accounts, they offered the promises of next month, or of selling realty and personalty. Workingmen, without property, without automobiles, and in commonplace circumstances, were less optimistic, less ashamed.[9]

While President Hoover and national business leaders gave the economy a clean bill of health, business and industrial activity in Ann Arbor contracted sharply. Construction during 1932 was 7 per cent of 1929. Retail sales from 1930 to 1933 decreased by over 50 per cent. By 1933 the large industrial firms were running in the red, and only one of the major corporations in the city paid dividends. While the industrialists and retailers could continue to live by dipping into capital, few workers had any reserves. From 1929 until the summer of 1933, the burden of unemployment and relief fell on the city government and the voluntary welfare associations.[10]

At first the burden fell on the Community Fund and its participating agencies. The Family Welfare Bureau (FWB) was the major relief agency, and the Community Fund gave priority to the FWB in allocating funds. Despite this, the FWB's budget was inadequate throughout the depression. In the late summer of 1930, the bureau was forced to restrict itself to cases within the city and to ignore the pressing needs of the surrounding villages. During 1931, while the Community Fund was able to sponsor clothing drives and soup kitchens, it was forced to cut back on all other relief activities. By the fall of 1931 the fund was borrowing on its 1932 income and was faced with tapping its endowment to meet current expenses. In addition to aiding at least one thousand indigent residents a month during the winter, the private agencies had to handle an average of two thousand transients monthly. In the fall of 1932, with the number of needy cases skyrocketing, the Community Fund faced a 20 per cent drop in contributions. With the fund unable to meet the needs of the community, the city assumed more and more responsibility, becoming the major relief agency during 1932.[11]

Prior to the depression, the city played an extremely limited role in local relief. Providing aid only to those unable to work, the city left relief for the unemployable to the private agencies. During the 1920's the mayor's office had been able to find jobs for unemployed residents, but by July 1930 he could do no more than give jobseekers letters of recommendation addressed "To Whom It May

Concern." This sharply contrasted with President Hoover's assurances of the adequacy of local resources.[12]

In late fall 1930, with unemployment mounting rapidly, Mayor Staebler followed the lead of Detroit's Mayor Frank Murphy and appointed an unemployment committee. Although the mayor's committee had no official status, it marked the beginning of the city's increased role in local relief activities and served to highlight the inadequacy of voluntary relief. Prior to the committee's appointment, city action had been limited to giving Ann Arbor residents job preference in the city school system and to banning outside labor on city construction projects. With the inauguration of the mayor's unemployment committee, the city sought to raise money for local relief agencies and find jobs for the unemployed.

Ann Arbor participated in the Michigan-Chicago charity football game, with the University of Michigan's share of the receipts being divided among the Michigan counties that sold tickets. Attendance at the November game had been disappointing, but, at $3 a ticket the mayor's committee had raised almost $2,400. This football game, like many Michigan relief activities, owed its origin to the young, ambitious, and somewhat mystical mayor of Detroit, Frank Murphy. Murphy's work in the metropolis forty miles eastward cast a giant shadow over Ann Arbor, and the smaller city, like dozens of others outstate, imitated the Murphy model.[13]

Five weeks after the charity football game, the committee sponsored a community dance, raising $1,900. Thus, through Mayor Staebler's initiative, over $4,000 was made available to the distressed Community Fund during the winter for the relief of the unemployed.[14]

Far more important than fund raising was the committee's direction of the employment bureau. Begun on November 24, 1930, two months after Detroit's bureau opened, the bureau sought to register all the unemployed in Ann Arbor and to find them jobs. If nothing else, it made the city aware of the severity of the problem. Within the first week, 385 unemployed had registered at the bureau. In February the total exceeded 800; in March, 1,000; and in April, 1,100. By June 10 the volunteers staffing the bureau had registered 10 per cent of the city's work force.[15]

Unfortunately, the mayor's committee and the unemployment bureau could do little more than find temporary jobs for the unemployed. In February it was reported that 603 jobs had been found and distributed among 240 workers. The city sought to create jobs. While the unemployed sold apples in the nation's largest cities, they cut wood and sold sandbags and onions in Ann Arbor. The demand for wood, sandbags, and onions was small, however, and the city was consequently forced to take an increasingly more active role in alleviating conditions. In the spring of 1931, probably more from frustration and desperation than from expectations of success, an "organized searching party," patterned on Detroit's door-to-door canvassing, was formed "to locate work for the city's unemployed." Men don't want charity, newly elected Mayor Newkirk explained. "They want work." [16]

Previously, in February, when the mayor's unemployment committee announced it would disband, Mayor Staebler had recommended to the Common Council that the employment bureau be continued. In noting that "the need for work is more acute than at any previous time," the mayor urged the council to study the formation of a permanent state employment office in Ann Arbor. The mayor also looked for assistance under the Wagner bill, soon to be vetoed by President Hoover. But with the state in financial difficulties, and the Wagner bill vetoed, the city had to forget about outside help.[17]

In May 1931 the city officially established the City Employment Bureau, with a full-time voluntary manager. At the same time, the city began to assume direct responsibility for providing work for the unemployed. During 1931, the city began construction of an eighteen-hole golf course and a new drain sewer in addition to hiring dozens of workers to improve city playgrounds and parks. Unemployment in the city was also relieved by the construction of the $1,400,000 Hutchins Hall at the university. Business picked up temporarily in the second half of 1931, highlighted by the establishment of the International Radio Corporation in Ann Arbor. Although the goal of employing two hundred workers was never attained, the radio manufacturer's employment level varied from 100 to 150, and in 1932 "a real old-time 1929 cash dividend" was paid. Increased business was reflected in the employment bureau's registration. During August the city reregistered the unemployed, and by October less than 500 men and women had been reregistered.[18]

Almost all the city's relief was in the form of work relief, and the result was serious division in the community's classes for the first time. In August, with relief expenses mounting, the city began paying scrip money instead of cash to all citizens obtaining employment and aid from the city poor commission and other welfare agencies. All able-bodied relief recipients were required to work out the relief they received, at the rate of thirty cents an hour in scrip money. The scrip could be used only at the city-owned store and coal yard. Rent, gas, and electricity were paid directly by the city and subtracted from the workers' wages.[19]

On November 16, 1931, the Ann Arbor Trades Council protested against the payment of work relief in scrip, against the city-owned store, and against the hiring by the city of an inspector to investigate Ann Arbor residents in need of help. Four days later the labor council clarified its position: men working for the city had earned their wages, and they should be able to spend them where they saw fit. The council also charged that the city store had higher prices than privately owned stores. Until the Ann Arbor Trades Council spoke out, there had been no spokesmen for the thousands of persons victimized by the economic depression.[20]

The Ann Arbor Trades Council, formed in 1907, consisted of representatives from the craft unions in the city. Prior to 1931, it had exhibited little interest in the abstract concept of workingmen, but devoted its energies to the advancement of the particular trades comprising construction work: carpentry, bricklaying, plumbing, plastering, and so forth. During 1931 the council broadened its interest and became the spokesman for labor in the city. Although the local labor leaders were particularly motivated because many craft union members were employed on local work relief projects, the labor leaders gave progressively more support to the growing Ann Arbor Socialist Party.

During 1932 and the first quarter of 1933 the friction between the workers and the city increased. Spurred on by the Trades Council, by speakers from various radical organizations, and by a series of newspaper articles examining Michigan unemployment, those on relief became more resentful. The articles concerning relief in the *Daily News'* series on Michigan unemployment probably caused more friction than any other single event. One article revealed that "landlords in Ann Arbor are drawing almost as much relief from the public treasury as members of unemployed families. . . ." Unlike most other Michigan cities, Ann Arbor concluded that rents from property occupied by the unemployed were as much an obligation as food and fuel. The result was that of every limited dollar spent for relief by the city, thirty-eight cents went to landlords, at the expense of aiding additional families or administering to the social needs of dependent families. Hundreds of men and women would crowd into the Common Council meetings on Monday nights to register their complaints.[21]

Although the New Deal would ameliorate the problems of relief in Ann Arbor, the inauguration of President Roosevelt and the emergency congressional session did little to stop the surge of social unrest. Three weeks after the inauguration, the conflict between the work-relief employees and the city came to a head. Two hundred workers went on strike. The Common Council had recently cut their wages, but the city action had merely added to the workers' grievances. On March 27, because it was raining, the workers were told to go home. Disappointed, they marched across town to the Trades Council's Labor Temple, where they elected a committee to present the workers' grievances to the city administration. The newspapers, which had generally ignored both the depression and labor in the city, gave excellent coverage to the workers for the first time, reporting the distressing conditions of some laborers. Erhart Bank, former proprietor of the Ideal Laundry and chairman of the laborers' committee, reported that he received $2.55 a week for groceries. Bank, his wife, and his daughter spent $.70 for milk and $1 for meat, leaving $.85 for all other food. Angelos Douvitos, another member of the committee, received $4.25 a week to feed his family of seven.[22]

The strike continued the next day, and the workers marched through the city from relief project to relief project, picking up supporters. The strike lasted four days, and the immediate objective of restoring the pay cuts was won. But the workers were still dissatisfied, and on April 1 they organized the City Workers of Ann Arbor. For the first time the laborers had formal representation.[23]

The growing dissatisfaction in the city was also reflected in the spring city elections. Although the Socialist party offered no citywide candidates and only ran aldermanic candidates in five of the six wards, it increased its vote from 4 per cent of the total in November 1932 to 6.2 per cent in April 1933. In the elections they contested, the Socialist candidates polled 7.3 per cent of the votes.[24]

Within a month of the strike the city's relief activities began to collapse. On May 3, 1933, the City Council announced that the men's dormitory for transients would have to be closed. Two days later the budget committee of the Common Council announced that allowances for welfare work would continue for only another week. The committee members, noting that the city had reached its legal debt limit, could find no funds for caring for the indigent. On May 13, the *Daily News* headlined, "City Welfare Fund Emptied," and the city decided that only cases of "dire necessity" were to be aided. During May the city's teachers had a payless payday in order to help balance the budget, although the teachers had already sustained a 21 per cent pay cut within the previous few months.[25]

If the Reconstruction Finance Corporation had not furnished the city with funds, the city's welfare activities probably would have halted before July 1933, when the State Emergency Relief Administration assumed responsibility for relief. On May 10, 1933, RFC money comprised $1,900 of the city's $3,100 welfare funds. Within two weeks the bankrupt poor fund received $9,946 from the RFC, and in June, $6,200 more.

The entrance of the RFC was a stopgap measure, but it signaled the end of an era. During the years of deepening economic tragedy, Ann Arbor had been able at least to alleviate much of the misery of the depression that was uncontrollable in most of the cities in Michigan and the United States. The city was able to continue local relief long after similar programs in most cities had collapsed, and relief lasted long enough so that the federal government's entry into welfare, under the RFC amendments during the Hoover administration, provided continuity until the New Deal welfare activities were inaugurated in July 1933.[26]

NOTES

1. U.S., Bureau of the Census, *Fifteenth Census of the United States: 1930, Population,* III, Part 1, 1164.

2. *Ann Arbor Daily News,* April 17, 1928, pp. 1, 3.

3. Edward Staebler Papers, Michigan Historical Collections, University of Michigan, Unemployment Committee to the Mayor and Council [1928], Unemployment File.

4. Staebler Papers, Edward Staebler to Portland Cement Association, December 17, 1928.

5. *Ann Arbor Daily News,* September 4, 1929, p. 1; October 31, 1929, p. 1; December 4, 1929, p. 1; November 15, 1929, p. 13.

6. *Ibid.,* January 18, 1930, p. 1; building permits issued for December 1929 were one-fourth of the dollar value for 1928. More important, December 1929 permits represented less than 1/2 of 1 per cent of the total year's valuation, whereas December 1928 represented 7 1/2 per cent of the 1928 permits issued; *Ann Arbor Daily News,* January 1, 1930, p. 1; September 12, 1929, p. 1; January 18, 1930, p. 1; Ann Arbor Community Fund, Board Minutes, 1921–1939, pp. 115–116, in possession of the Community Fund Association, Ann Arbor; *Ann Arbor Daily News,* December 10, 1929, p. 1; December 27, 1929, p. 1.

7. Rudolph E. Reichert Papers, Michigan Historical Collections, University of Michigan, Rudolph E. Reichert to C. L. Brooks, January 7, 1930; Mack & Co. Papers, Michigan Historical Collections, University of Michigan, Thomas J. Rice to Mack & Co., January 21, 1930; G. W. Fletcher to Mack & Co., May 2, 1930, Credit Office Correspondence.

8. Mack & Co. Papers, Mrs. E. H. Wirt to Mack & Co., January 6, 1930; Mrs. Paul Laughlin, notes on dunning letter, September 10, 1930, Credit Office Correspondence.

9. Mack & Co. Papers, Mrs. G. C. Drake to Mack & Co., February 1, 1930; Mrs. F. Lirette to Mack & Co., July 30, 1930; Fannie J. Drake to Mack & Co., September 19, 1930, Credit Office Correspondence.

10. *Ann Arbor Daily News,* January 1, 1930, p. 1; December 31, 1932, p. 6; U.S., Bureau of the Census, *Fifteenth Census of the United States: 1930, Distribution,* I, 532–533; U.S., Bureau of the Census, *Census of American Business: Retail Distribution: 1933,* VIII, 84; the International Radio Corporation was the firm that paid the dividends.

11. Ann Arbor Community Fund, Board Minutes, p. 126; John Andrews, "History and Functions of the Ann Arbor Community Fund" (unpublished seminar paper, Institute of Social Work, University of Michigan, 1947), in possession of the Ann Arbor Community Fund; Ann Arbor Community Fund, Board Minutes, pp. 144, 146; *Ann Arbor Daily News,* August 3, 1932, p. 1; Ann Arbor Community Fund, Board Minutes, pp. 161–162; miscellaneous financial records in possession of the Ann Arbor Community Fund.

12. Staebler Papers, Edward Staebler to Hoover Steel Ball, April 21, 1928. The Hoover general superintendent replied: "We are always glad to help worthy citizens in their efforts to find steady employment and want you to call on us at any time that we can be of any assistance in this way." D. N. Saxton to Edward Staebler, April 23, 1928.

In July 1930 the following letter was typical:

To Whom It May Concern:

The bearer . . . is seeking employment. For the past six months he has had very little work and, having a wife and two small children, one of them a helpless cripple, dependent on him, he is extremely anxious to earn money to take care of them.

. . . is a willing worker and if you can use him, you will be doing him and his family a favor which will be appreciated by all of them and,

Yours truly,

Mayor

Staebler Papers, letter of July 5, 1930.

13. Staebler Papers, Edward Staebler to Don Clement, December 5, 1930; Fred Green to Edward Staebler, November 11, 1930; Fred Green to Edward Staebler, December 19, 1930.

14. Staebler Papers, financial report of the mayor's unemployment committee, May 27, 1931.

15. *Ann Arbor Daily News,* November 24, 1930, p. 1; November 29, 1930, p. 1; February 9, 1931, p. 1; March 16, 1931, p. 1; April 4, 1931, p. 3; June 17, 1931, p. 1.

16. *Ibid.,* February 5, 1931, p. 1; Staebler Papers, Edward Staebler to the Householders of Ann Arbor, January 3, 1931; January 6, 1931; Irving Bernstein, *The Lean Years* (Boston: Houghton Mifflin, 1960), p. 294; *Ann Arbor Daily News,* March 20, 1931, p. 1; June 12, 1931, p. 1. The new mayor was H. Wirt Newkirk, a Republican. Democratic Mayor Edward Staebler did not run for reelection in the spring.

17. Staebler Papers, Edward Staebler to the Common Council, February 28, 1931.

18. *Ann Arbor Daily News,* May 25, 1931, p. 1; Hutchins Hall represented 60 per cent of all Ann Arbor construction dollars in 1931; *ibid.,* April 17, 1931, p. 1; December 19, 1931, p. 1; Shirley Smith Papers, Michigan Historical Collections, The University of Michigan, Shirley Smith to James Craig, December 19, 1931; *Ann Arbor Daily News,* October 3, 1931, p. 3.

19. *Ann Arbor Daily News,* August 22, 1931, p. 1; August 3, 1931, pp. 1, 11.

20. *Ibid.,* November 17, 1931, p. 1; November 21, 1931, p. 1.

21. *Ibid.,* August 3, 1931, pp. 1, 11. There was no pressing need for the city to assume the rent of relief workers. Since evictions in Ann Arbor were infrequent and landlords could not lease apartments in any case, they, like their tenants, could only wait for better times to return. Above all, they had a social conscience and were unwilling to evict the unemployed. Reichert Papers, Rudolph Reichert to E. F. Lloyd, June 7, 1932.

22. *Ann Arbor Daily News,* March 27, 1932, pp. 1, 10. During the 1930's, Ann Arbor had two newspapers: the biweekly, later triweekly, *Washtenaw Tribune* and the daily (except Sunday) *Ann Arbor Daily News.*

The *Tribune* was locally owned and covered news of the entire county to the exclusion of state and national news. During the late 1920's and early 1930's, the *Tribune* covered all business expansion and ignored unemployment and community problems. The paper encouraged local optimism, and was in the absurd position of continually forecasting the end of a depression which its pages never reported even existed.

The *Ann Arbor Daily News,* owned by the Booth chain, was the most important newspaper in town. The front page was generally given to state, national, and international news. The *Daily News* also covered a wider variety of local news than did the *Tribune.*

Although more reliable and less optimistic than its rival, the *Ann Arbor Daily News,* like the *Tribune,* failed to cover the most important news story during the 1930's, the depression. During the 1920's, the paper headlined the record profit reports of the city's industrial corporations, whereas in the 1930's, the *Daily News* failed to report dividend omissions and income statements. Unemployment and layoffs entered the pages of the *Daily News* only when the paper announced the reopening of the city's factories.

The coverage of the mayor's employment bureau was a notable exception, but eventually it was buried in inside pages, then disappeared altogether. Although the coverage of the 1933 relief workers' strike was excellent, the *Daily News* used this event to show that the workers were ordinary local citizens and had rejected outside radical agitators. Overall, the newspaper coverage for the period was seriously misleading.

23. *Ann Arbor Daily News,* March 28, 1933, p. 1; March 30, 1933, p. 1; April 1, 1933, p. 1.

24. *Ibid.,* April 4, 1933, p. 10.

25. *Ibid.,* May 3, 1933, p. 1; May 5, 1933, p. 1; May 10, 1933, p. 1; May 11, 1933, p. 1.

26. *Ibid.,* May 10, 1933, p. 1; May 19, 1933, p. 1; June 10, 1933, p. 1. RFC funds were available under the Emergency Relief and Construction Act of 1932.

Unemployment Relief in Philadelphia, 1930–1932: A Study of the Depression's Impact on Voluntarism

Bonnie Fox Schwartz

In Philadelphia, President Hoover's theory of local responsibility for relief probably had as fair a test as was possible under the circumstances. The city had suffered serious unemployment before 1929, and by 1930 it ranked third among nineteen major cities in unemployment. Having discontinued public outdoor assistance in 1879, Philadelphia had a strong tradition of private philanthropy. In November 1930 a Committee of One Hundred paved the way for the establishment of a private agency, the Committee for Unemployment Relief. When the state authorized the city to borrow $3 million for relief, the distribution of this fund was assigned in June 1931 to Horatio Gates Lloyd, chairman of the Committee for Unemployment Relief.

The Lloyd Committee, employing new coordinative methods, undertook the "most imaginative and effective of municipal relief programs in the early years of the depression." Five subcommittees were responsible for relief, work, maintenance loans, care for homeless men, and breakfasts for needy schoolchildren. Yet despite efficient management—overhead charges amounted to only 6.85 per cent of the total outlay—the Lloyd Committee continually exhausted its funds as the number of applicants for aid steadily grew (at the rate of two thousand families per week by February 1932). The city's $3 million was gone in a year. An allocation of

[Reprinted from *Pennsylvania Magazine of History and Biography*, XCII (January 1969), 86–108.]

$5 million from the United Campaign Fund lasted three months —until April 1932, when relief payments were suspended for eleven days. $2.5 million in state aid then became available. This sum lasted two months. Beginning in mid-June 1932, 57,000 families were left to shift for themselves. By this time formerly staunch advocates of local responsibility were calling for federal assistance.

(Lloyd, who received a dollar a year for his fourteen-hour daily schedule of community service, insisted that there be no political interference with his disbursement of public funds. A different situation is described in a prize-winning article largely devoted to post-1932 developments: Raymond L. Koch, "Politics and Relief in Minneapolis During the 1930's," Minnesota History, *XLI [Winter 1968], 153–170).*

A relevant urban study, Roman Heleniak, "Local Reaction to the Great Depression in New Orleans, 1929–1933," Louisiana History, *X (Fall 1969), 289–306, focuses on relief activities, which began on March 6, 1930, when Mayor T. Semmes Walmsley called a conference of labor leaders and businessmen to deal with the problem of unemployment. Five subcommittees were created, one of which registered the unemployed. A total of 10,345 registered, a figure Heleniak considers low because of the reluctance of the jobless to sign up. The city government gave little assistance to the needy through 1930.*

In January 1931, civic leaders and businessmen formed the New Orleans Welfare Committee, with the city providing $10,000 in ready funds. This Committee raised about $500,000 in a year, the chief source of funds being a contribution by city employees of 5 per cent of their salary. By the end of March 1932, the New Orleans Welfare Committee was on the verge of collapse. In May a bond issue of $750,000 passed by a vote of 12,000 to 2,000, and in the summer of 1932 the New Orleans Welfare Committee replaced job-finding efforts with work relief, giving part-time work to about two thousand persons. This program "could not begin to solve the problem of unemployment in New Orleans." Some additional help was received from the State Unemployment Relief Committee when it obtained from the Reconstruction Finance Corporation a loan of $1 million, part of which was allocated to New Orleans. At the end of 1932 the State Unemployment Relief Committee employed more than seven thousand persons in the Orleans district, *and 8.3 per cent of the population benefited from this assistance. The State Unemployment Relief Committee figures suggest that New Orleans was far better off than the rest of the state, but they are misleading because the city did not receive a proportionate allotment from the Huey Long–dominated state government.*

The year 1932 "appeared to be the crucial period of the depression for New Orleans." The school system and the city government were in extremely difficult straits despite drastic fiscal belt-tightening, and the Community Chest's revenues were declining while demands for its services were increasing. Nevertheless, in the period 1930–1933 there was a minimum of protest, and the depression did not hit New Orleans as hard as it struck many other cities in the nation.

The idea of self-help has historically permeated American attitudes toward social welfare. Nineteenth-century "scientific philanthropy" implanted a basic hostility toward public outdoor relief in the Progressive mind. And throughout the prosperous twenties, social workers believed that only private charity should provide for the needy who did not require institutional care.[1] Staunchly adding support to this doctrine of voluntarism, President Hoover voiced his confidence in the superiority of the "American way" from the outset of the Great Depression.[2] Hoover's Quaker upbringing and previous successes in voluntary relief work—in Belgium, Russia, and along the banks of the Mississippi—helped convince him that "voluntary cooperative action would accomplish the dual purpose of relieving distress and exercising vital national traits." [3] In opposing paternal statism, he expressed the fear that any transfer of individual responsibilities and local obligations would undermine the safeguard "against overwhelming centralization and degeneration of that independence and initiative which are the very foundations of democracy." [4]

Although voluntarism was not as strongly emphasized in the twenties as before, it faced no serious challenge prior to 1930. In the two years following the Great Crash, urban settlements began struggling with mounting case loads and diminishing revenues. Questioning the validity of Hoover's doctrine, social workers rapidly lost any lingering aversion they may have felt toward "official assistance." By 1932 most welfare spokesmen asserted that unemployment relief could no longer be regarded as a form of charity. They recognized it as a public obligation to which the jobless were entitled as a matter of right. When the resources of local communities broke down, social workers did not hesitate to solicit from the states, and even the national government, additional funds for the emergency.[5]

Philadelphia's experience during this period provides an excellent case study of a "breakdown of local resources." [6] This metropolis had always taken pride in its impressive private philanthropic and settlement work, which dated back throughout the Gilded Age. When the city suffered the severe effects of economic depression even before the Great Crash, its welfare leaders instinctively reacted as they had in all previous panics. Initiating the most imaginative and efficient program of private community service, they made Philadelphia a model to other cities and future inspiration for New Deal projects. Both contemporary observers and subsequent historians have highly praised its unemployment relief organization. President Hoover congratulated the city, and depression historian Broadus Mitchell characterized it as "the utmost local effort." [7] Yet despite the strong traditions, ingenious leadership, and effective execution, Philadelphia's experiment in local cooperation completely failed by June 1932.

To cast back, a cursory glance at Philadelphia in the 1920's would convey the image of a prosperous metropolis. The City of Brotherly Love ranked as the third largest city in the nation and was a major industrial, financial, and distribution center. Almost half its 2,000,000 inhabitants depended on manufacturing and construction enterprises for their livelihood. Of all the assessed valuations in the city, nearly one third were in industry. A Federal Reserve Bank and a United States mint contributed to Philadelphia's financial prominence. And in addition to seaport facilities, numerous railroad terminals situated in or near the city handled the trade for the entire Delaware Valley.[8]

A closer examination, however, reveals that Philadelphians did not share in the national economic boom of the twenties. During this decade, the city's industries (as a whole) suffered a relative decline in importance compared with other production centers.

The biennial manufacturing census, taken in 1919 and alternate years, showed a substantial decrease in the number of wage earners employed by Philadelphia manufacturers.[9] A federal survey of unemployment made the following introductory comment:

> The existence of unemployed labor and unemployed productive equipment in such a highly industrialized community as Philadelphia . . . is not confined to these periods of cyclical depression [1914 and 1921]. Even in years of prosperity much of industry's manpower is idle and unproductive.[10]

This study, made in April 1929, revealed 10.4 per cent of Philadelphia's labor force unemployed—three quarters were idle because they could find no work.[11] Men constantly begged the welfare societies for any kind of jobs, not for relief. One man pleaded:

> Have you anybody you can send around to my family to tell my wife you have no job to give me? Because she does not believe that a man who walks the street from morning till night, day after day, actually can't get a job in this town. She thinks I don't want to work.[12]

Dr. J. Frederick Dewhurst, director of the federal survey, observed: "It seems significant that this unemployment, surveyed in good times, matched that of 1915, a period of severe depression and desperate idleness." [13]

Declines in textile mills and building contracts during the mid-twenties contributed especially to this local depression.[14] In the early summer of 1927, cloth manufacturing became irregular. Orders came so slowly that one would be completed before another arrived. Plant workers began losing a day occasionally. As the depression continued, laborers missed two and three days a week. A loom operator told a Lighthouse welfare worker that two of her four machines stood idle, and she remarked sadly, "Where there were formerly sixteen weavers employed, there are now but four." [15] St. Martha's House in South Philadelphia reported many cases of unemployment due to "the general business depression." [16]

Family and neighborhood life consequently suffered the effects of these industrial stoppages in the twenties. When more than 4,000 families were evicted as early as 1926, social workers lamented the irony of Philadelphia's reputation as a city of homes. By 1929 the figure doubled, as unemployed families continuously "felt the sheriff's hammer" and lost all the equity invested in their homes.[17] While those who had houses sheltered their evicted friends, caseworkers marveled at "the humanity of the poor toward the poor." So-called "combined families" comprised 30 per cent of the families on relief.[18] A welfare investigator reported:

> People slept on chairs; they slept on the floor. A case of a family of ten moving into a three-room apartment with a family of five was not exceptional. Daily calls came into the social agencies for beds and chairs. The demand for boxes on which people could sit was almost unbelievable.[19]

The sheer magnitude of distress exposed the inadequacy of unorganized private relief. Individual families, neighbors, landlords, and employers, even when they wished, proved incapable of grappling with relief on this scale. As the burden shifted to private neighborhood agencies, social workers questioned their capability of meeting future needs.[20] The Philadelphia Family Society, for example, had reached its maximum capacity of caring for 750 families a month by 1929. Unless an old case closed or some benevolent individual made a contribution, it could offer no further assistance.[21] Helen Hall of the University Settlement wrote:

> We like to feel that no neighbor knocks in vain at the settlement door, but these days . . . these knockings reach a crescendo. In years of apparent prosperity, they have become insistent.[22]

By 1930, a study of nineteen major cities revealed that the severity of Philadelphia's unemployment exceeded that of all others except Detroit and Cleveland.[23] *Business Week* reported in June 1930 that a count of the city's jobless "ran 40 per cent heavier than a year ago." [24] Although some explained their idleness by sickness or old age, 11.7 per cent of the labor force were unemployed because they could find no work.[25] The Great Crash of 1929 had aggravated Philadelphia's previous local decline; and the formation of eighty breadlines and soup kitchens signalized industrial failures and future hard times.[26] Because of the shortcomings of private relief programs, many jobless flocked to City Hall. Huddled in the corridors of the public mansion, Philadelphia's destitute waited their turns at the welfare application desk.[27] Since no tax revenues had been allocated for public assistance, the City Council had no funds to offer them.[28] This embarrassing display, however, forced the city fathers to abandon their policy and appropriate $150,000. In a few weeks, this small sum became exhausted, and Philadelphia approached the winter of 1930–1931 with a deficit.[29]

Although municipal officials lacked the foresight needed for concerted action, other individuals recognized the emergency. Jacob Billikopf of the Federation of Jewish Charities and Karl de Schweinitz of the Community Council of Philadelphia had been preaching "unemployment as an industrial and social disease to be attacked with measures for prevention and control." [30] By emphasizing coordinated activity and a steady enlargement of area cooperation, they stimulated public interest in organized relief. A plan for a council of social agencies in 1929 illustrated the influence of this growing trend.[31] Since that time, social workers, university professors, and businessmen had continued to support integrated welfare service. Their efforts culminated in the formation of the Committee of One Hundred with Jacob Billikopf as chairman.[32] On November 7, 1930, this committee initiated community action at a luncheon in the Bellevue-Stratford Hotel. The meeting attracted more than 200 persons of the city's leadership in industrial, professional, and business life.[33] And in an opening rally, the president of Strawbridge and Clothier declared: "The situation calls for the same spirit of fighting as that which engaged Philadelphia during the World War!" [34]

The conference first considered the possibility of extending the activities of the Municipal Department of Public Welfare.[35] But such an action would signify a radical departure for Philadelphians, who had discontinued public outdoor assistance in 1879.[36] Since that time, the city was known as one of a few metropolitan areas with practically no public relief disbursements.[37] During a recession (1914–1915), however, a private agency administered some appropriations.[38]

Clinging to the orthodox belief that there was something sinful about public relief, the city fathers thoroughly agreed with Herbert Hoover's theory of local responsibility.[39] Karl de Schweinitz, a longtime political reformer and public servant, stated: "My belief is that relief is normally a neighborhood affair. I would say first the neighborhood, then the municipality, then the state." [40] In a letter to the *Public Ledger* entitled "How to Help Philadelphia Relieve Unemployment," Constance Biddle suggested:

> Institutions have been built up by Philadelphians in their own city over long years. They have grown with the growth of the city and are ready and willing to serve this great need.[41]

Although severe unemployment created a grave emergency, most people doubted the depression would continue for a long time or that it would prove extensive or devastating.[42] Philadelphians thus adhered to their traditional attitudes toward relief and proceeded to remedy the present distress in accordance with President Hoover's philosophy. A comprehensive program of *private* rather than public participation unfolded, resulting in the establishment of the Committee for Unemployment Relief. Horatio Gates Lloyd, a partner of Drexel and Company (the Philadelphia branch of the House of Morgan), accepted the chairmanship and abandoned his lucrative business for a fourteen-hour daily schedule of community service.[43]

With a conservative outlook toward the Great Depression and its own welfare role, the Lloyd Committee considered its immediate task merely to raise sufficient funds from the people of Philadelphia "to tide over the temporary distress." [44] With this goal, the committee conducted a campaign which collected $4,000,000 in private donations.[45] Fearing the eventual exhaustion of this money, the members suggested a small municipal appropriation to supplement these funds. After months of numerous conferences between committee representatives and city and state officials, the Pennsylvania General Assembly passed the Sterling Bill, which authorized the city to borrow $3,000,000 for relief.[46] Despite many fears of the "iniquitous dole system" penetrating the community, the City Council yielded by adopting an ordinance creating a Bureau of Unemployment in the Municipal Department of Public Welfare.[47] Instead of the council's distributing its appropriation, however, Horatio Lloyd himself was appointed by the city as special administrator to disburse the public funds. He agreed to take this additional position provided there be no political interference.[48]

Philadelphia, therefore, functioned as a "community" during the winter of 1930–1931 largely through the coordination of voluntary private organizations.[49] Strictly in line with tradition, the municipal government, up to the middle of 1931, took only a minor part in the relief program. A *Survey* editorial commented:

> Thus Philadelphia steps out, first among large cities with its unemployment relief program geared to its revealed needs, freed through Mr. Lloyd's captaincy of any political entanglements. . . . The line between public and private responsibility is clearly drawn with complete confidence on both sides. Here, if ever, would seem to be a demonstration worth watching.[50]

With adequate financial support, the Lloyd Committee embarked upon "the most imaginative and effective of municipal relief programs in the early years of the depression."[51] This organization represented the greatest array of lay service and coordinated social work that Philadelphia ever experienced. Both the University of Pennsylvania and Swarthmore College sponsored research programs; and the entire press, especially J. David Stern's *Philadelphia Record*, vigorously supported Lloyd's organization. All the business, political, and welfare forces in the city rallied behind his leadership to serve in a single integrated movement.[52]

The establishment of the Lloyd Committee as a central planning organization represented a new coordinative method in private social work. Each settlement house, however specialized its immediate task, began to realize that its own work impinged upon many other undertakings. Individual caseworkers came to appreciate their role as part of "a great network serving the welfare of the people of Philadelphia."[53] Traditionally autonomous local agencies now participated in a cooperative movement.

Lloyd and his associates felt that "social planning based upon the scientific method" was the only means of coping with city-wide unemployment.[54] Sociological investigations, conducted by university professors, revealed valuable data which aided in forming the welfare programs.[55] Committee members examined these studies, considered past experiences, and eventually devised effective means of coping with the emergency. They undertook to provide for direct relief, made-work relief, a revolving loan fund, shelter for homeless men, and breakfasts for schoolchildren. Because these five programs made Philadelphia a model for other communities during the early years of the depression, they are worth considering in greater detail.[56]

For each activity, the Lloyd Committee created subcommittees to decide on policies and direct the actual procedures. A Subcommittee on Relief, for example, consisted of ten executives from private agencies engaged in family service. This group believed that direct relief had to be decentralized and disbursed through the existing local agencies. Where no agency existed, the committee itself assumed the responsibility by using the services of trained personnel.[57] The Subcommittee on Relief formulated a program to deal with the local settlements and also created a special unit of fifty social workers. This relief corps, paid from the committee's own funds, assisted in disbursing private contributions and special city appropriations among the needy.[58]

The actual distribution was highly coordinated. It involved the opening of four application centers located in different areas and staffed with workers directly employed by the committee. When private agencies lent their personnel, the committee paid a fixed sum toward their salaries; and the agency made up the balance.[59] A Social Service Exchange immediately cleared all the applications (received at the centers) through direct wire connections or by messengers.[60] Additional file clerks and typists, furnished by the committee, handled the increased volume of work. No relief was given out by the application centers. After an interview and report from the Exchange, an applicant received advice on his problem or was referred to a relief-dispensing agency. This reference was final, and the application center registered the family with the Social Service Exchange in the name of the agency to which it was assigned.[61]

Through a special voucher system, the committee reimbursed the local agencies for the funds expended. In the same manner, the committee assumed responsibility for the salaries of the additional personnel. This left the local agencies, with their original staffs and regular budgets, free to handle the burdens they had previously assumed. The Lloyd Committee paid all the added expenses due to the recent unemployment.[62]

The relief dispensed was "scarcely lavish." [63] For the most part, it consisted of weekly grocery orders which ranged in value from a dollar and a half for two adults to five dollars for a family of six. A sadly limited amount of coal, shoes, and second-hand clothing was also provided. Young children received milk only in cases of illness.[64] And the committee paid no rents at all, so that 25 per cent more food orders could be distributed in corresponding measure. The members believed: "It is more essential that the unemployed at least get something to eat." [65]

To employ the able-bodied of families that would otherwise require direct relief, the Lloyd Committee appropriated funds for a work program. The members intended that this form of assistance be as extensive as possible.[66] A Subcommittee on Work, supported by the Chamber of Commerce Committee on Unemployment, designed the details for this program. A prominent businessman assumed the chairmanship, and an Emergency Work Bureau was created. The director, a man of wide experience in industrial and personnel management, had previously visited several cities for possible suggestions. And his three chief assistants, who served as department heads, were also highly skilled and experienced in their several duties.[67] While welfare agencies loaned a number of social workers, business firms offered executives, personnel, and clerical workers who formed a nucleus for the bureau's organization. The made-work program involved an administrative staff of 300 persons, half being part-time volunteers. The majority of the remainder came from personnel departments and clerical forces of public service corporations and other large firms, like Sears, Roebuck.[68]

The Subcommittee on Work held certain positive convictions: "that the work should be decentralized, that alarming publicity should be avoided, and that time should be allowed for developing a sound scheme and organization." [69] Within a few weeks, however, the bureau received applications (only through local agencies), arranged for jobs, and actually put men to work. The most striking feature of this experiment, aside from its size, was the wide diversity of work provided. Not only did the program utilize common labor, but even skilled and professional workers found opportunities. The only criteria were that the work be something for which no money was available and which would not be accomplished without the labor supplied by the bureau.[70]

Manual labor engaged in more clean-up and repair work than in new construction. Demolition of buildings was avoided because of the danger of accident. The Division of Housing and Sanitation of the Department of Health used more than 1,200 men, whose wages amounted to $120,000, in jobs like removing rubbish from vacant lots, boarding up slum dwellings, cleaning alleys, and posting signs. While landscape gardeners trimmed and planted trees and hedges, the Department of Public Works and the Park Commission employed men to lay walks and drives, build and paint fences, and clean the woodlands. In private institutions, men made repairs and renovations, while women were assigned as domestic servants.[71]

Philadelphia offered more original employment for white-collar workers than any other city at this time. The local chapter of the Institute of Architects, for example, surveyed the city's colonial landmarks by using unemployed architects and draftsmen. For this job, each one received twenty dollars a week.[72] Expert typographers set Braille type for the blind, while dietitians and cooks participated in school feeding experiments. More than 118 jobless entertainers, musicians, and recreation leaders brought their talents to settlements, playgrounds, hospitals, and children's institutions. Their visits had a special value as a morale builder, both for the unemployed and for those whom they served.[73]

The Lloyd Committee tried to fashion its forms of assistance to complement the varied needs of the unemployed. While the work program and direct payments provided for the most impoverished, families with available resources were urged to negotiate a commercial loan. The committee believed, however, that there still existed an area of need intermediate between complete destitution on the one hand and unused credit resources on the other. The members considered the welfare of families which would fall in neither of these classes—"Working people who, except for the present crisis, would not be dependent and who would be too proud to accept charity, but whose needs are desperate." [74]

At the suggestion of Judge Horace Stern, a fund was created to issue loans to such families.[75] Since its primary purpose was to prevent the necessity of appealing for relief, the fund attempted to preserve the self-respect and prevent the keen mental suffering of those families which would feel humiliated by having to make such an appeal.[76] The committee hoped these loans might prevent families of proved financial integrity and responsibility from lapsing into a dependent state.

Loans from this revolving fund differed materially from those previously in existence sanctioned by the Small Loans Act of Pennsylvania. They were issued upon the personal signatures of the husband and wife with no interest or an optional maximum rate of 3 per cent net. After the borrower obtained a job or found other resources, he repaid the money in weekly installments. During the period from January to May 1931, a total of 563 loans ranging from $18 to $175 each were granted to 517 families. This particular program was one of Philadelphia's unique experiments that received national attention.[77]

Another nationally publicized program, and one that effected dramatic changes, involved the care of homeless men. Prior to the committee's attention, the city had grossly neglected the transients who roamed the streets.[78] By the fall of 1930, more than 500 men spent each night sleeping on the bare concrete floors of police station cellars.[79] Mayor Harry Mackey commented on this tragic inadequacy: "These men, who through no fault of their own are out of work, . . . are not to be classified with the 'down and outer' as we know him in normal conditions. . . . They sought relief only when all efforts failed to procure employment." [80] Alarmed by this fact, the Lloyd Committee took immediate action and appointed a special planning committee. A mission superintendent with unusual executive ability, community leadership, and years of experience in dealing with transients became the chairman. His Subcommittee for the Homeless included religious leaders, social workers, business executives, and recreation organizers.[81]

The core of their program centered about an emergency shelter in an enormous eight-story building loaned by the Baldwin Locomotive Works. Crews of homeless men, from the missions and police stations, rapidly removed the accumulated grease and grime and installed plumbing and heating. While the superintendent secured 3,000 cots from the War Department, the Red Cross furnished commissary equipment. Before opening the shelter, the Committee decided not to replace the work of existing missions, but to handle only additional transiency caused by the depression. The members also agreed that every man should work for three or four hours a day in exchange for meals and lodging.[82]

The committee anticipated that no more than 500 would need shelter, but when the lodge opened on November 28, 1930, 831 men applied. Although they originally intended to use only three floors, all eight stories were eventually equipped for service. At its peak, the shelter handled nearly 3,000 men a night, while regular missions continued to house their capacity loads.[83]

Mayor Mackey took a particular interest in the shelter. Disguising himself as a vagrant, he spent several nights there to see how the homeless men fared. Reporters, who compared his make-up talents to Lon Chaney's, wrote: "Unshaven and roughly dressed, wearing a bushy false mustache and sideburns and using a red bandana handkerchief, Mayor Mackey has been eating and sleeping frequently of late with the penniless unemployed men." [84] Each Friday night, the mayor provided entertainment for the lodgers. In addition, Charles H. English, executive secretary of the Playground Association, taught the men how to entertain themselves. As a result of his suggestions, the men staged "everything from boxing bouts to minstrel shows." [85] These activities played a vital role in maintaining morale and keeping the transients mentally fit for their return to industry.

A citywide provision of breakfasts to needy schoolchildren represented another of Philadelphia's innovations in social welfare. Nowhere else in the United States was this particular form of relief so extensively applied. Remarking that school breakfasts "represented an excursion into a hitherto unexplored field of relief giving," teachers and social workers watched the committee's procedures with special interest.[86]

Because evidence had shown increased malnutrition among schoolchildren, the Lloyd Committee decided to introduce a breakfast program. Economic need, however, became the sole basis for selecting the participants. Philadelphia school authorities decided to assist in this project as an "expedient means of meeting an emergent need." [87] They held no conviction that relief measures were a function of the Board of Education.

The comprehensive program, designed by an appropriate subcommittee, attempted to provide breakfasts for every needy child. While an average of 8,000 were fed each school day, almost 4,500 also received breakfasts on Saturdays and Sundays. These meals were provided under the direction of the Division of School Medical Inspection, and principals and teachers personally supervised the activities in each school. The enterprise cost approximately $100,000, one-third assumed by the Lloyd Committee. Unsolicited private subscriptions and actual food donations made up the balance.[88] Under the supervision of the Diocesan Superintendent of Schools, breakfasts were extended to parochial schoolchildren of the Roman Catholic Church. Following similar arrangements as those made with the public schools, the Lloyd Committee contributed toward this work also.[89]

These five programs illustrated the intimate working relationship that existed between businessmen, social workers, school personnel, and city officials. From these various projects, the Lloyd Committee acquired a fund of knowledge and experience which would affect measures for alleviating distress in years to come. Businessmen assumed a greater social responsibility in meeting the present needs than ever before. And their future role in these relief activities would surely increase.[90] Because the Lloyd Committee fostered citywide cooperation, it created a new coordinated network for Philadelphia's welfare programs. Karl de Schweinitz felt that a precedent had been established for future settlement work in all large urban areas:

> Out of our present misery . . . will come a better organization of society. Social work was never in a better position to assume leadership and to influence the course of events. Not in a generation have we experienced such an integration of social work, business, and politics. Social work will be modified in its expression by the institutions through which it will now operate.[91]

The Lloyd Committee served as both a financial and coordinative body. Relief distribution was completely in Lloyd's charge.[92] As its five major programs illustrate, the organization supervised and coordinated all the city's private agencies also. To staff all these projects, Lloyd built a corps of 250 workers "beholden to no political machine or privileged group." [93] And these extensive efforts were accomplished in an efficient manner with a minimum overhead expense. *The Philadelphia Record* commented that the committee

> struck the happy mean in administering relief to the unemployed. A larger staff would have cost more in administrative expenses than would have been saved by closer investigation. And fewer workers would have permitted many families not entitled to aid to receive relief funds.[94]

In fact, the committee's overhead charges, including general supplies and the workers' payroll, averaged only 6.8 per cent of its total outlay. The remainder of the funds could thus go toward all the relief projects. Startled by such efficiency, a journalist in *The Nation* stated, "This is probably a better record than can be shown by any similar organization in the country." [95]

The Lloyd Committee's highly organized program made Philadelphia a national model. But despite this remarkable achievement and efficient management, its financial resources quickly reached the point of exhaustion. By the end of the first year, the city's $3,000,000 appropriation was gone, and Lloyd's organization "resorted to panhandling on a large scale." [96] Joining the Welfare Federation and the Federation of Jewish Charities, the committee helped to launch a "United Campaign" in November 1931.[97] The three groups set a combined goal of $9,000,000 to be proportionally divided between them. To arouse the public to the tragedy in their midst, the committee used shocking human-interest stories for propaganda purposes.[98] Mayor Mackey dramatized the appeal by warning the wealthy to "give for their own safety." [99] At a fund-raising dinner he told the audience:

> Empty stomachs cry for food, scantily clad people demand clothing, and cold men, women, and children must have fuel. . . . The responsibility of the moment knocks at our door. Today marks the hour for performance, while tomorrow must take care of itself.[100]

The campaign officials at first doubted that such a large sum was attainable. But as public enthusiasm grew, many corporations, firms, and individuals of all classes made contributions. *The Philadelphia Record* reported: "In a scene reminiscent of the war chest campaigns of 1917–1918, $255,000 was raised in ten minutes yesterday for the relief of distress among the unemployed of Philadelphia." [101] The final results demonstrated Philadelphians' strong adherence to the theory of private local responsibility. By accumulating more than $10,000,000 in cash and pledges, the United Campaign eventually exceeded its goal. This drive collected "the largest sum ever raised in Philadelphia for charitable work." [102] Karl de Schweinitz rejoiced: "I do not recall an occasion when the citizenship at large rose to such emotional heights as it did on that particular day when it announced that $10,250,000 had been raised." [103]

Upon receiving its $5,000,000 share from the United Campaign collection, the Lloyd Committee felt more optimistic.[104] But amid this slight ease of tension, grave statistical realities pointed toward an uncertain future. When the campaigners projected their drive, 2,700 families were relying on the committee for support. By December 1931, when President Hoover and POUR (President's Organization on Unemployment Relief) officials congratulated Philadelphia on its "charitable performance," the number had reached 4,000.[105] And in early February 1932, Karl de Schweinitz reported to the House Committee on Labor: "We are spending at the rate of thirty-five thousand dollars a day, which is over a million dollars a month. You can see that the figure is going up." [106] Lloyd addressed an urgent appeal to Governor Gifford Pinchot:

> With forty-eight hundred families now receiving assistance and an additional two thousand coming under its [the Lloyd Committee's] care each week, Philadelphia is rapidly approaching a situation where, unless help comes speedily, thousands of men, women, and children will actually face starvation. . . . The money from the recent United Campaign will be exhausted by May.[107]

The $5,000,000 barely lasted three months! By April 1932, the committee had almost completely expended its allotment.[108] In an emergency meeting, Lloyd and his associates quickly adopted three temporary measures to give them a reason for existence. With their few remaining dollars, they supplied milk to families with infants and small children. The shelter remained open on a day-to-day basis. And since the National Red Cross had donated government flour, the committee took charge of its distribution.[109] But now more than 5,000 families actually faced starvation. Their funds exhausted, the Lloyd Committee discontinued regular food orders.

Testifying before the LaFollette-Costigan Committee, Karl de Schweinitz related an "intensified picture of human misery" when he described how these families managed:

> One woman went along the docks and picked up vegetables that fell from wagons. Sometimes fish vendors gave her fish at the end of the day. On two different occasions the family was without food for a day and a half. . . . Another family did not have food for two days.

Then the husband went out and gathered dandelions and the family lived on them.[110]

The only hope for the future lay in possible state aid. Anxiously reading the daily papers, the starving families prayed for headlines announcing the constitutionality of the Talbot Act.[111] This law, which had passed the Pennsylvania General Assembly in December 1931, appropriated $10,000,000 to be allotted to the State Department of Welfare for distribution to the "poor districts" of Pennsylvania.[112] The act was promptly challenged on the grounds that the state constitution prohibited such charitable grants to individuals. In April 1932—just when the Lloyd Committee ran out of funds and unemployed families faced starvation—the state supreme court began deliberating the test case to decide the constitutionality of the Talbot Act. Finally, on April 7, 1932, by a four-to-three vote, the court upheld the appropriation: "There is no direct prohibition against the use of state money to pay for the care and maintenance of indigent, infirm, and mentally defective persons, without ability or means to sustain themselves. . . ."[113] The court stretched the police powers to sanction this state aid as part of the protection of the health, safety, and welfare of the people. This incident illustrates the constitutional limitations and long, devious channels that confronted such bills and frequently delayed funds from reaching the needy unemployed.[114]

Eleven days after the Lloyd Committee suspended relief payments, Philadelphia received its share of the state fund, $2,500,000.[115] An administrative disagreement arose when a few local poor boards in the city insisted on their right to handle their individual shares. Except in four districts, where neighborhood agencies held their ground, differences were finally resolved.[116] Lloyd again administered the money, except for these four areas. He insisted upon the same condition as before—that there be no political interference.[117]

When the Lloyd Committee resumed its work, families received food orders once again, but welfare officials clearly realized the severe limitations of the small appropriation. Where would they turn when these Talbot funds ran out? Karl de Schweinitz considered alternatives: "The financial situation of Philadelphia is such that no great help can be hoped for from the city. Since pledges to the United Campaign continue to fall due until next October, it is difficult to see how additional private funds could be raised. . . . Taking the community as a whole there seems to be no united sentiment in favor of federal relief." [118]

The Talbot funds barely lasted two months. "An army of grim hunger and agony was invading" Philadelphia; on June 20, 1932, it attacked 57,000 defenseless families.[119] *The Philadelphia Record* headlined the frightening details that morning:

> The Lloyd Committee is through. For fifty-seven thousand families to whom the Committee has meant life itself, STARVATION is "just around the corner." The Committee for two years has fought the wolf away from the doorsteps of Philadelphia's worthy poor. It has tapped and exhausted every available source of succor. And now its funds are gone.[120]

The Lloyd Committee decided to disband. Fearing it would cruelly mislead dependent families to believe that help was in sight, the organization stopped dispensing all forms of assistance and closed the shelter.[121]

For ten agonizing weeks, 57,000 families were left to shift for themselves in the summer of 1932. Philadelphians wondered "what was happening to these families? There were no reports of people starving in the streets, and yet from what possible source were they getting enough food to live on?" [122]

A survey of 400 representative families provided tragic answers to these questions. These people lived from one day to another with no dependable income and all possible credit exhausted. While shelter was assured as long as landlords remained lenient, the question of food required more drastic remedies. A common source of food was the docks, where fruit and vegetables were sold for market. People gathered around stalls and snatched at anything cast out. Hunger occasionally motivated street begging and petty thievery of milk and groceries from doorsteps. Playing on the sympathy of storekeepers, children forced tears down their cheeks to induce them to offer a little food.[123] After citing these examples, the study concluded:

> Families visited did not starve to death when relief stopped. They kept alive from day to day, catch-as-catch can, reduced for actual

subsistence to something of a stray cat prowling for food, for which a kindly soul sets out a plate of table scraps or a saucer of milk.[124]

Philadelphia's critical emergency shocked its most traditionally oriented citizens and aroused them to advocate *direct federal* relief. Despite its drive and ingenuity, the Lloyd Committee had fought a losing battle. Although it had made innovations in social work techniques, the local effort could not meet the needs of Philadelphia's unemployed. The number of destitute families continuously outgrew the available resources. The city itself was so bankrupt that the mayor had to declare that no one was starving to bolster the courage of reluctant bankers to buy municipal bonds.[125] The Pennsylvania legislature also failed to rectify the situation quickly. Other constitutional limitations still remained which prevented the state from incurring large debts.[126] A social reformer remarked: "When that constitution was framed, they had no thought of any such emergency as this arising." [127] As a final consequence, Billikopf, de Schweinitz, and even Lloyd led Philadelphians in becoming insistent champions of direct federal relief.

As early as 1931, Jacob Billikopf had recognized the enormity of the unemployment relief problem when he stated: "Private philanthropy is no longer capable of coping with the situation. It is virtually bankrupt in the face of great disaster." [128] And Karl de Schweinitz also realized the practical ineffectiveness of the theory of local responsibility: "We do not pretend to be perfect in the administration of unemployment relief in Philadelphia, but humanly speaking I do not see how we could have done anything better. . . . It was physically impossible to handle this great number of people." [129]

The most exemplary change in approach, however, was that of Lloyd, the chairman. He had previously been characterized as a conservative banker, typical of his class, with little concern for the masses. But after his experience with the Unemployment Committee, he also acknowledged the limitations of private charity and the American tradition of self-help.[130] As his committee disbanded Lloyd made a final statement:

The situation today is quite different from what it appeared to be when the Committee was first formed. The duration of the depres-

> sion, the vast and increasing numbers of unemployed, and the general economic conditions are such that it requires no argument for the realization that the situation has progressed far beyond any possibility of relief from sources of private philanthropy, even for the most primitive necessities of life.
>
> The present need is on a scale that calls not for more charity but for governmental action to save the health and indeed the lives of a large portion of the citizenry.[131]

Philadelphia's experience during 1930–1932 illustrated the practical failure of Hoover's theory of local responsibility. When faced by a crisis of such magnitude, private and municipal resources broke down. The needs of the unemployed overwhelmed traditional community institutions even when organized at peak efficiency. A national problem could not be managed with local means, and unemployment relief had ceased to be "an emergency to be dealt with by stopgap measures." [132]

NOTES

1. Merle Curti, "American Philanthropy and the National Character," *American Quarterly,* X (1958), 427–428; Robert H. Bremner, *From the Depths: The Discovery of Poverty in the United States* (New York, 1956), pp. 261–262.

2. Richard Hofstadter, *The American Political Tradition and the Men Who Made It* (New York, 1948), p. 295.

3. Albert U. Romasco, *The Poverty of Abundance: Hoover, the Nation, the Depression* (New York, 1965), p. 143.

4. Quoted in Irving Bernstein, *The Lean Years: A History of the American Worker, 1920–1933* (Boston, 1960), p. 287.

5. Bremner, pp. 261–262; Frank J. Bruno, *Trends in Social Work, 1874–1956* (New York, 1957), pp. 330–331.

6. Bernstein, p. 287.

7. *New York Times,* December 9, 1931, p. 3; Broadus Mitchell, *Depression Decade: From New Era Through New Deal, 1929–1941* (New York, 1947), p. 100.

8. U.S. Bureau of Labor Statistics, *Bulletin,* No. 520, "Social and Economic Character of Unemployment in Philadelphia," prepared by J. Frederick Dewhurst and Ernest A. Tupper (Washington, 1930), pp. 5–6; U.S. Bureau of Labor Statistics, *Bulletin,* No. 555, "Social and Economic Character of Unemployment in Philadelphia," prepared by J. Frederick Dewhurst and Robert R. Nathan (Washington, 1932). p. 7.

9. U.S. Bureau of Labor Statistics, *Bulletin,* No. 520, p. 6.

10. *Ibid.,* p. iii.

11. *Ibid.,* p. 17.

12. Harry L. Hopkins, *Spending To Save: The Complete Story of Relief* (New York, 1936), p. 84.

13. Clinch Calkins, *Some Folks Won't Work* (New York, 1930), p. 14.
14. Karl de Schweinitz, "Philadelphia Takes Heart," *The Survey,* LXVI (May 15, 1931), 217.
15. Marion Elderton, ed., *Case Studies of Unemployment* (Philadelphia, 1931), p. 47.
16. *Ibid.*, pp. 147–148, 234–235.
17. Jacob Billikopf, "The Social Duty to the Unemployed," *The Annals of the American Academy of Political and Social Science,* CVIV (1931), 67.
18. This term referred to a situation where two to four families lived under one roof as one household. Florence Peterson, "Unemployment Relief—Local and State," in John R. Commons, ed., *History of Labor in the United States, 1896–1932* (New York, 1935), p. 234.
19. Maxine Davis, *They Shall Not Want* (New York, 1937), p. 24.
20. Bernstein, p. 291.
21. Gertrude Springer, "The Burden of Mass Relief," *The Survey,* LXV (November 15, 1930), 201.
22. Helen Hall and Irene Hickok Nelson, "How Unemployment Strikes Home," *The Survey,* LXII (April 1, 1929), 51.
23. De Schweinitz, *The Survey,* LXVI, 217.
24. "Philadelphia's Survey Shows Peak of Unemployment Passed," *The Business Week,* June 11, 1930, p. 10.
25. U.S. Bureau of Labor Statistics, *Bulletin,* No. 555, p. 17; Calkins, p. 13.
26. Community Council of Philadelphia, *A New Approach to Social Problems* (Philadelphia, 1932), p. 3; Harry A. Mackey, "Stop! Look! Listen!" (a radio address), November 3, 1930, Gifford Pinchot Papers, Box 2523E17, Library of Congress.
27. Calkins, pp. 9–10.
28. Joanna C. Colcord, William C. Koplovitz, and Russell H. Kurtz, *Emergency Work Relief as Carried Out in Twenty-Six American Communities, 1930–1931* (New York, 1932), p. 166.
29. Peterson, p. 228.
30. Colcord, Koplovitz, and Kurtz, pp. 166–167; De Schweinitz, *The Survey,* LXVI, 217.
31. "A Council for Philadelphia," *The Survey,* LXVI (May 15, 1930), 181; "Philadelphia's Council," *The Survey,* LXII (April 15, 1929), 110.
32. De Schweinitz, *The Survey,* LXVI, 217.
33. *Philadelphia Public Ledger,* November 8, 1930, p. 3.
34. *Philadelphia Inquirer,* November 8, 1930, p. 2.
35. De Schweinitz, *The Survey,* LXVI, 217.
36. In the crisis of 1894, Philadelphia relied entirely upon private contributions and private agencies. Leah Hannah Feder, *Unemployment Relief in Periods of Depression: A Study of Measures Adopted in Certain American Cities, 1857 Through 1922* (New York, 1936), pp. 104, 126.
37. Davis, p. 24.
38. The City Council's appropriation of $150,000 in 1930 represented another exception. Feder, p. 310.
39. U.S., Congress, Senate, Subcommittee of the Committee on Manufactures, *Hearings, Unemployment Relief,* 72nd Cong., 1st sess., 1932, p. 52.
40. *Ibid.*, p. 137.
41. *Philadelphia Public Ledger,* November 14, 1930, p. 12.
42. *Philadelphia Record,* June 20, 1932, p. 1.

43. For this position, he received a dollar a year. De Schweinitz, *The Survey,* LXVI, 217.

44. *Philadelphia Public Ledger,* June 20, 1932, p. 4.

45. Joanna C. Colcord, *Cash Relief* (New York, 1936), p. 132; Bruno, p. 301.

46. *Philadelphia Record,* March 27, 1931, p. 1; "Shaking Hands with Starvation," *The Survey,* LXVI (June 15, 1931), 301.

47. Jacob Billikopf, "What Have We Learned About Unemployment?," *Proceedings of the National Conference of Social Work* (Chicago, 1931), p. 37; "Cities Watch Capital But Push Own Winter Programs," *The Business Week,* August 26, 1931, p. 7.

48. *New York Times,* June 30, 1931, p. 2.

49. Ewan Clague and Webster Powell, *Ten Thousand Out of Work* (Philadelphia, 1933), p. 87. The Russell Sage Foundation figures showed that in the spring of 1931 the country as a whole had 72 per cent of its unemployment relief coming from public sources and 28 per cent from private. In Philadelphia, the proportions at this time were 45 per cent public and 55 per cent private.

50. "Forehanded Philadelphia," *The Survey,* LXVI (August 15, 1931), 459.

51. Bernstein, p. 298.

52. *Ibid.*

53. Community Council of Philadelphia, pp. 2–3.

54. *Ibid.*

55. Ewan Clague, "Philadelphia Studies Its Breadlines," *The Survey,* LXVII (November 15, 1931), 197.

56. Copies of the studies and outlines of the programs were requested by officials of the President's Organization on Unemployment Relief (POUR). Karl de Schweinitz to Fred C. Croxton, November 7, 1931, POUR Papers, National Archives; Olga A. Jones to Karl de Schweinitz, November 16, 1931, and Karl de Schweinitz to Olga A. Jones, November 23, 1931, *ibid.*

57. Colcord, Koplovitz, and Kurtz, p. 180.

58. Harry A. Mackey, *Great Characters the Spirit of Giving Has Revealed in Philadelphia, 1930–1931,* p. 8.

59. Colcord, Koplovitz, and Kurtz, pp. 180–181.

60. De Schweinitz, *The Survey,* LXVI, 218.

61. Colcord, Koplovitz, and Kurtz, p. 181.

62. *Ibid.*

63. Davis, p. 24.

64. *Ibid.*

65. Mauritz A. Hallgren, "Mass Misery in Philadelphia," *The Nation,* CXXXIV (March 9, 1932), 277.

66. Clague and Powell, p. 135.

67. Colcord, Koplovitz, and Kurtz, p. 167.

68. De Schweinitz, *The Survey,* LXVI, 218.

69. Colcord, Koplovitz, and Kurtz, p. 167.

70. *Ibid.*

71. *Ibid.,* p. 172.

72. H. Louis Duhring to Herbert Hoover, June 9, 1932, POUR Papers.

73. Colcord, Koplovitz, and Kurtz, p. 173.

74. Community Council of Philadelphia, *Personal Loans in Unemployment Relief* (Philadelphia, 1932), p. 4; Davis, p. 25.

75. Judge Stern subsequently headed the subcommittee for this program. "Revolving Loan Fund Suggested for Philadelphia's Unemployed," *The Business Week,* November 19, 1930, p. 18; de Schweinitz, *The Survey,* LXVI, 218.

76. Community Council of Philadelphia, *Personal Loans in Unemployment Relief*, p. 40.
77. *Ibid.*, p. 5.
78. De Schweinitz, *The Survey*, LXVI, 217–218.
79. *Philadelphia Public Ledger*, November 8, 1930, p. 3.
80. Mackey, p. 8.
81. Charles H. English, "Recreation in the Unemployment Relief Program," *Recreation*, XXV (December 1931), 493.
82. Robert S. Wilson, *Community Planning for Homeless Men and Boys: The Experience of Sixteen Cities in the Winter of 1930–31* (New York, 1931), p. 102.
83. *Ibid.*
84. *Philadelphia Record*, February 26, 1931, p. 1; *New York Times*, February 26, 1931, p. 4.
85. De Schweinitz, *The Survey*, LXVI, 218.
86. Community Council of Philadelphia, *A Cooperative Study of School Breakfasts* (Philadelphia, 1932), p. 1.
87. *Ibid.*
88. *Ibid.*, p. 3; James M. Williams, *Human Aspects of Unemployment and Relief* (Chapel Hill, 1933), p. 199.
89. De Schweinitz, *The Survey*, LXVI, 217.
90. *Ibid.*, p. 219; English, *Recreation*, XXV, 492.
91. Quoted in Gertrude Springer, "The Challenge of Hard Times," *The Survey*, LXVI (June 15, 1931), 385.
92. Hallgren, *The Nation*, CXXXIV, 276.
93. *Ibid.*
94. *Philadelphia Record*, April 16, 1932, p. 6.
95. Hallgren, *The Nation*, CXXXIV, 276.
96. *Ibid.*
97. Billikopf, *Proceedings of the National Conference of Social Work*, p. 37.
98. Williams, p. 185.
99. *Philadelphia Record*, February 16, 1931, p. 1.
100. Remarks of Mayor Harry A. Mackey before a United Campaign dinner, November 9, 1931, Gifford Pinchot Papers, Box 2523E17.
101. *Philadelphia Record*, February 12, 1931. p. 1.
102. U.S., Congress, House, Subcommittee of the Committee on Labor, *Hearings, Unemployment in the United States*, 72nd Cong., 1st sess., 1932, p. 94; telegram from L. H. Kinnard to W. S. Gifford of POUR, December 8, 1931, POUR Papers.
103. Committee on Manufactures, *Unemployment Relief Hearings*, 1932, p. 116.
104. *Ibid.*
105. *Ibid.*, *New York Times*, December 9, 1931, p. 3; Walter S. Gifford to Philip C. Staples, Vice-President of the Bell Telephone Company of Pennsylvania, December 8, 1931, POUR Papers.
106. House Committee on Labor, *Unemployment Hearings*, 1932, p. 93.
107. *Ibid.*
108. H. L. Lurie, "Spreading Relief Thin," *The Social Service Review*, VI (June 1932), 232.
109. *Philadelphia Record*, April 12, 1932, p. 1.
110. *Ibid.*, May 10, 1932, p. 1; U.S., Congress, Senate, Subcommittee of the Committee on Manufactures, *Hearings, Federal Cooperation in Unemployment Relief*, 72nd Cong., 1st sess., 1932, pp. 20–26.

111. *Philadelphia Record,* April 11, 1932, p. 1; *ibid.,* April 12, 1932, p. 6; Arthur Dunham, "Pennsylvania and Unemployment Relief, 1929–34," *The Social Service Review,* VIII (June 1934), 249.

112. Edith Abbott, *Public Assistance* (Chicago, 1940), p. 256; Richard C. Keller, "Pennsylvania's Little New Deal" (unpublished Ph.D. dissertation, Columbia University, 1961), pp. 75–76.

113. Quoted in Dunham, *The Social Service Review,* VIII, 250.

114. Peterson, p. 231; Romasco, p. 171.

115. "Pennsylvania's Ten Millions," *The Survey,* LXVIII (May 15, 1932), 178.

116. *Ibid.*

117. *Philadelphia Record,* April 16, 1932, p. 1.

118. "How the Cities Stand," *The Survey,* LXVIII, 75.

119. *Philadelphia Public Ledger,* June 20, 1932, p. 1.

120. *Philadelphia Record,* June 20, 1932, p. 1.

121. *Ibid.; Philadelphia Public Ledger,* June 20, 1932, p. 4.

122. Ewan Clague, "When Relief Stops What Do They Eat?," *The Survey,* LXVIII (November 15, 1932), 583.

123. *Ibid.,* 584.

124. *Ibid.,* 585.

125. Subcommittee of the Committee on Manufactures, *Hearings, Federal Cooperation in Unemployment Relief,* 1932, p. 22.

126. Romasco, pp. 170–171.

127. From statement of Fred Brenckman, Washington representative of the National Grange, Committee on Manufactures, *Federal Cooperation Hearings,* 1932, p. 13.

128. Billikopf, *Proceedings of the National Conference of Social Work,* p. 39; Jacob Billikopf to Walter S. Gifford of POUR, August 27, 1931, POUR Papers.

129. U.S., Congress, Senate, Subcommittee of the Committee on Manufactures, *Hearings, Federal Aid for Unemployment Relief,* 72nd Cong., 2nd sess., 1933, pp. 115–116.

130. Hallgren, *The Nation,* CXXXIV, 276.

131. Quoted in Gertrude Springer, "Getting the Most from Federal Relief," *The Survey,* LXVIII (July 15, 1932), 325.

132. *Ibid.;* Gifford Pinchot to Jacob Billikopf, January 11, 1932, Gifford Pinchot Papers, Box 2561E25.

Communists and Fascists in a Southern City: Atlanta, 1930

John Hammond Moore

The developments described in this selection encompassed the new and the old. A new element was the Communist activities that triggered the sequence of events recounted here, activities for which another new element, the Great Depression, provided the occasion. The old, overriding factor was race relations: repression of radical or pro-Negro activity accompanied by protests against repression, and toleration of anti-Negro activity accompanied by condemnation were familiar pairings. Also familiar was the kind of white organization that emerged, although its adoption of black shirts and its name were a departure from the dress and appellation of the sheeted Ku Klux Klan. The impact of the depression was evident in the Black Shirts' threat to replace Negro workers with whites. Officially, the organization, under pressure, modified this threat, denying any intention of displacing Negroes already at work. In any event, the Black Shirts did not match the terrorism practiced by whites in Mississippi, where systematic brutality, including seven murders by mid-1933, was employed to force Negro locomotive firemen out of their jobs on the Illinois Central (Irving Bernstein, The Lean Years *[Baltimore: Penguin Books, 1966], p. 423).*

Some economic arguments against the Black Shirts were of a general kind, referring to mutual dependence and efficiency. The Macon Telegraph *declared, "If the Negro doesn't work and make*

[From *South Atlantic Quarterly,* LXVII (Summer 1968), 437-454.]

his living. the white man must work and make it for him," while the Atlanta Journal *pointed to the inefficiency of replacing experienced Negro workers with inexperienced whites. The* Bainbridge Post-Searchlight *offered a precise, personal argument that indicated the Negro's status in the South's economy: "Mr. Black Shirt man, we hereby invite you down here to take the nigger's place in the cotton patch. . . . Eighty per cent of the Negro jobs would not be accepted by white folks. . . ."*

The emergence of communist and fascist groups in Georgia's capital city represents a weird mixture of both national and international tensions. Benito Mussolini, Joseph Stalin, the Ku Klux Klan, economic troubles, and a drive to unionize Southern industry are all part of this complex tale. The Duce unwittingly gave the Atlanta "Fascisti," or Black Shirts, their name, but little more. It is apparent they knew practically nothing about Italy, its leader, or his program; and it is most unlikely that Mussolini ever heard of his Georgia contingent. Stalin, while probably equally ignorant of the Black Shirts, was more directly involved. For had he not goaded American Communists into taking an active interest in the Southern Negro, this short-lived band of reactionaries might never have appeared.

The potential of the Negro as a Communist was discussed by both Lenin and Stalin in the early twenties, but because of the turbulence of Russian life no firm policy was established.[1] In 1925 Stalin told a group of American Negroes that the "Black South" possessed some of the characteristics of a nation, and three years later "black nationalism" became an avowed goal despite the misgivings of American Communists.[2] Resolutions of the Executive Committee of the Communist International emphasized that the Negro worker in the Eastern and Northern United States was now able to play "a considerable role" in the class struggle against American imperialism and could also aid his oppressed brother in the South.[3] The committee vigorously attacked Jim Crow practices, made a strong plea for trade unions among Negroes, and stressed that the American Negro question was part of a worldwide problem. More important, it sketched plans for black revolution in the

South and ordered American Communists to end "white chauvinism." Resolutions specifically censured Party members of Detroit and Gary for refusal to associate with Negro comrades.

During 1929, although details are wrapped in obscurity, it is obvious the dictates of Moscow were being followed, and by 1930 a variety of booklets and pamphlets had translated the dry verbiage of the Communist International into phrases which startled and infuriated white Americans, especially Southerners. Those who saw *The Communist Position on the Negro Question* found it particularly offensive. The cover of this booklet clearly indicated black counties and carried this subtitle: *Self-Determination for the Black Belt.*

> In the South the fi[g]ht must be fearlessly developed against the thievery and robbery of the Southern capitalists and landlords; against the lynch terror. We must fight not merely inequality, but against the whole system by which this inequality is enforced.
>
> In the first place, our demand is that the land of the Southern white landlords for years tilled by the Negro tenant farmers, be confiscated and turned over to the Negroes. This is the only way to insure economic and social equality for the tenant farmers.
>
> Secondly, we proposed [*sic*] to break up the present artificial state boundaries established for the convenience of the white master class, and to establish the state unity of the territory known as the "Black Belt," where the Negroes constitute the overwhelming majority of the population.
>
> Thirdly, in this territory, we demand that the Negroes be given the complete right of self-determination; the right to set up their own Government in this territory and the right to separate, if they wish, from the United States. . . .[4]

This booklet conceded that within the limits of the proposed Negro nation "there will of course remain a fairly significant white minority which must submit to the right of self-determination of the Negro majority. There is no other possible way of carrying out in any democratic manner the right of self-determination of the Negroes."

Faithful to the words of the Kremlin, American Communists concentrated their first efforts among Negro and white tenant farmers and workers in industrial centers such as Birmingham and Chattanooga. Of course, rural campaigns elicited little support and encountered violent opposition from landlords. Within a short time urban authorities were applying their own unique brand of legal pressure and harassment. Although Atlanta was not a prime center of Communist interest, by January 1, 1930, city police were alert to the first stirrings of activity.[5] Their task was made easier some six weeks later when a disillusioned Negro turned informer.[6]

R. C. Miller, a Spanish-American War veteran, claimed to be the first member of his race to join up during the 1929 drive. He became associated with the Party at the Jewish Workers' Club, 473 Capitol Avenue, and was subsequently named organizer for the sixteenth district with headquarters in Charlotte. Miller told the Fish Committee at hearings held in Atlanta on November 15, 1930, that he attended several meetings, but became disgusted and quit in February of that year.[7]

> After finding out a great many secrets in the Communist Party that I didn't approve of, as being an American citizen, I did not feel it would exactly suit me and I knowed it would not suit my country, and that was swearing my allegiance to the Soviet Government against any wars or any Soviet. I knew that I was a little out of place, as I had been an American citizen, to swear against my flag. I knowed I could not carry out my promise successfully with the organization. I quit the organization after returning from Charlotte and refused to go to the national convention which was in Pittsburgh. I sent in my resignation, which has never been accepted; if it has, they have never communicated with me, but yet they still send me literature.

Miller supplied the committee with some of this "literature," commenting that not *all* Party plans were printed—some were merely "handed from bosom to bosom." The main goals in the South were, he said, to organize Negroes at all costs so as to overturn the American government and also to organize the textile mills, for they were "the pivot wheel to our future wars."

When asked specific questions, Miller said the Party was supposed to have 100,000 Negro members in the South, but admitted he knew only nine who belonged.[8] There were, however, perhaps a hundred more associated with groups such as the International Labor Defense and the Trade Union Unity League. Miller stressed that Red literature was being "strewed" about the Negro district every Saturday night, and it *was* being read with considerable interest.[9] An exchange between Chairman Fish and this witness concerning Party growth is especially revealing.

Miller: The onliest thing that keeps them [Negroes] from coming to be members is they are not having any meetings regularly.
Fish: But [the] Communist Party teaches hatred of God . . . and colored [people] are deeply devout Christians. . . .
Miller: Well, I want to say my race is not all that wrapped up; his conditions will make him lay his religion aside.

Fish emphasized loyalty to flag, country, and American institutions. Miller agreed such ties existed and were strong, but stoutly maintained, "He wants to better his conditions." He agreed the Negro did not put much faith in the Party's "social equality" doctrine, but reiterated that the black man simply wanted better working conditions.[10]

Following Miller's disenchantment, early in 1930 American Communist leaders dispatched two young organizers to Atlanta. M. H. Powers, who represented the Party, was from Minnesota.[11] Joe Carr, a Wheeling, West Virginia, youth, was organizer for the Young People's League. During these same weeks still another force became evident in Atlanta: the American Federation of Labor's drive to recruit Southern workers, especially in textile mills.[12] It was inevitable that these attempts to improve the plight of workers (one by the Reds and the other by the AFL) would become hopelessly intertwined—if not in fact, at least in the public mind. Textile executives, with the aid of the Atlanta newspapers and city police, made certain such confusion was not easily resolved.

On Sunday, March 2, William Green spoke at Atlanta's Paramount Theatre, where he was heckled by an organizer for the National Textile Workers' Union, Mary Dalton, who charged him with "selling out to the bosses." [13] Four days later, as Communists staged widespread "Red Thursday Marches," the police expected Miss Dalton to cause trouble. However, only a few "long hairs" showed up at the city hall to distribute literature and there were no disturbances. Apparently disappointed, on March 9 police finally were able to make the arrests they so desired. Circumstances were confusing and testimony before the Fish Committee contradictory. Powers and Carr were to address an integrated meeting in Rucker's Hall at the corner of Piedmont and Auburn avenues ("up there over a Negro undertaker's parlor") on city grafters, unemployment, and the next war. On some pretext—a tear-gas bomb, failure to get a permit, the nature of the topics, or disorderly conduct—police entered and arrested the two young Communists and three other whites, including the person who was presiding, an Emory student named Robert H. Hart. When the chief of police refused to detain them, Powers and Carr tried to resume the meeting; but, as they called to individuals milling about the sidewalks near the hall, they were again arrested and originally charged with luring customers into a place of business—"spieling." Testifying before the Fish Committee some months later, Captain Grover C. Fain remarked that the pair was held without bond. When asked why, he replied, "Well, we got a lot of paraphernalia, circulars, and things." Pressed to explain the technical charge, Fain said, "I cannot think of what it is; it is a great big word." That "big word" was *insurrection.*

On May 21 six more persons were arrested at an integrated meeting attended by some forty-five persons. They included Miss Dalton; Ann Burlak, an International Labor Defense worker; Gilmer Brady (Negro), organizer for the American Negro Labor Congress; Henry Story (Negro), a local printer; and Mr. and Mrs. Julius Klarin, also of Atlanta.[14] The Klarins, thanks to political pressure and testimony of their landlady, were soon released. Mrs. J. E. Andrews said they were courteous, industrious, and charitable. She conceded the pair did not believe in divine guidance, but added that recently she had noted "a consecration to the spirit of service as they see it that indicates a gradual unfolding of the knowledge of God through the spirit of Christ." [15]

On May 30 the four remaining Reds were also charged with insurrection under statutes passed in 1866 and amended in 1871. Anyone guilty of insurrection or an attempt to incite insurrection might be put to death. If a jury recommended mercy, an individual might get five to twenty years in prison. If anyone merely circulated insurrectionary materials he could receive a similar prison sentence.[16] Despite loud protests from reactionary circles the "Atlanta Six" were eventually released under heavy bond. These outcries were answered by a stern statement signed by sixty-two prominent Atlantans, among them Emory's president and numerous faculty members.

> The undersigned do not indorse the revolutionary philosophy and tactics of the Communist Party and its affiliated organizations. Yet we believe Communists should be protected in their constitutional rights of free speech and free assemblage.
>
> Raids, prosecutions, and imprisonments will only give added weight of evidence to the claims that a "capitalistic" society is oppressing the working classes. Furthermore, a policy of repression will exaggerate the importance of false ideas, and is likely to open the floodgates for future repression of progressive social movements. This is an extremely important consideration. If the precedent of repression of new ideas is once established, who can prophesy what good ideas may in the future be repressed merely because they are new.[17]

Apparently satisfied that the Red threat had been nipped in the bud, authorities in Atlanta relented somewhat. However, two years later, as the depression worsened, they again formally indicted the "Atlanta Six" for making speeches ("the contents of which are unknown") to individuals ("unknown") and for soliciting membership of various persons (also "unknown"). The grand jury could cite specific pamphlets which the "Six" had in their possession when apprehended in 1930, but no one had actually seen them circulating those materials.[18] The "Six," who scurried beyond Georgia's borders as soon as released on bond, were never brought to trial; and, as the result of a United States Supreme Court decision (*Lowry v. Herndon,* 1937), charges were finally dropped on August 30, 1939.

Yet the most spectacular reaction to Red activity in Atlanta was not the tactics of the police or the anguished cries of Emory intellectuals. It was the rise of the Black Shirts. Admittedly, the group only existed for about ninety days, but during the hot summer of 1930 its leaders could count some 40,000 followers. Made up of Klansmen, jobless whites, and restless youths, the Black Shirts enjoyed the tacit approval of the city's power structure—at least they faced no opposition when they marched through the streets and used the steps of the state capitol, the city auditorium, and numerous public school buildings as meeting places. In fact, the ease with which the Fascisti congregated would make one wonder if Atlanta police did not have a double standard: one for groups they liked and another for those they did not like. This movement, once under way, was also aided by increasing economic distress and tension created by the murder of an innocent Negro youth.

The initial gathering of the Black Shirts (strangely inspired by Mussolini, who was anathema to the anti-foreign, anti-Catholic Klan) was held on June 10 at the Junior Order United American Mechanics Hall on Flat Shoals Avenue.[19] Some four hundred disgruntled whites met and formed a secret order "to combat the Communist Party and to discourage the teachings of Communism and foster white supremacy." Holt J. Gewinner, Dewey Smith, and J. O. Wood were named as a committee to perfect permanent plans for an organization to be supported by "voluntary contributions." [20] Five days later Dennis Hubert, a sophomore at Morehouse College, was brutally murdered by T. L. Martin, a white gas station attendant. Hubert, son of a respected minister, was on a playground near his home when Martin and six companions drove up, accused the fifteen-year-old youth of insulting a white female, and after a brief conversation shot him in the head.[21]

Martin and several associates were indicted for murder on June 25. The following day the Hubert home was burned to the ground, and a subsequent Negro protest meeting was dispersed by a tear-gas bomb. Within hours an attempt was also made upon the life of the dead boy's cousin.[22] While Martin awaited trial, Black Shirt leaders emphasized that a white man might soon be convicted of killing a Negro, and they hit upon a theme which found sympathetic response: "If white men would assert their rights there would be no unemployment in Atlanta and the other cities of the South." [23]

On July 24 the *Atlanta Constitution* reported that a Black Shirt rally had been held at the English Avenue School. Resolutions were passed urging hotels to substitute white bellboys and attendants for Negroes. Members also scored a pasteurized milk ordinance being considered by the city council. Among the speakers were Wood, E. C. Metz, R. S. Gulledge, and City Councilman Ellis B. Barrett. The following day, as Martin's fate was being debated, this handbill appeared in some sections of the city: "If you love your life, your home, your country, come to the Georgia Avenue High School tonight at 8 o'clock and listen to matters discussed that can't be put on paper." [24]

When a copy was brought to the offices of the Commission on

Interracial Cooperation (predecessor of the Southern Regional Council), members decided to send a representative who was accompanied by a reporter from "a leading newspaper," presumably the *Constitution.* There they heard Negroes referred to as "burr heads" and "nuts." One man spoke of "buck niggers bellyin' down the streets pushin' white women off the side-walks." Others talked of Reconstruction days "when millions of black heels were placed upon the necks of the white people of the South." Listeners were reminded of how the Ku Klux Klan threw off this "yoke," and they were told that if they wanted jobs or feared the labor competition of Negroes *all* they had to do was *organize.*

Realizing only a spark was needed to set off serious disorders, the Commission approached local authorities and various civic and religious leaders. During the weekend of the 27th, Negro and white ministers urged caution. G. Everett Millican (acting mayor) assailed rumors of racial turmoil and appealed to "all good citizens to set their faces against every person and faction seeking to embroil the races in trouble." [25] According to Commission records, members were stationed at potential danger spots during late July and early August. They were in constant contact with city and county officials; and there was no trouble when Martin was found guilty on the 28th. It seems unlikely that these efforts alone kept the peace. Certainly Judge E. Earl Camp made his views clear when passing sentence upon Martin: "It is only the lowest type of our citizenship that causes racial difficulties and we are determined that this class of citizens shall not disturb the orderly processes of our courts." [26]

What is certain, however, is that the Fascisti were making a concerted effort to capitalize upon these tensions. On the same day that Martin was sentenced, the *Atlanta Journal* carried this brief notice: "Fascist Body Plans East Point Meeting." Readers were told to gather at Russell High School at 8 P.M. to hear speeches opposing communism. Wood, who as regional director of the group would preside, reiterated that anyone interested in fighting the Red menace could join. There were no dues, no fees—all contributions were voluntary. "Several well attended meetings have been held recently in various parts of the city," he added with a note of pride. Then, in its Sunday edition (August 3), the *Journal* carried this remarkable ad:

Black Shirts

American Fascisti: We have just what you want!

Why not wear one at the meeting Monday night at Lakewood Heights. The price is very reasonable, but immediate supply is limited. Better get yours Now.

Allen M. Pierce
9 Edgewood Ave.[27]

Following publication of this ad, Black Shirt activity was enveloped in secrecy. For nearly three weeks no newspaper had any comment concerning the Fascisti despite numerous parades and meetings and formal application for a charter. On August 8, R. A. Gordon, Gulledge, and Gewinner applied to Fulton County Superior Court for a twenty-year charter, summarizing the aims of the "American Facisti [*sic*] Association and Order of Black Shirts" in this manner:

> That it is the purpose of said organization to inculcate and foster in the minds of its members and the public generally, white supremacy; charity among its members, and fellowship; the obedience to law and order; the upholding of the Constitution and laws of the United States and the several states thereof; the instruction of its members in the fundamental principles of free government; the combating of all influence that seeks to undermine and overthrow the principles of Democracy and the Republican form of government; to promote friendship and good fellowship among its members and the public generally; care for its sick, bury its dead, and do any other act of charity and benevolence which its governing board or members of its different lodges and subdivisions may decide to do.[28]

Six days later the *Constitution* noted that J. O. Wood, candidate for the state legislature, would speak at a rally; however, it failed to mention his Fascisti connections, which may have been rather tenuous at best, for sometime during the month of August Gewinner proclaimed himself "adjutant-general" of the Black Shirts, instituted regular dues, and ousted several of the original leaders. Among these was Wood, who ostensibly was repudiated for organizing a woman's auxiliary—the Black Skirts! Finally, on August 23, unable to ignore the group any longer, the *Constitution* mentioned that a parade had been held the previous evening in downtown Atlanta. Escorted by city police and marching with full approval of Mayor I. N. Ragsdale, the Fascisti made their way from Peachtree and Baker streets to the state capitol where, flanked by huge banners attacking communism and white unemployment, speakers demanded prosecution of all Reds and jobs for out-of-work whites.

It was the *Macon Telegraph*—ever eager to embarrass the Atlanta press—which at last rose to the attack. Ably edited by W. T. Anderson, a true liberal and an outstanding crusader for justice, the *Telegraph* ridiculed the Fascisti as a "get-rich-quick" scheme, another attempt by Atlanta city slickers to take money from honest Georgians. According to a front-page story (August 24) the Black Shirts had enlisted 21,830 members during the preceding three weeks at $1.00 per head. This report exposed the group as little more than a makeshift employment agency which merely offered to "try" to find jobs. It was no secret that corridors leading to the little office at 218 Peters Building were congested with throngs of young white men clamoring for application blanks. The *Telegraph* claimed the group had branch offices in Macon, Savannah, and Columbus, and planned to expand to Chattanooga and Knoxville. It quoted one Atlantan who predicted it would be "a hard winter" for Negroes. "Before Christmas there isn't going to be a black bell boy or black truck driver in Atlanta. . . . This is white man's country and there are too many Negroes in jobs and too many white men out of jobs." The Fascisti were already busy compiling lists of vacant rural tenant houses to be offered to city Negroes.

In an editorial appearing in the same issue Anderson blasted the Black Shirts as "a blood brother to the Ku Klux Klan and to the Supreme Kingdom and to Essekay and all those other grandiloquent orders which have originated in Atlanta in the fertile minds of the best aggregation of sucker trappers ever foregathered in America." [29] The truly discouraging element, wrote Anderson, was that there were 21,830 Georgians "who believe they can save the nation by taking jobs away from Negroes."

On Tuesday, August 26, the *Telegraph* featured an unusual two-column, front-page editorial: "CRACK THE HEAD OF THIS NEWEST NASTY THING." This scathing account explained in simple terms the aims of the Black Shirts:

> it may be stated that they want to run all the Negroes out of their jobs in cities and towns and give these to white people. The reason is that America is a "white man's country, and the Negro must get out, and go out in the country." The order will assist the Negro to get himself a piece of land in the country where he may work until the order decides that he is doing too well there and then the by-laws and constitution may be amended. Here we have been thinking all these centuries that if we could only get the Negro to go to work, to hold his job, all would be well with the white man—that the latter could rest. And now that the Negro has gone to work, up jumps an order to put the white man to work again. We don't think the thing is going to be popular for very long. For if the Negro doesn't work and make his living the white man must work and make it for him. A fine program the black shirts have mapped out.

The Black Shirts, said the *Telegraph,* were like a man who stubs his toe. He looks around to see who is to blame. In this case, Wood, Gewinner, and their followers had made the Negro responsible. The *Telegraph* credited Atlanta and its press for the sudden expansion of the group, for had the *Constitution, Journal,* and *Georgian* given them proper publicity there would not have been even 2,100 Black Shirts—let alone 21,000!

During the last days of August and the first ten days of September the Fascisti tried to hold meetings in Griffin, Athens, Barnesville, Newnan, Marietta, Rome, Decatur, Lawrenceville, and Macon. However, once they ventured outside of the security of Atlanta, the group encountered stiff and immediate opposition from ministers, civic leaders, editors, and lawmen. The *Griffin Daily News* (August 29) said a man attending a rally there remarked that what the nation needed was "not black shirts, but dirty shirts—shirts made dirty by the wearer working hard and long." On Saturday, August 30, men wearing black shirts emblazoned with white sergeant chevrons appeared in Macon distributing applications and selling the *Black Shirt* at five cents per copy. (This weekly sheet explained that "Fascisti" meant "my country.") Mayor A. G. Dudley halted sale of the publication in Athens, terming the Black Shirts "a dangerous, if not vicious, organization."

The *Constitution* (August 31) and the *Journal* (September 2) finally concluded the Fascisti might cause trouble. In keeping with Atlanta's tender regard for the business community, the *Journal's* principal complaint was that these new doctrines might be economically unsound. After all, throwing a thousand experienced Negroes out of work so as to employ a thousand inexperienced whites did not really make much sense. Yet while detailing increasing difficulties faced by the Black Shirts, these newspapers hardly launched a true campaign against the Fascisti. Only the *Macon Telegraph* maintained the constant glare of publicity; and during the opening weeks of September there was substantial grist for the mill. In addition, both federal and county grand juries were scrutinizing the Black Shirts. U.S. officials suspected the group was breaking federal law. Also, they were interested in the activities of Holt Gewinner, who was on probation following conviction for tax evasion. Fulton County authorities had a more mundane concern: Fascisti threats to businessmen and housewives were creating havoc among cooks, nurses, domestics, all types of Negro workers. Early in September the county grand jury passed a resolution deploring the methods of the Black Shirts as "inimical to the best interests of the white and colored races" and strongly urged that the pending charter be denied.[30]

Meanwhile, federal officials questioned Gewinner (somewhat belatedly) concerning payment of a North Carolina bond with a fraudulent check. In November 1928 he had been involved in an auto accident near Greenville, North Carolina, and posted bond with a false draft on the Lu Max Grease & Oil Company of Atlanta. To add to the Black Shirts' woes, early in September J. T. Lee, a former member, obtained a court order temporarily denying a charter to the group. Lee said Gewinner and others seized control illegally and instituted a $1.00 membership fee. According to Lee, each member who paid his fee then got an application for admission to the Ku Klux Klan. He accused Gewinner of spelling the name of the association "Facisti," not understanding its true principles, and converting the body into a military order when no such purpose was intended.[31]

Yet the Black Shirts doggedly faltered forward. Dewey Smith, editor of the *Black Shirt*, wrote to the *Constitution* (September 2) praising a recent editorial entitled "Aiding Business Revival." This, he emphasized, was precisely what the Fascisti were trying to do. The Black Shirts were only interested in fighting communism and putting white men to work. They were not trying to stir up racial turmoil. The Reds, on the other hand, were preaching rebellion, social equality, and placing "the germs of riot" in Negro minds. The Fascisti, he said, only wanted to put white men to work "where practicable . . . not in the place of Negroes already employed."

Two days later, while addressing about one hundred Macon citizens, Black Shirter Travis Lamar told the horrors of communism in Atlanta and reiterated that his organization's attitude toward the Negro worker was being distorted.

> They're [the Communists] telling the Negroes they ought to marry white folks. They're telling them they ought to go into their homes. They're talking that stuff to them, and we're here to fight it. We respect the flag. We salute it.
>
> We've got much good publicity in the papers, and we've got much bad. But we haven't tried in any case to force a Negro out of a job. We've just asked for the jobs that white men might be filling, and in one month we've gotten 1,000 white men jobs.[32]

Lamar claimed 40,000 members, but quickly added that did not mean $40,000. If employed, a member paid $1.00. If not, he was accepted on credit and given ninety days' grace. If he got a job within that period he was expected to pay the admission fee; if not, another grace period was granted.

Four days later the Black Shirts—perhaps frustrated—resorted to one of the few acts of violence which can be charged against them. William G. McRae, a young lawyer who had signed the Emory protest of August 3, was assaulted and beaten in his Hurt Building office. The attack was noted briefly in the Atlanta papers, but at the time the Black Shirts were not mentioned. McRae refused to press charges and was subsequently elected to the state legislature.[33]

By mid-September the Fascisti were in deep trouble. They faced increasing hostility from the press, and even Atlanta's civic and religious leaders, who had watched the growth of the group with benign awareness, were becoming wary. Lee's injunction was dismissed on the 16th, but Gewinner was now in difficulty because of another bad check. He had rented the city auditorium for a rally held on September 3 and had given officials a personal check for $40 drawn on Citizens & Southern—a bank in which he did not have an account. The Black Shirts' adjutant general claimed he thought the check "a mere formality." He wrote it, he said, only after the custodian refused to open the building, emphasizing that the Black Shirts had used the facility on several occasions free of charge.[34]

Gewinner promised to pay up as soon as possible, but the future of both the Fascisti and their leader looked bleak. On the 19th the *Constitution* said Black Shirt headquarters at 202 Whitehall Street were virtually deserted, and a week later four Atlantans (J. O. Wood, James R. Venable, Raymond V. Berger, and Thomas B. Vest) announced they had chartered a *new* Black Shirt group in Orlando, Florida. This came as a distinct surprise to both Gewinner and the Florida secretary of state, who branded the report false. Meanwhile, the Fulton County Grand Jury urged Mayor Ragsdale to deny an application for a parade permit which was on his desk. "Someone has said that Americans have no objection to Black Shirts in Italy or even to Red Shirts in Russia, but we insist that this particular kind of haberdashery be worn in the home land of fascism and not in America, as our people could be at better business than aping the reactionary institutions of Europe, and we coincide in this opinion." [35]

On October 17, Judge G. H. Howard denied the Black Shirts' application for a charter, pointing out that "white supremacy" as described in the proposed rules and bylaws was too vague and probably not within the purview of state and local law. The judge noted that signs and banners used in parades clearly indicated that a large number of members did not understand the term and would quickly misconstrue the proposed charter to unlawful ends.[36] The following day Gewinner filed an amendment to the charter, but to no avail. And on October 31 the county grand jury expressed the hope and belief that "the danger of this threatened menace to the peace and security of our community has passed away." [37] As for Holt Gewinner, on November 5 federal authorities asked him to account for his recent activities—fraudulent checks, drunken driving charges, and failure to pay back taxes. Five days later he was fined $500 and sentenced to six months in prison.[38] With Gewinner behind bars, Atlanta's Black Shirts passed into oblivion.

Ironically, despite the valiant efforts of the *Macon Telegraph,* it was the tiny *Bainbridge Post-Searchlight* which wrote the group's epitaph.[39]

> We got one of their *Black Shirt* papers and all we could see to it was that the Black Shirt fellows wanted all the jobs and did not want the nigger to have any. About the most illogical mess we ever read. Mr. Black Shirt man, we hereby invite you down here to take the nigger's place in the cotton patch, also you can have his job cutting cross ties, dipping turpentine, bell hopping, feeding the hogs, plowing the corn, hoeing, pulling fodder, and if those are not enough you can come down here and dig in the fuller's earth mines and do everything else that a nigger does.

But, said this south Georgia weekly, "Mr. Black Shirt man" would not show up because he was looking for "easy" work.

> The Black Shirts won't thrive in the country worth a barbee. It has been hard enough to get the Negroes to pick cotton and we know well that the white men of Atlanta belonging to this thing could not be gotten into a cotton patch with a ten-ton tractor. . . . But this thing will die right where it is. Eighty per cent of the Negro jobs would not be accepted by white folks because it is real work and the bunch we saw in line there in Atlanta surely did not look like a gang that was hunting any nigger's work or white man's either as far as that matter[s]. This is one movement that will die of its own tail weight.

Of course, sadly, the movement did not really "die." The sentiments of the Fascisti were still alive and would emerge from time to time under a variety of names and symbols. In fact, in the desperate summer of 1932 a social worker reported that "the K. K. Klan and a black shirt organization" were being fanned to life among unemployed mill workers in the northwest section of Atlanta.[40] There was also sporadic Communist activity in that city after 1930, the most notable incident being the Angelo Herndon case (1932–1937). To Herndon, a young Negro Party worker from Ohio, goes the dubious honor of actually being tried and convicted under Georgia's insurrection laws.[41]

With the rise of Roosevelt's New Deal, extremist groups found it increasingly difficult to attract a following in Atlanta; and at the same time that the Squire of Warm Springs was changing American life, communism with its "popular front" efforts was becoming somewhat more respectable and Fascism/Nazism less so. In a sense, then, just as domestic and international tensions caused a weird ideological outburst in Atlanta in 1930, changes in national and world politics eased or altered the direction and nature of those tensions as that troubled decade advanced toward Munich, Danzig, and Stalingrad.

NOTES

1. American Communists were certainly aware of the Negro and from their inception promised him "active support"; but, weakened by factional splits and caught up in the Jim Crow mind of the twenties, they did nothing.

2. Theodore Draper, *American Communism and Soviet Russia: The Formative Period* (New York, 1960), pp. 333–334. Draper concludes this was largely "wasted effort." More Negroes joined the Party, true, but most of them were living in the North. Also, the Southern "peasant" Negro in whom Stalin was especially interested tended to migrate to cities and to other parts of the nation. As official policy the idea of a Negro nation was abandoned in 1943, revived in 1946, and jettisoned again in 1958. See Draper's Chap. XV, "The Negro Question," and James S. Allen, *The Negro Question in the United States* (New York, 1936), esp. Chaps. IX and X.

3. See *The Communist International (1919–1943): Documents,* edited by Jane Degras, 2 vols. (London, 1960), II, 552–557.

4. Quoted in "Herndon *v.* State," *Reports of Cases Decided in the Supreme Court of the State of Georgia,* CLXXVIII (Atlanta, 1934), 860–865; this pamphlet was originally published in 1930.

5. There was a full slate of Communist Party electors on the Georgia ballot in 1928, but it seems unlikely that these individuals had any valid commitment to Communist doctrine or the American Communist Party to them. According to the records of the secretary of state, they included L. W. Warr, C. S. Knight, Ernest Carl Fullerton, Max Singer, Denny G. Katz, S. J. Letheis, Nathan Mazer, Adam Wehmer, Sam Nasson, F. C. Boatner, Harry Haranis, M. G. McCoy, G. R. Hutchinson, and J. K. Kiseler. The ticket received sixty-four votes.

6. *Investigation of Communist Propaganda: Hearings Before a Special Committee to Investigate Communist Activities in the United States of the House of Representatives,* 71st Congress, 2nd sess., Part 6, I (Washington, 1930), 218–229. This group, headed by Hamilton Fish, Jr., of New York, held rather superficial hearings in five Southern cities, November 13–18, 1930. In addition to Atlanta, they met in Chattanooga, Birmingham, New Orleans, and Memphis.

7. The *Southern Worker* (January 10, 1931) denounced Miller as "a scoundrel, stool pigeon, and spy." This Birmingham publication edited by James S. Allen said Miller had been expelled "about a year ago" after only a brief association with the Party.

8. In 1929 the American Communist Party had some nine thousand members. and this total more than doubled by 1933. See Edward W. Palmer, *The Communist Problem in America* (New York, 1951), p. 128.

9. During the fall of 1930 the *Southern Worker* claimed twenty-five paid subscriptions in Atlanta and weekly sales of about 150 copies. See issues of October 11 and 25.

10. Others who testified included Fulton County's assistant solicitor general John H. Hudson and several policemen. They presented additional literature, identified a hall at 348 Fair Street as Party headquarters, and told of efforts to break up the group.

11. Powers was from either St. Paul or Duluth, but Atlanta authorities insisted he was a "Russian Jew" masquerading under an alias.

12. See files of Atlanta's *Journal of Labor* for a description of this campaign.

13. *Atlanta Constitution,* March 10, 1930. Miss Dalton was arrested, but soon released.

14. See Walter Wilson, "Atlanta's Communists," *Nation,* June 25, 1930, pp. 731–732, for a contemporary account.

15. *Atlanta Journal,* May 22, 1930.

16. When asked about these arrests, Captain Fain told the Fish Committee these were the only persons apprehended for Red activity in Atlanta in 1930. "When they have a Communist meeting here," asked one committee member "you lock them up?" "Yes, sir," replied Fain. The "Six" were originally charged with violating section 58 of the state penal code (circulating insurrectionary materials).

17. *Journal,* August 3, 1930.

18. These items included copies of the *Daily Worker, Labor Defender, Out of a Job* by Earl Browder, *What Every Worker Should Know About the Communist Party, An Appeal to the Southern Workers,* and *Against the Bosses' War! Defend the Soviet Union.* See these cases in Criminal Bench Dockets, Criminal Minutes, Fulton County Superior Court, Atlanta: Carr *et al.*—#33291, XXII, 194; #37116, XXV, 37, XXVI, 54, 259, 528; Dalton *et al.*—#33515, XXII, 222, XXVI, 253; #37299, XXV, 59, XXVI, 54, 417.

19. *Constitution,* September 2, 1930.

20. Gewinner, who would emerge as the leader of the group, was at this time a salesman living in southeast Atlanta. During the twenties he promoted prize fights in Atlanta, failed to pay federal taxes on receipts, and was free on extended probation. Smith would become editor of the *Black Shirt,* a weekly which appeared in August and September 1930. Wood, a onetime Ku Klux Klan candidate for governor and once editor of the Klan's *Searchlight,* would break with the Fascisti sometime in August.

21. According to the *Savannah Tribune* (July 24, 1930), Mr. and Mrs. J. G. Garvins and a Mrs. Harmon were drinking near the playground. As they crossed the area one of the women fell and Hubert remarked, "You better take the drunk lady home." This apparently constituted an "insult." The Klan claimed in its *Kourier* (August 1930) that Hubert tried to rape a white woman, and that Martin and his friends saved her and had to shoot the young Negro when he tried to escape before police arrived. The *Kourier,* published in the Buckhead section of Atlanta, said it did not condone such actions, but since the Negro was now demanding "social rights" extreme measures might be necessary.

22. See "The Black Shirts Meet Defeat," a confidential report in the files of the Commission on Interracial Cooperation, Atlanta University. This survey, while revealing, credits the commission with the breakup of the group. Inept leadership and stern (if belated) opposition from the press and the courts really sealed the fate of the Fascisti, not action by the commission. During these weeks both Negroes and whites collected funds to help rebuild the Hubert home.

23. *Ibid.*

24. *Ibid.* This was apparently the fifth regular meeting held in the Atlanta area. According to one source a total of fourteen meetings and rallies were held there during the summer of 1930. .

25. *Constitution,* July 29, 1930. Nevertheless, this was the only Atlanta newspaper giving even halfhearted support to efforts to avert trouble. It gave Millican's plea front-page coverage and editorially praised his actions. Hearst's *Georgian* was too busy battling United States membership in the World Court and advocating restrictions on immigration to give much attention to local matters. Interestingly, William Joseph Simmons of Klan fame chose the weekend of the 27th to launch his "Caucasian Crusade," also known as the "White Band." To the embarrassment of some prominent Atlantans he cited their endorsement. These leaders included Dr. Sam W. Small, William Schley Howard, Congressman Robert Ramspeck, and James I. Lowry (sheriff of Fulton County). Lowry denied formal endorsement, but conceded he had "approved a proposal to join a movement for racial purity." See *Journal,* July 27, 1930.

26. *Journal,* July 28, 1930.

27. This shop was located near Five Points, the traditional heart of the city. The advertisement was two columns wide, and "Black Shirts" appeared in letters one inch high. Ironically, this same issue carried the Emory University protest concerning suppression of free speech.

28. Charter application #12246, Charter Book F, p. 276, Fulton County Superior Court. The attorney for the Black Shirts was Walter A. Sims, mayor of Atlanta from 1923 to 1927.

29. The Supreme Kingdom, inspired by the Scopes Trial, was the brainchild of Edward Young Clarke, member of a distinguished Atlanta family. It was formed to fight atheism and evolution, but never attracted much of a following. Eventually Clarke transferred the Supreme Kingdom to Oklahoma under the name of Essekay, (S-K), where it apparently died a quiet death.

30. *Journal,* September 5, 1930.

31. Commenting editorially upon Lee's injunction, the *Macon Telegraph* (September 4) suggested these words be inscribed over the door of the Fascisti's Atlanta headquarters: "If I was so soon to be done for, what was I ever begun for?"

32. *Macon Telegraph,* September 5, 1930. The following day this newspaper blasted Atlanta and its press: "Come on, you Atlanta, with your next sucker-bait! South Georgia is fertile field for your schemes, your seven secret orders in the incubator. You have a grand hot-house in Atlanta in which to grow your plants and bring them to sturdiness and virility, then to set them out all over the state like poison ivy and rake in the dollars as they flourish. The Atlanta newspapers will see that you are protected."

33. See Edwin Tribble, "Black Shirts in Georgia," *New Republic,* October 8, 1930, pp. 204–206. This report, a good analysis of the movement, fails to name McRae, but gives enough information to make identification possible. While Tribble wrote before the story of the Fascisti was complete, he noted that Georgia Negroes were alarmed by this group, which made a more direct appeal to bigotry than the Klan. The latter sought only to keep the Negro from participating in government. "This new organization," he said, "touches the lean pocketbook of the white and lays the cause of his unemployment directly at the door of the Negro."

34. *Constitution,* September 19, 1930.

35. *Ibid.,* September 26, 1930.

36. Charter application #12246, Fulton County Superior Court.
37. Miscellaneous Grand Jury file #10, Fulton County Superior Court.
38. Case #8550, U.S. District Court, Northern District of Georgia, Atlanta.
39. Quoted in the *Macon Telegraph,* September 5, 1930.
40. *Community Life,* July 1932, p. 3.
41. Herndon was eventually freed by a decision of the U.S. Supreme Court in May 1937.

The Depression in Harlem

Federal Writers Project (Roi Ottley and William J. Weatherby, editors)

For Negroes, "last hired, first fired," the depression was particularly severe, and for a significant number of Harlem Negroes unemployment was a familiar condition before the Great Crash. The observation that many families in Harlem "existed in squalor approaching that of the Arkansas sharecroppers" indicates that the blacks of the rural South suffered along with their urban brothers. Ironically, many Negroes had left the South for the cities out of desperation, only to join the ranks of the destitute.

This selection also identifies an aspect of Negro urban life in the depression that has had an enduring impact on black family relationships: the high rate of unemployment among Negro males and the dependence for income on female employment. That Negro protests of the 1960's often are reminiscent of protests in the 1930's —against discrimination by employers and the police, for example —suggests that there has been continuity as well as change in Negro life.

Black Harlem, 1929–1935.—Hand-to-mouth living had been the rule in Harlem for many years. Though some had tasted of the

[Reprinted from *The Negro in New York: An Informal Social History, 1626–1940* (New York: Oceana, 1967), pp. 265–280. Copyright © 1967 by the New York Public Library, Astor, Lenox and Tilden Foundations. Reprinted by permission of the publisher.]

fatted calf during lush days, more than two thousand Negro families were destitute at the height of prosperity.[1] Before the full effects of the depression were felt, the average weekly income of a Negro workingman had been eighteen dollars. Sixty per cent of the married women worked, a figure four times higher than that of the native-born white Americans.[2] In twenty-five years Harlem's population had increased more than 600 per cent to more than 350,000 (equal to the total population of Rochester, New York), with an average density of 233 persons per acre compared with 133 for the rest of Manhattan. The community had become a vast swarming hive in which families were doubled and trebled in apartments meant for one family.[3] But with the financial collapse in October 1929, a large mass of Negroes were faced with the reality of starvation and they turned sadly to the public relief. When the few chanted optimistically, "Jesus Will Lead Me and the Welfare Will Feed Me," the many said it was a knowing delusion, for the Home Relief Bureau allowed only eight cents a meal for food; meanwhile men, women, and children combed the streets and searched in garbage cans, many foraging with dogs and cats.

TENEMENT DWELLINGS

The crashing drop of wages drove Negroes back to the already crowded hovels east of Lenox Avenue. In many blocks one toilet served a floor of four apartments. Most of the apartments had no private bathrooms or even the luxury of a public bath. Wherever a tub was found it usually had been installed in the kitchen. Without exception these tenements were filthy and vermin-ridden. Along Fifth Avenue, between 135th and 138th streets, were flats with old-fashioned toilets which rarely flushed and, when they did, they often overflowed on the floors below. In the winter the gaping holes in the skylights allowed cold air to sweep down the staircase, sometimes freezing the flush for weeks. Coal grates provided the only heat. The dwellers scoured the neighborhood for fuel, and harassed janitors in the surrounding districts were compelled to stand guard over coal deliveries until they were safely stored in the cellars. Landlords in this section hired a janitor for nothing more than a basement to exist in, for which he had to clean six floors, take care of sidewalk and backyard, haul garbage, make minor repairs, and where a house had a hot-water furnace he had to stoke it.[4]

Many families had been reduced to living below street level. It was estimated that more than ten thousand Negroes lived in cellars and basements which had been converted into makeshift flats. Packed in damp, rat-ridden dungeons, they existed in squalor approaching that of the Arkansas sharecroppers. Floors were of cracked concrete and the walls were whitewashed rock, water drenched and rust streaked. There were only slits for windows. A tin can in a corner covered by a sheet of newspaper was the only toilet. There was no running water in some, and no partitions to separate the adults from the curious eyes of the young. Packing boxes were used as beds, tables, and chairs. In winter rags and newspapers were stuffed into the numerous cracks to keep out the wind.

I wish the rent
Was Heaven sent
—Langston Hughes

Shunted off into these rundown sections, Negroes were forced to pay exorbitant rents while landlords relaxed supervision and flagrantly violated the city building and sanitary codes. Compared with 20 to 25 per cent of their income generally paid by white families for rent, Negro tenants paid from 40 to 50 per cent.[5] More than half of the Negro families were forced to take in lodgers to augment the family income. Frequently whole families slept in one room. Envied was the family who had a night worker as a lodger. He would occupy a bed in the day that would be rented out at night—same room, same bed, same sheets, and same bedbugs. This was described as the "hot bed." If the family had a bathtub, it, too, after being covered with boards, would be rented out.

The artificial scarcity of dwellings was accentuated by white property owners who in making a Negro district had heightened the housing problem of Negroes and thus were able to maintain high rents. A prominent member of the New York City Realty Board is quoted as saying:

> I believe a logical section for Negro expansion in Manhattan is East Harlem. At present this district has reached such a point of deterioration that its ultimate residential pattern is most puzzling. Many blocks have a substantial section of their buildings boarded up

or demolished and a goodly percentage of those remaining are in disrepair and in violation of law. . . . An influx of Negroes into East Harlem would not work a hardship on the present population of the area, because its present residents could move to any other section of New York without the attendant racial discrimination which the Negro would encounter if he endeavored to locate in other districts.[6]

"LAST HIRED, FIRST FIRED"

Discrimination against employment of Negroes had practically closed the doors to any and all types of occupations. Generally, the poorer half of the colored population lived on an income which was only 46 per cent of that of the poorer half of the white population.[7]

The people of Harlem regarded the public utilities and trade unions as the chief agencies of discrimination. Particularly were these barriers extended to white-collar employment. During the period 1930–1935 the Consolidated Gas Company employed 213 Negroes as porters among its ten thousand employees; the New York Edison Company, with the same number of employees, had only sixty-five Negroes, all of whom were porters, cleaners, and hall men. The New York Telephone Company had a similar situation. The Interborough Rapid Transit Company had 580 Negroes employed as messengers, porters, and cleaners, out of ten thousand employees. The Western Union Telegraph Company had two clerks and two operators and a few messengers employed in Harlem. Except for this office, Negroes employed by this corporation occupied the same menial positions as colored employees had in the other public utilities. The Fifth Avenue Coach Company's policy of excluding Negroes had assumed the aspects of a caste system.

These companies had already placed themselves on record. In January 1927, the *Messenger* published a reply to an inquiry made by the magazine concerning the employment of Negroes in the Consolidated Gas Company. The letter, signed by the company's vice-president, H. M. Bundage, said:

> Replying to your favor of November 23rd, have to advise that Negroes employed by us render common labor, maid service and the like. We do not assign Negroes as stenographers, clerks or inspectors.

The New York Telephone Company in response to this same inquiry wrote:

> As to the question of employment by the company of persons of known Negro descent, we might say that we do employ such persons, having some on our payroll at the present time assisting us in the conduct of our restaurant and lounge facilities.

The trade unions, particularly the craft unions, were active in keeping the large employment fields barred to Negroes. In 1936 Charles L. Franklin, in his book, *The Negro Labor Unionist of New York,* listed twenty-four international unions which excluded Negroes by initiation rituals. Out of the sixteen of these unions, covering a membership of 609,789 workers, that answered Franklin's inquiries concerning racial discrimination, thirteen said their restrictions remained. One answered that its constitution had been changed to include Negroes. Another reported that the word "white" had been removed from the constitution, but that this was meaningless since there were no colored telegraphers. Still another declared it had changed its policy and admitted colored lodges but would not have colored representation at its conventions.

SLAVE MARKET

After 1930 wage standards all but disappeared. This was particularly true of domestic work, which absorbed the vast majority of Negro women workers who, with the almost complete unemployment of Negro men, were becoming the sole support of the family. Unable to find positions through regular employment agencies or newspaper advertisements, many of them traveled to the Bronx in search of a day's work.[8] Frequent complaints of exploitation caused two young Negro women, Ella Baker and Marvel Cooke, to visit the area and describe their experiences in a magazine article. Here, they said, was "a street corner market where Negro women are 'rented' at unbelievably low rates for housework. The heaviest traffic is at 167th Street and Jerome Avenue where, on benches surrounding a green square, the victims wait, grateful at least for some place to sit. At Simpson Street and Westchester Avenue they pose wearily against buildings and lampposts or scuttle about in an attempt to retrieve discarded boxes upon which to sit. Not only is human labor bartered and sold for the slave wage, but human love is also a marketable commodity. Whether it is labor or love, the women arrive as early as eight A.M. and remain as late as one

P.M. or until they are hired. In rain or shine, hot or cold, they wait to work for ten, fifteen, and twenty cents per hour. They wash floors, clothes, windows, etc. Some had been maids and domestics in wealthy homes. Some were former marginal workers." [9]

Unemployed, the last refuge of these people was the relief offices, but here, they complained, they were often met with red tape and prejudice. At this time it was estimated that more than fifty thousand Negroes were neither working nor receiving relief.

I went to see my investigator.
She smile and say
Come back later, come back later.
—Abe Hill

Negro sharecroppers of the South who had lost their land drifted into the big cities and thousands found their way to Harlem, swelling the total of destitutes. Before the relief system was instituted, Negroes had tried every device from "Hoover block parties" [10] to "house rent parties" to tide over the bleak times. Negro churches took an active part in the feeding of many of the people, for private welfare agencies were flooded with pleas for aid. There was bitter waiting and more bitter street fighting.

In the first month in 1933 the Home Relief Bureau opened its doors and was immediately deluged with thousands of demands for food, clothing, and employment; some even asked for transportation to the South and the West Indies. Nine months later more than twenty-five thousand Negro families were receiving unemployment relief from the city, almost 50 per cent of all the families in Harlem. By 1936 the figure had become 21 per cent of the city's entire relief rolls. But Negroes had only nine per cent of the work relief jobs allotted by the Home Relief Bureau.[11] At the same time, the Welfare Department allowed $4.15 for food for two weeks to a male over sixteen years old, an increase over the $3.30 allowed in 1934 and $3.55 in 1935.[12]

Negroes made considerable complaint against the manner and the amount of relief distributed. But discrimination is a wisp which cannot be nailed down, and investigations of it were never very fruitful, though standardized relief under Mayor La Guardia's administration (1934–40) reduced the number of complaints. When

Negroes received work relief they were assigned chiefly to menial jobs and were given an inferior status despite their previous training and experience.[13]

THE "LUNG BLOCK"

Unemployment, congestion, and substandard dwellings took their toll of Negro health. In 1934 a survey of twenty thousand residents of Negro Harlem, chiefly on the relief rolls, revealed 3 per cent suffering from pulmonary tuberculosis, comprising 5 per cent of the city's deaths from this disease. One block, especially, was known as the "lung block," where more than three thousand persons resided. The death rate there was twice that of white Manhattan.

"Tuberculosis," wrote Dr. Louis T. Wright, a Negro, fellow of the American College of Surgeons and surgical director of Harlem Hospital, "we all know, is a disease that is rampant among the poverty stricken of all races. Colored people, therefore, show high morbidity and mortality rates from this condition alone, due to bad housing, inability to purchase food in adequate amounts, having to do laborious work while ill, little or no funds for medical care and treatment." But most hospitals treating T.B. refused to admit Negro patients or limited the type of ward service available, except Sea View Hospital in Staten Island.

The story was the same with social diseases. For the five-year average from 1929–33 there were more than three thousand venereal cases among Negroes per hundred thousand, twice that among whites.[14] "It is not due to lack of morals," said Dr. Wright, "but more directly to the lack of money, since with adequate funds these diseases could have been easily controlled." The real dread of Harlem was, and still is, pneumonia, from which the death rate was double that among whites. More dreadful was infant mortality, which took a toll of one in ten, twice that of the city as a whole. Twice as many Negro women died in childbirth as white women. A vital commentary on Harlem's health was the Central Harlem Health Center's report that it had filled approximately twenty thousand cavities in children's teeth in a six-month period.

THE MORGUE

Only one hospital in the city was, and is, concerned with the health of Negroes—Harlem Hospital, a public institution which has been a sore aggravating the life of the community for many years. Situated in the heart of the Harlem area, it attempted to care for more than 350,000 Negroes and all Puerto Ricans, Italians, and Jews living in East Harlem. Harlem Hospital contained 273 beds and 52 bassinets in 1932. Investigators for the Mayor's Commission discovered that "patients were forced to sleep on the floor, on mattresses and on benches, even in the maternity wards. Patients recently operated upon slept on benches or on chairs." Besides being the only city hospital in the community, Harlem Hospital also received Negro patients routed from other institutions in the city.

In 1932 proportionately twice as many people died at Harlem Hospital as at Bellevue Hospital.[15] It was for this reason that Negroes feared going to Harlem Hospital and referred to it fiercely as the "morgue" or "butcher shop." Many cases were refused admittance because of overcrowding; sometimes there were as many as fifteen patients waiting for attention in the emergency clinics. Only three ambulances were available for calls in Harlem in 1932. Most of the other hospitals refused to admit Negroes, and the few that did allow them to enter practiced segregation. In March 1937 the wife of W. C. Handy, composer of "St. Louis Blues," lay critically ill in an ambulance more than an hour before the doors of Knickerbocker Hospital while the hospital officials debated whether or not a Negro should be admitted.

The city lacked also sufficient facilities for the training of Negro physicians and nurses. Negro interns were admitted in only three hospitals and Negro staff members only in hospitals "where there was a predominance of Negro patients." The medical staff of Harlem Hospital, Negro newspapers charged, pursued a policy of preventing Negro doctors and nurses from serving. In 1929 there were fifty-seven white doctors and only seven Negroes on the staff, though there were almost three hundred Negro physicians from whom to draw. The problem was identical for Negro nurses; they were admitted to only two training schools in the city—Lincoln Hospital and Harlem Hospital—and these had no white students. Even certain specialized sources were frequently not opened to them.[16]

BITTER BLOSSOM [17]

Crime was the bitter blossom of poverty. The evil effects of bad housing and the lack of recreational facilities caused an alarming increase of juvenile crime. There were more Negro children in New York City than in any other city in the world.[18] In 1919, the first year that the Courts of Domestic Relations kept special records of children, a little more than 4 per cent of the cases arraigned were Negroes. The ratio of Negro children arraigned in the Children's Court increased from 4.2 per cent in 1919 to 11.7 per cent in 1930. By 1938 almost 25 per cent of the cases were Negroes. This occurred while the total number of white children arraigned decreased 38.3 per cent.

The overwhelming bulk of Negroes are Protestant, and since the provisions of the New York State law insist upon neglected children being fostered only within their own religion, this left most of them without care. Only six out of thirty-four Protestant agencies cared for Negro children, though Roman Catholic care was found to be more adequate. During the five-year period 1931–1935, the Children's Court adjudged more than three thousand Negro children to be neglected and assigned most of them to a state institution to solve the problem of food and shelter. More than a third of the boys arrested were charged with offenses involving property, though most of them were arrested for hitching on trolleys, stealing subway rides, selling newspapers after 7:00 P.M., and shining shoes on the streets.[19]

Negro adults were chiefly arrested for their participation in the "policy racket"; a little less than 8 per cent were women. Almost 50 per cent of the women arrested in the city during the period 1930–1935 were Negro and 80 per cent of these were charged with prostitution. The widespread operations of the "policy racket," which extracted so much money from the community for the benefit of racketeers, were due to a large extent to the desperate economic conditions of the people who had hoped to gain through luck what had been denied them through labor. A percentage of

Negro arrests was the result of "the unconscious or deliberate discrimination on the part of the police force against Negro people." [20]

. . . WHILE ROME BURNS

Unemployment mounted to staggering totals as the country sank deeper in the mire of depression. The federal, state, and city administrations failed to act in the unemployment crisis at a time when the *New York Times* was acknowledging that bread lines were feeding thousands of people a day. Regarded as only a temporary situation, the relief financing began with popular contributions, for private charity had been overtaxed. When the depression still did not pass, the city assumed partial support of the unemployed on a pay-as-you-go basis. A day did not pass without demonstrations in front of Harlem's Home Relief offices because of this unhappy plan.

Meanwhile, the affairs of the city had gone from bad to worse. The Seabury investigation began its hearings and turned up evidence which made it apparent that Mayor Walker was in a highly vulnerable position. Particularly was Harlem stirred when Seabury uncovered a vice ring which framed innocent women, a fact that Negro women knew only too well. There were many Negroes with friends who had been so victimized.

After Mayor Walker's resignation in 1932, the new city administration was faced with a relief problem that clamored for attention. It first threatened to tax the Stock Exchange and then borrowed money for relief. The point had been reached where the richest city in the richest country in the world could barely meet the needs of the emergency. Two vital things then happened: Roosevelt was elected President in 1932, and with his support La Guardia became mayor in 1934. But an impenetrable wall of discrimination and segregation, of despair and unhappiness, had sprung up around Harlem. The appalling specter of sickness, poverty, and death grimly faced the Negro.

PROTEST

The long-expected explosion came on March 19, 1935, when ten thousand Negroes swept through Harlem destroying the property of white merchants. At the time, the outburst was labeled incorrectly a "race riot." White New York was almost panic-stricken as a nightmare of Negro revolt appeared to be a reality. In the very citadel of America's New Negro, "crowds went crazy like the remnants of a defeated, abandoned, hungry army." So formidable did the demonstration become that the Harlem Merchants' Association, a group of white shopkeepers, demanded unsuccessfully that Governor Lehman send troops to patrol the district.

An absurdly trivial incident furnished the spark. On the afternoon of March 19, a Puerto Rican lad was caught stealing a ten-cent penknife from the counter of a five-and-ten-cent store at West 135th Street. In resisting his captors, the boy hit them. Incensed at what appeared to be a retaliatory display of brutality by the store's white male employees, the Negro shoppers attacked them. Others spread the alarm that a Negro boy was being beaten. A general alarm brought police reserves. Rumor then followed that the boy had been beaten to death, and Negroes rushed to the scene intent upon "avenging" the "murder."

The police estimated that by 5:30 P.M. more than three thousand persons had gathered. Several stepladder speakers addressed the crowds, charging the police with brutality and the white merchants with discrimination in employment. They were pulled down by the police and arrested. Two hours later protest leaflets were hurled through the neighborhood by members of the Young Communist League.

Large detachments of uniformed police, plainclothesmen, and mounted police charged the crowds. Radio cars were driven on the sidewalks to disperse the people. Instead of withdrawing, the crowds grew in numbers and in hostility. Stirred to traditional anger against the police, they surged through the streets smashing store windows, hurling bricks, stones, and other missiles at the police. The mob broke into bands of three and four hundred and looted stores owned by whites. An anecdote is told of a Chinese laundryman who rushed out on the street and in self-defense hurriedly posted a sign on his store window which read: "Me colored too." On Lenox Avenue, the scene of most of the disorder, laden rioters emerged from shattered shop windows, while women stood on the fringe of crowds and shouted their choice of articles. A more humorous side of this was the case of a ragged youth who entered a wrecked tailor shop and outfitted himself with a new spring coat, complaining bitterly that he would be unable to return for alterations.

Sporadic outbursts continued until the early hours of the morning. Five hundred uniformed policemen, two hundred plainclothesmen and mounted police, and fifty radio cars were active in quelling the outburst. At least two hundred stores owned by white merchants were smashed and their goods carried away. The total damage was estimated at more than two million dollars. Three deaths —all Negroes—were reported. Thirty-odd people were hospitalized for bullet wounds, knife lacerations, and fractured skulls, and more than two hundred persons received minor injuries, cuts, and abrasions. Some one hundred persons, the majority of them Negroes, were arrested on charges of inciting to violence, unlawful assemblage, and looting. The boy, in the meantime, had actually been released, after the manager had refused to press charges.

". . . FOAM ON TOP THE BOILING WATER"

Many reasons were offered for the uprising. The daily papers were particularly alarming in their reports, characterizing it as Harlem's worst riot in twenty-five years. The *Daily News* said that "Young Liberator orators whipped the fast-gathering crowds into a frenzy of hysteria . . . apparently to seize the opportunity to raise the issue against the store which had been picketed (by Negroes) for its refusal to hire colored clerks." The *Evening Journal,* manifestly incensed, traced its cause directly to "Communistic agitators circulating lying pamphlets." The *Post* said editorially that it would have been impossible to inflame Harlem's residents "if there had not been discrimination in employment and on relief, and justifiable complaints of high rents." The *New York Sun* derided the district attorney's (Dodge's) attempt to find Red propaganda behind the disturbance. "Actually," said the *Sun,* "Communists are more likely to have been passengers on the ebullience of a volatile population than authors of its effervescence."

Harlem's Negro leaders said that "seeing Red" was an official privilege and divergence, for the disorder had deep social, economic, and political roots. The Reverend William Lloyd Imes, pastor of St. James's Protestant Episcopal Church, felt that the white merchants were "reaping a harvest that they had sown," because of their refusal to employ Negroes. Channing Tobias, Negro field secretary of the YMCA, summed up the situation in this manner:

> It is erroneous and superficial to rush to the easy conclusions of District Attorney Dodge and the Hearst newspapers that the whole thing was a Communist plot. It is true there were Communists in the picture. But what gave them their opportunity? The fact that there were and still are thousands of Negroes standing in enforced idleness on the street corners of Harlem with no prospect of employment while their more favored Negro neighbors are compelled to spend their money with business houses directed by white absentee owners who employ white workers imported from every other part of New York City.

The views of the Negro leaders followed almost a uniform pattern. For example, George W. Harris, publisher of Harlem's *News*, said: "They [the rioters] were inspired because the colored people have been denied a decent economic opportunity. Private business, public utilities and the city government have oppressed a despondent Negro population and the result is a magazine of dynamite which it is only too easy to set off. The City of New York has consistently denied positions to colored boys and girls. . . . The riots were born of impatience at segregation, dominations of underworld leaders, who have found a fertile field for their activities among the credulous Negroes of the neighborhood." Roy Wilkins, editor of the *Crisis*, felt that it was a great mistake to dismiss the riot as the demonstration of a few agitators and attributed it to "a demonstration induced by discrimination against the Negroes in economics, employment and justice, and living conditions." In a series of articles for the *New York Post*, the Reverend Adam C. Powell, Jr., pastor of the Abyssinian Baptist Church, sought to prove that the outburst was essentially a social protest.

PEOPLE'S COURT

Mayor La Guardia immediately named an investigating committee composed of prominent citizens, of which seven were Negro and five whites.[21] It was known as the Mayor's Commission on Conditions in Harlem, and its report was prepared by E. Franklin Frazier, a professor of sociology at Howard University. The public, anxious to air its grievances, appeared at the public hearings which were conducted by the commission at the Harlem Heights Court. Officials of large firms and utilities were placed on the stand and interrogated by the public and the commissioners alike. The witnesses who appeared also represented welfare and civil employee groups and labor unions. Anyone who had a complaint was welcome to take the stand. This privilege often caused heated demonstrations by Negroes.[22]

On Saturday afternoons the Mayor's Commission held its public hearings. Hundreds of Negroes would crowd into the small municipal courtroom at West 151st Street, and before a member of the commission who presided as chairman the people presented their case. Often emotional and incoherent, some timid and reticent, some noisy and inarticulate, but all with a burning resentment, they registered their complaints against the discriminations, the Jim-Crowism, and all the forms of oppression to which they had been subjected.

The testimony carried, despite its tragic character, an undertone of humor when expressed in the Negro idiom. In the relating of a story of the killing of a Negro youth by a white policeman, several Negroes who had been eyewitnesses to the incident were called to the stand. The first witness was a man who approached the stand reluctantly and in a lowered, muffled voice, as though he feared too open a discussion of the shooting or too blatant a knowledge of it might involve him unpleasantly with the police authorities, recounted what he had seen. His impatient audience punctuated his testimony with encouraging shouts of "Aw, man, talk up, you ain't down South!" This cooperation failed to help and the man completed his mutterings and sat down. A clean-cut, aggressive, sharp-tongued youth succeeded him. In clear, resonant tones he measured out his answers. When the chairman asked, "Did you see anyone throw any milk bottles at the police?," the boy answered, "Man, you know ain't nobody gonna throw no milk bottles at a cop who's got a forty-four [gun] staring him in the face . . . people ain't crazy!" Suddenly remembering the difficulty that the audience had had in hearing the testimony of his mouselike predecessor, he good-naturedly bellowed out, "Am I talkin' loud enough?" and the courtroom displayed its approval with a howl of laughter.

The city's commission turned over its report to Mayor La Guardia in March 1936, one year later. The 35,000-word document was published by the *Amsterdam News,* July 18, 1936. Whereas columns and columns of material appeared in the daily press during the riot, the same papers published only sedate accounts of the report. The *Amsterdam News's* "scoop" went practically unnoticed, except by the *Daily Worker.*

During the 1937 session of the legislature, a commission was named to submit a report on the condition of the urban colored population in New York State before March 1938.[23] The commission submitted its first report in March 1938 and had its tenure extended in order to submit a second report in February 1939. Lester B. Granger, industrial secretary of the National Urban League, who served as executive director of the commission, was assigned the task of preparing the first report. Many private agencies launched investigations on various phases affecting Negro life.

DEEP SOCIAL ROOTS

Both investigations concluded on one note: a Harlem riot in 1935, at the height of modern times, in the great city of New York, must have had deep roots. The conditions confronting Negroes were found to spring from several distinct and closely related causes. As a population of low income, it suffered from conditions that affected low-income groups of all races, but the causes that kept Negroes in this class did not apply with the same force to whites. These conditions were underscored by discrimination against Negroes in all walks of life. The rumor of the death of a boy which spread throughout the community had "awakened the deep-seated sense of wrongs and denials and even memories of injustices in the South." The Mayor's Commission reported as the riot's cause "the smouldering resentments of the people of Harlem against racial discrimination and poverty in the midst of plenty." Together with the diminished wage scale, the relief standards had further lowered the already degraded position of these people. Poverty, it was claimed, had taken its toll in the Negroes' health, morale, and general living conditions. The riot was, in the New York State Temporary Commission's view, "a spontaneous and an incoherent protest by Harlem's population against a studied neglect of its critical problems."

NOTES

1. The New York Charity Organization Society reported 592 Harlem Negro families under their care from 1927 to 1928, and these comprised only 24.7 per cent of all Negro families receiving charity.

2. Beverly Smith, *New York Herald Tribune,* February 10, 1930.

3. State of New York, *Report of the New York State Temporary Commission on the Condition of the Urban Colored Population to the Legislature of the State of New York* (Albany: J. B. Lyon, 1938), pp. 44–56.

4. More than 85 per cent of these buildings were old-law tenements.

This information—and much of this chapter—is derived from the report of the Mayor's Commission on Conditions in Harlem, "The Negro in Harlem: A Report on Social and Economic Conditions Responsible for the Outbreak of March 19, 1935" (La Guardia Papers). Although the report was not published at the time, the *Amsterdam News* (July 18, 1936) later printed a summary, and some of the commission's findings were also reported in E. Franklin Frazier, "Negro Harlem: An Ecological Study," *The American Journal of Sociology,* XLIII (July 1937), 72–88.—Ed.

5. Mayor's Commission Report. (See preceding note.—Ed.)

6. *Report of the New York State Temporary Commission,* p. 49.

7. Including relief and employed families of all classes together, one-half of all native white families of New York City had incomes of less than $1,814 yearly, but one-half of all Negro families had incomes of less than $837.

8. "The practice of hiring for housework Negro women who congregate on street corners in the Bronx, known as 'domestic slave markets,' was severely condemned by the Bronx Citizens' Committee for the Improvement of Domestic Employees meeting. . . . It was proposed that centers of special agencies be established in the sections where they congregate in order to shelter them in severe weather and also see that prospective employers pay them fair wages."—*New York Times,* December 1, 1939.

9. Ella Baker and Marvel Cooke, "The Bronx Slave Market," *Crisis Magazine,* XLII, No. 11 (November 1935), 330.

10. President Hoover called for neighborhood endeavor to raise relief funds for the unemployed. This resulted in numerous "street" or "block" parties at which money was raised.

11. Mayor's Commission Report.

12. The city's relief allowance for a male adult was raised to $6.25 by 1939.

13. Mayor's Commission Report.

14. New York Department of Health, Vital Statistics, December 1938.

15. Harlem Hospital reported an 11.2 mortality, Bellevue 5.7, and Coney Island Hospital 5 per cent in 1932.

16. *Report of the New York State Temporary Commission,* p. 31.

17. Note on draft: "Call it *Crime* (less flowery but better)."—Ed.

18. The U.S. Census of 1930 reports 75,123 Negro children under fifteen years of age in this city, 46,580 in Manhattan. Under twenty there were 60,402 in Manhattan and 96,243 in the five boroughs. Owen R. Lovejoy, *The Negro Children of New York* (New York: The Children's Aid Society, 1932), p. 5.

19. Mayor's Commission Report.

20. *Ibid.*

21. Its members included Dr. Charles H. Roberts, Oswald Garrison Villard, Mrs. Eunice Hunton Carter, Hubert T. Delany, Countee Cullen, A. Philip Randolph, Judge Charles E. Toney, William Jay Schieffelin, Morris Ernst, Arthur Garfield Hays, Col. John G. Grimley, Rev. John W. Robinson, and Rev. William McCann.

Seven Negroes and five whites make twelve. There are 13 names here. Presumably the final draft would have corrected this arithmetic.—Ed.

22. Interview with Arthur Garfield Hays, November 22, 1939.

23. The commission was composed of Harold P. Herman, chairman, William T. Andrews, Reverend Michael Mulvoy, John J. Howard, Leon A. Fischel, Walter J. Mahoney, Robert W. Justice, Henry Root Stern, Francis B. Rivers, Mrs. Elizabeth Ross Haynes, Reverend John H. Johnson, and Henri W. Shields.

Country II

Frantic Farmers Fight Law

Frank D. DiLeva

In the general introduction I focused on the protest of the Midwestern farmer, the subject of this selection and the next. The "Cow War" in Cedar County, Iowa, in 1931 showed that much more was involved in the farmers' problems, as they saw them, than the tuberculin test, which had been mandatory since 1925. "In reality it was the economic question and not the tuberculin test that was chiefly responsible for resistance on the part of cattle owners." Farmers concluded from the "Cow War" that in order to express their grievances effectively they needed more than a local organization. This would be provided by the Farmers' Holiday Association, the direct-action affiliate of the National Farmers' Union, which helped to initiate and direct the rural rebellion against low farm prices and farm foreclosures that swept across Iowa, Nebraska, and Minnesota beginning in the summer of 1932.

In the years immediately following the financial crash of 1929, there came a series of disturbances in Iowa in which farmers were the aggressive participants. These disturbances appeared in three distinct phases: opposition to the tuberculin test law, known as the "Cow War," the Sioux City "Milk Strike," and the "Farm Holiday."

[From *Annals of Iowa,* XXXII (October 1953), 81–109.]

The first of these disorders, which usually was designated as the "Cow War," took place in Cedar County in eastern Iowa and had its main focal point in the locale of Tipton.[1] Designed as a protest against enforced testing of cattle for bovine tuberculosis, it reflected the attitude of many farmers in the year 1931. The presence of bovine tuberculosis was widespread in the state and every conceivable effort was made to stamp it out, but a combination of events led the Iowa farmer to believe that enforcement of the test required by law cheated him of a just return from his cattle; therefore in his mind the protest was justified.

The Sioux City "Milk Strike," which was organized and directed by the Sioux City Milk Producers' Association, was of shorter duration and involved fewer persons than the "Cow War." It also served, however, to reveal and to publicize the farmers' economic situation.

Running contemporaneously with the "Milk Strike" and at times joining with it was the "Farm Holiday." The longest and most violent of the disturbances, it involved more persons and issues than had either of the preceding revolts. The "Farm Holiday" had its beginnings in the summer of 1932 and did not end until late in 1933.

In their attempts to block the duly constituted agencies of law and order, the farmers appeared to be acting out of character as stable, conservative, law-abiding citizens. To the contemporary observer, these disturbances may have seemed to be extremely violent, radical, and directed against the basic institutions of our country. Yet even a hasty examination of the history of the United States reveals precedents of far more extensive unrest, a greater degree of violence and a more direct challenge to established authority which offer no evidence of left-wing tendencies. . . .

As is true of most historical phenomena, the "Cow War" in Iowa had its roots in conditions developing some years before its actual outbreak in 1931. While to the country at large the full effects of the 1929 crash did not appear until the middle of 1930, or in some cases even later, to the farm population the depression was a living, crushing thing long before 1929. It affected agriculture shortly after World War I and, though farm commodities had brief periods of higher levels during the twenties, there was nothing like the prosperity which had existed during the war years.

During the years 1926 to 1931, through overextension of credit, one Iowa farmer out of every seven lost his land.[2] In addition, of the 111,333 farms in Iowa which were being operated by private owners, by 1930, 64,425 were mortgaged.[3] This meant that 57.9 per cent of the farms in Iowa were mortgaged. In 1925, only 53.7 per cent of the farms had been mortgaged. Each of the farmers in 1930 paid an average of $1.37 per acre in real estate taxes and carried a debt of $9,626.[4] The total mortgage burden was equal to 48.5 per cent of the value of the farms—not excessive or unusual, however.

These were some of the factors facing the farmer as he went into the year 1931. He had mortgaged his land either in its purchase or to buy additional acres. Whether it was due, as many have said, to the fact that he had overexpanded during the boom years of 1919 and 1920, speculated in land purchases, and borrowed far beyond his means of repaying is a moot point.

No doubt this had to do with the farmers' plight, but it was not the entire cause of his economic difficulties. The farmer found himself in the situation of having borrowed cheap money and of becoming confronted with a tremendous debt in a time of scarce money. The reasons for the scarcity of money become obvious with the following statistics:

In 1919 the average value of cattle was $44.53 per hundredweight and the average value of hogs was $23.28 per hundredweight. By 1925 the price of cattle had declined to $22.52 per hundredweight and the average price of hogs had dropped to $13.05. Corn, the largest money crop for the farmer, had suffered the same type of collapse. From a high in 1919 of $1.513 per bushel it fell to $0.699 per bushel in 1925, and, after a few fluctuations, by 1931 the average price for the year had dropped to $0.318 per bushel and the market had not yet ceased its decline.[5] Faced with this situation, it was a rare person among the farmers who was not convinced that the time for drastic action had arrived. Most of those seeking relief were disgusted with investigations, promises, and governmental inaction.

One should not overlook the efforts made to obtain relief for the farmers' plight through the federal government. Attempts at relief were brought up in Congress, but they met a fate in many cases which showed a definite lack of foresight on the part of both legislators and presidents. One of the more important of these bills, known as the McNary-Haugen Bill, was brought before the legislators in Washington every session from 1924 to 1927 and finally, after many revisions, was passed in 1927, only to be vetoed by President Coolidge.[6] The bill with its "equalization fee" was designed to appeal to the Midwestern farmer who was traditionally a supporter of high tariffs. It was this fee which was to pay for the project, but the bill was vetoed, not once but twice, in successive years. Other bills were proposed, investigated, and in most cases defeated during the "farmers' administration." Bills which were designed to give the farmer benefits similar to those received by industry through the protective tariff seemed doomed to failure.

It is evident that the actual reasons for the "Cow War" rested on the general economic conditions of agriculture, although the immediate reasons were attributed to the tuberculin test. This was aptly put by Jay N. Darling: "The real problem was the collapse of farm prices and tumbling land values. Bank failures, mortgage foreclosures and prohibitive taxation added to the misery of being caught between a crash of price and a rise of dollars." [7]

This combination of circumstances explains the situation that faced numbers of farmers by 1931, and why in March of that year the outbreak of the "Cow War" was precipitated by the enforcement of the unpopular tuberculin test.

This test was designed to prevent the spread of bovine tuberculosis by the detection of the disease and condemnation of affected cattle. This usually meant a loss to the farmer, since the condemned value of the diseased animal was never its true worth. One could not expect the farmer in the face of a grave economic crisis to be jubilant concerning the condemnation of his cattle for a mere fraction of their former worth, and to the farmer, the tuberculin test seemed to bring about this very thing.

In the weekly *Tipton Advertiser,* published in the very center of the agitation area, there appeared on March 5, 1931, an article which stated that the Cedar County State Bank of Tipton failed to open its doors. This was the first of many bank failures in Cedar County and heralded an era of bank failures The effect of such a closing was tremendously important to the farm population, for the bank held notes which automatically became due and consequently money became more difficult to obtain. With the banks closed and income threatened by the tuberculin test, the farmers were desperate.

The state of Iowa had made provisions for the testing of cattle as early as 1919, when the legislature appropriated $100,000 to be spent in a coordinate program with the United States Department of Agriculture.[8] By 1925, the test had been made mandatory and its administration proceeded slowly but surely throughout the counties of Iowa.

In the initial stages, after 1919, the work of tuberculosis eradication went rather slowly, since the state required 51 per cent of the owners of breeding and dairy cattle to sign a petition asking the county board of supervisors to make application for the enrollment of the county in the program.[9] The supervisors were then authorized to levy an assessment of three mills to cover the expenses and indemnities.[10] Earlier, under a voluntary program set up in 1923, twenty-five counties had signed up for the test.

A county or district was considered accredited by law under one of two types of action: (a) a modified accredited area was one which had reduced tuberculosis to .005 per cent; (b) an accredited area was one which had 25 per cent of the cattle owners petitioning for the test.[11] The one-half of 1 per cent specified for a modified accredited area was not as great a reduction as the figures seem to indicate, for bovine tuberculosis had not reached any truly great proportions.[12]

The law for testing was revised and altered, amended and added to every two years from 1925 to 1931. At this latter date it read:

> It shall be the duty of the department of agriculture to eradicate bovine tuberculosis in all the counties of the state in the manner provided by law in this chapter. Said department shall proceed with the examination including the tuberculin test of all such cattle as rapidly as possible.
>
> It shall be the duty of each and every owner of dairy or breeding cattle in the state to conform to and abide by the rules laid down by the state and federal departments of agriculture and follow their instructions designed to suppress the disease, prevent its spread and avoid reinfection of the herd.[13]

Upon the surface, this enactment would normally seem to all farmers to be a desirable thing, and to a degree it was. By 1926, twenty-seven counties had become accredited areas and each year saw more added to the total. The testing continued until in 1930 there were a total of fifty-eight counties declared as accredited.[14] The slowness of testing was due to lack of funds and lack of trained personnel for administering the test.

Specific problems faced the Iowa farmer in the early months of 1931. The bovine tuberculosis test was nothing new. It was not something designed to hinder the farmer's way of life, although in a short time he came to feel that it was unfair, corrupt, and designed to rob him of a portion of his livelihood. But prior to 1931 there had been little or no controversy about the matter, although a test case in court resulted in the upholding of the constitutionality of the law by the state supreme court.[15]

The procedure carried out in administering the test was generally as follows: A veterinarian hired by the state inoculated a farmer's cattle with a solution containing inert tuberculin bacilli. After a short period he returned to the cattle and tested their reaction to the inoculation. If an animal reacted unfavorably, it was termed a "reactor" and by law condemned to be destroyed.[16] The farmer received a certain amount of salvage remuneration, and therein lay the beginnings of the "Cow War," for the salvage return realized on his sale of the condemned animals was not equal to the worth of the cattle or to the expected return. The following formula was devised by the state for estimating the farmer's total remuneration:

> The sale price or salvage goes to the owner. That amount is subtracted from the appraised value. Of the remaining sum the state pays the farmer one-third, the national department of agriculture pays the farmer one-third and the farmer himself must stand for one-third of the loss.[17]

To illustrate, if a farmer had a reactor with an estimated value of $400, which was condemned and sold to a packer for perhaps a quarter of a cent a pound, the owner would receive about $22.50. This sum would then be subtracted from the appraised value of the cow, leaving a total of $377.50. The federal government would then pay one-third of this amount, the state another third, and the farmer would lose a third. The farmer's total return would then equal $273.66 for an animal appraised at $400 and probably worth more.

To the farmer, perhaps already in dire economic straits, having no control over the price paid by the packer or the appraised value, this situation seemed designed to cheat him out of his just return. It may be argued that the farmer received a fair compensation for a "reactor," but to the farmer nothing could be fair about losing approximately $130 of an animal's worth. In his financial plight the loss of even one dollar would no doubt have been felt, and the loss of $130 on each "reactor" could well have been a major catastrophe. In many instances a single animal may not have been important, but, if multiplied by five or six or twelve, the total sum would assume staggering proportions. Thus twelve animals would mean a loss of $1,500 or more, based on the above estimate. At any time this would be a substantial loss to a farmer, but in the year 1931 he felt it could well place him in bankruptcy.

It was this situation which caused the actual outbreak of the "Cow War." The anticipated loss, to the "embattled" farmer of Iowa, was the "shot heard 'round the world."

The reasons for the outbreak are subject to conjecture. It may have been that the farmer in his economic distress could no longer hope. He was involved in a depression which, publicly recognized since 1929, struck the farmer as early as 1920. By 1931 he may have reached the end of his patience.

Another possible factor was the type of personality that appeared among the active members of the revolt. The leaders had dropped the cloak of conventionality and had become insistent and violent in their demands for a favorable solution. The active leaders were straightforward and uncompromising men, and in them the beginnings of the struggle may be found.

The actual rebellion started on the fifth of March 1931. At this time it was announced that the cows of William Butterbrodt, who lived six miles northeast of Tipton, would be tested. The group of state agents and veterinarians who were to conduct the test were met by approximately two hundred farmers,[18] who objected to the test but who did not commit any acts of violence. The tuberculin was injected into the cattle and the state men left. The following day a group of farmers met at Tipton to send a petition to Governor Dan Turner and the state legislature asking that the tests be discontinued and the law repealed.[19] Three days later the state veterinarian returned to the Butterbrodt farm to read the results of the tests or to check the reaction.

Upon arrival at the farm, the veterinarians found nearly five hundred farmers waiting to prevent them from reading the results of the test.[20] After being blocked at the Butterbrodt farm, the state agents and veterinarians proceeded to the farm of E. C. Mitchell, only to be met by another group of irate farmers. It became apparent at this point that a considerable portion of the farmers of Cedar County were firmly opposed to the testing. Estimates of the number of those in open opposition vary widely. Those who supported the state government definitely made the estimate as low as possible. The test objectors for the most part were in the eastern section of Iowa, centering around Tipton.

The tenth of March saw five Cedar County farms picketed by the objectors. A warning system apparently had been arranged for the purpose of summoning farmers in case an attempt was made to carry out the scheduled testing.[21] For the next week the testing rested in a state of suspended animation, pending orders from the state testing offices.[22] The farmers in the interim were being organized by J. W. Lenker of Wilton Junction, who, as president of the Farmers' Protective Association and a cattle raiser, had a definite stake in the problem. Lenker led his group of one thousand to fifteen hundred men to Des Moines on the nineteenth of March.[23] There they stormed the statehouse and demanded that they be heard by the General Assembly in open session. The capitol grounds were jammed to overflowing, and the crowd became so unwieldy that all legislative business other than the discussion of the tuberculin test was suspended.[24] In response to demands made by the farmers, they were granted a hearing by the legislature.

Lenker explained the actions of the farmers during the hearing. He said:

> We are here primarily to demonstrate against compulsory tuberculosis testing and to urge the passage of the house bill making tuberculosis testing optional and making the county the unit of determination whether testing shall be undertaken.[25]

The bill approved by Lenker, known as the Davis bill, earlier had been introduced by Lawrence Davis, representative from Delaware County. It was designed to repeal the compulsory provisions of the testing law and make it a matter of choice. Not only did the farmers' group discuss the tuberculin test law, but they also included in their grievances such matters as the establishment of a state police system, which they opposed. They condemned compulsory military training at the state university and state college. They also attacked the county assessor bill, a minimum wage law for teachers, and tax-free securities. The addition of various grievances other than the tuberculin test is a fair indication that the farmer's problems, as he conceived them, involved far more than the tests.[26] The temper of the farmers was shown by the placards carried during their visit to the statehouse. Such rhymes as these were numerous:

Fake, fake, fake,
Vets condemn our cattle
And to the packers take
Fake, fake, fake.[27]

The invasion of the statehouse could not help coming to the attention of the governor, since it was held almost literally upon his front doorstep. Governor Dan Turner spoke to the farmers during the afternoon session of the hearing, and his speech was to become a key to all his subsequent dealings with the farm problems. His statement seemed to sum up his complete philosophy concerning the testing and the objectors. Although it allowed for little constructive action, it epitomized the cautious executive going to all lengths to carry out his oath of office.

> "A test of representative government is involved in this matter," he [Governor Turner] said, "and I ask you, as you cherish your own right, that you aid me in carrying out the plain provisions of the law, and I herewith guarantee to you so far as lies within my power your rights shall be maintained, your lives and property protected." [28]

So far as J. W. Lenker and the rest of the farmers in the statehouse on that day were concerned, the above statement was merely a mouthing of platitudes. They felt that it gave them no reassurance and left them in the same position they had held before their demonstration.

Following the demonstration at the state capitol, the testing went on with a certain degree of smoothness, for noncooperating farmers had been summarily threatened with a quarantine. To the farmer this was the equivalent of losing a cow, for under the provisions of the quarantine law no meat or milk could be sold from that animal. The statute clearly provided for this contingency: "If he refused to confine the cattle, the department may employ sufficient help to properly confine them and the expense of such help shall be paid by the owner or deducted from the indemnity if any is paid." [29]

The lack of any voiced resentment against the testing in the three weeks following the visit to the statehouse prompted state authorities to issue a statement that the objections had died away. This mistaken conclusion was based on the belief that since E. C. Mitchell, one of the leaders of the opposition, had allowed his cattle to be injected, the testing of his cattle would go to completion. However, the test readings were the crucial phase of the entire process, and Mr. Mitchell soon proved to be very uncooperative at the time of the attempted readings.

The official statement concerning the withdrawal of opposition to the test must necessarily have been made the day before its appearance in the evening papers, for on the day of its publication, April 10, the call had been sent over the rural party line for all objecting farmers in the Tipton area to assemble at the Mitchell farm to prevent the test readings.[30] A group of newspapermen who [had managed to learn of the situation] arrived at the farm in search of firsthand news and were forcibly ejected. At the entrance to the property were seventy-five farmers who refused admittance to any person not personally known to them.[31] The arrival of Dr. Malcolm, chief of the division of animal industry of the State Department of Agriculture, did little to soothe irritated tempers. His appearance signaled an attempted stampede of the Mitchell herd; when this failed, he was asked by Mitchell to leave the property. Two men in the group asked Mitchell's permission to throw Dr. Malcolm from the property and, after receiving an affirmative reply, proceeded to aid the doctor in making an unceremonious exit.[32]

The reaction to this incident was soon evident. Norman Baker, proprietor of Station KTNT and a staunch supporter of the resistance group, stated: "The farmers are only asking for their rights." [33] Sheriff Foster Maxson of Cedar County stated that the situation was out of control. In talking to Governor Turner he made a formal request for troops.[34]

Accordingly, the state's National Guard was ordered by the governor to stand by, and two companies were alerted at 1:30 A.M. the morning of April 13.[35]

Into this explosive situation, seemingly made to order for him, stepped a dynamic personality, Milo Reno. Reno was an ordained minister,[36] but he did not have charge of a church. He had been a farmer in his early youth,[37] but no longer did he farm. His talent seemed to lie in the field of farm problems. As president and controlling factor in the Farmers' Union from 1921 until his death,[38] he carried on activities concerning farmers and their problems that were varied and numerous. As a private citizen interested in the struggle of the farmers engaged in the tuberculin disorders, he elected himself a personal intermediary between the farm group and the governor.

Reno had not been asked to accept such a position, but he talked to the governor and proceeded to talk to the representatives of the farmers to see if an effective settlement could be reached. His motive in the situation remains unclear, for it is difficult to determine whether he was simply attempting to further his own political ends, thus supporting his own ego, or acting as a man who felt that his experience and background made him the answer to the farmers' prayers. Regardless of his reasons, he did enter into the "Cow War," though his entry did little to effect a real peace.

The first public act of Milo Reno was to ask the governor to hold up the calling out of the guard until a conference could be held; he suggested Iowa City as the place for the meeting.[39] The governor agreed to Reno's suggestion upon the condition that the testing of the E. C. Mitchell herd be completed. The farmers then elected J. W. Lenker as their committee head to meet the governor.[40] Mitchell agreed to the tests and, after they were completed, he stated, "I don't care so much about the testing but I object to the principle of the test." [41] One animal reacted. The testers met no opposition even though Mitchell faced the loss of the "reactor."

Reno met with the group of farmers prior to the governor's conference at Iowa City. Included in the group were J. W. Lenker; Paul Moore; William Butterbrodt; Lawrence Davis, author of the bill to repeal the test law; Robert Moore, who was state secretary of the Farmers' Union; and H. R. Gross, press representative of the Farmers' Union. The unofficial conference brought about no change, and J. W. Lenker summed up the attitude of the group when he said to Reno: "We are just where we started." [42]

The meeting with the governor took place at the Jefferson Hotel in Iowa City at 1:15 P.M. on Monday, April 13, 1931. It was a closed session, and the words spoken behind the closed doors were known only to those in attendance. The governor arrived accompanied by Attorney General John Fletcher and Colonel Grahl of the Iowa National Guard.[43] Colonel Grahl was there in an unofficial capacity, since the calling out of the National Guard seemed likely. The farmers were represented by Paul Moore and Jake W. Lenker.

For some unknown reason Reno did not put in an appearance but, in commenting later concerning the whole problem, he ably summed up the farmer's position in opposing the tests. According to Reno: "The intradermal test is not dependable. Those cattle in which tuberculosis is present to the greatest extent will not show reaction to the test. You see, there is enough tuberculin in their system to set up a wall of resistance against the serum injected." [44]

Although the reasoning has been proved false, it did express the views of the farmer. But there were enough veterinarians who believed the test invalid to support the farmers in such a view, although the test had been used for many years previous to the controversy and little or no question of its validity had been raised. In another statement, however, Reno came closer to the heart of the farmer's problem. Speaking through the *Des Moines Tribune-Capital,* he said:

> The condemned cattle are purchased by the packer at his own price—two cents is a good average—ninety per cent of the meat bought by the packer is passed as fit for human consumption by a federal inspector. The present test is unfair to the farmer and the public alike. It robs the farmer and does not protect the public.[45]

In reality it was the economic question and not the tuberculin test that was chiefly responsible for resistance on the part of cattle owners. The farmers put forth three compromise provisions and presented them to the governor at the meeting in Iowa City. They were:

> A. The farmers were to be permitted to use accredited veterinarians of their own choosing.
>
> B. The state should withdraw all forces engaged in testing at the time.
>
> C. The governor was to exercise every effort toward bringing to a vote the Davis bill.[46]

Governor Turner would not agree to call off the state agents, but he did permit the farmers to choose their own veterinarians, if accredited by the state. Since he felt that coercion was being used to bring about support of the Davis bill, he therefore refused to use his influence in the matter. An attempt in the legislature to bring about passage of the bill was defeated by a vote of 80 to 22.[47] Governor Turner gave as his reason for refusing to call off the state officials that more people supported the test than objected.[48]

The governor's acceptance of the proposal authorizing farmer-selected veterinarians seemed rather onesided. However, the farmers agreed to call a truce, as for the most part they seemed to expect their demands to be met. At any rate they interpreted the truce to be the end of the rebellion and were satisfied with the outcome as they saw it.

The final termination of the "War" lay in the disposition of information for assault and violations of the state quarantine act, which had been brought against twenty-three of the men in the early days of the struggle. These were for the most part dismissed or suspended.

But the final shot of the first phase of the "Cow War" was fired by the farmers. J. W. Lenker and E. C. Mitchell attempted to obtain an injunction restraining the state from further testing; this was denied by Judge Moffit of Tipton. An appeal was filed, though there seemed little possibility that it would be granted.[49] The second attempt at forestalling the state by legal action was a similar petition filed by Arthur Fogg and other farmers around Tipton against the State Department of Agriculture. Eleven hundred farmers signed the petition to restrain the department, but again Judge Moffit refused to grant the injunction.[50] Though in effect the failure to secure injunctions against the state ended the war for a time, the state itself discontinued the test for a period. Quiet remained on the Tipton front, however, only as long as the state's efforts were discontinued.

The months of June and July 1931 saw no cattle testing and consequently no opposition. The state tolerated a truce of sorts and the farmers ostensibly had come to the realization that violence was not the answer to the problem. Events, however, soon again disturbed the surface calm. On the fifth day of August, the state was granted an injunction restraining J. W. Lenker and forty-four others from obstructing the agents in their administration of the tuberculin test.[51] The injunction meant little in itself, for the state already was empowered to act; nevertheless it must have irritated some of the farmers, for on the twentieth of the month war flared anew and law and order were disrupted.

Dr. Malcolm ordered the state veterinarians to resume testing, presumably to determine if those farmers who had previously objected would now give their consent. The veterinarians conducting the tests were given specific instructions to withdraw from any farm where violence or objection was met.[52] Perhaps Dr. Malcolm had not really expected the farmers to change their minds; at any rate objections became evident almost as soon as he started to work. The first protest came in the form of the violent expulsion of a state agent from the farm of Arthur Fogg, just north of West Liberty. Dr. A. H. Joehnk of Iowa City visited the Fogg farm for the purpose of testing his cattle and found the owner more than reluctant to allow the testing. The doctor was met with a shower of eggs and water thrown by the wife and daughter of Fogg, who himself threatened to use a shotgun.[53] The doctor claimed to have been injured not by water and eggs, but by something else which presumably was thrown by the women.[54]

Similar series of incidents were repeated at two other farms, though there were individual variations. William Butterbrodt, who resided about six miles northeast of Tipton, assisted a state agent in his hurried exit from the farm by a well-placed kick,[55] according to the doctor, who no doubt made a reliable though prejudiced witness. The third dissenter was William Hogan, living north of Durant, who forbade the testing of his cattle but did not attempt any act of violence.[56]

Thus Dr. Malcolm learned the true temper of the farmers. They were not ready to concede that the testing should be allowed to continue without a challenge. The state immediately counter-challenged with an injunction it had previously obtained and the three resisting farmers were served with the proper papers and told to appear in court.

Thus in the first attempt at a retest, nine other farmers had been visited; of these nine, one was sick, one submitted, five were not at home, and two asked to be allowed veterinarians of their choice.[57]

Hogan and Butterbrodt pleaded not guilty when brought into court and were released upon eight hundred dollars' bond. Fogg also pleaded not guilty but changed his plea to guilty when told of the maximum sentence which could be imposed.[58] Fogg was fined fifty dollars and had a one-day jail sentence suspended. The proceedings, though without violence, brought forth many well-wishers and sympathizers. At the time of the Butterbrodt hearing at least one hundred farmers accompanied him to the courtroom, and for a time violence was feared.[59]

Faced with open and outright violation of the law, Governor Dan Turner authorized the appointment of sixty-five state agents and sheriff's deputies to aid in the enforcement of the cattle-testing law. The first place chosen was to be the farm of Jake Lenker of Wilton Junction.[60]

Notification of the testing set rumors into rapid circulation. Reports that 325 farmers from Des Moines and Lee counties were on their way to assist the protesting farmers spread rapidly throughout the area.[61] No verification for the report could be found immediately, but the rumor persisted. Another rumor was that masses of farmers were moving on the Lenker farm to forestall state action.[62] Still another story held that the farmers were driving their cattle out of the county in an effort to prevent the test.

> Rumors reaching Tipton this morning were to the effect that objecting farmers were driving their cattle out of the county. One observer reported that a herd of twenty head were driven to the Cedar county line near Wilton last evening by a man on horseback during a downpour of rain.[63]

These two reports were verified to a certain extent by later happenings though neither achieved the expected proportions.

In response to Governor Turner's move to resume the testing program, Dr. Malcolm personally on September 21 had gone to the farm of Jake Lenker to perform the tests and had taken with him approximately sixty-five deputies and various state agents. This group was met by at least four hundred farmers, and though the deputies used tear gas, a shower of clubs, mud, and "Irish confetti" caused them to perform a strategic withdrawal.[64] Several deputies were injured and their cars smashed. Dr. Malcolm was attacked and bruised, the radiator of his car was filled with mud, the gas line was broken, tires were slashed, and windows knocked out.[65]

Governor Turner had only shortly before this incident returned from Washington, D.C., where he had attended a conference concerning the price of corn. Although the conference solved nothing, it had been important enough to take him from the state. His almost immediate reaction to the mishandling of Dr. Malcolm and the deputies was the calling out of the National Guard. He justified his position with the following statement: "Where men are organized against government, there is only one thing to do, and that is to put down the insurrection. That is exactly what I propose to do in Cedar county." [66]

Regardless of the political consequences—and that seems to have been the governor's attitude in the whole matter—the troops moved into Tipton. The town soon became an armed camp and the soldiers, in all the joviality of an outing, affectionately named the encampment grounds Camp Bovine or Cow Camp.[67] The troops mobilized were the 168th Infantry, the 133rd Infantry, and the 113th Cavalry, which brought no horses.[68] These three regiments and the headquarters staff brought the total to nearly two thousand troops.[69]

The troops arrived amid a small amount of heckling, but no violence. Groups of farmers gathered on street corners to speak in hushed tones of their coming, and the townspeople watched with something like relief. The guardsmen accepted the duty as a joke and entered Tipton in a happy mood. With the troops came an order from the governor, enlisting the aid of seventy-five veterinarians to complete the testing. Machine guns lined the roads of Cedar County at strategic points; only persons with military passes were allowed to travel in or out of the area.[70] No farmer was allowed out of the area under any circumstances without military escort,[71] and the region quickly took on the look of an encampment.

Quickly, efficiently, the troops (some of them men of Cedar County) went into operation, and their first objective was the farm of Jake Lenker. Under command of General Park A. Findley, Colonel Glenn Haynes was sent to the Lenker farm with a detachment of men and a veterinarian. Upon their arrival they found that Lenker had removed his cattle from the premises, and Colonel Haynes immediately arrested him.[72] He was charged with moving his cattle illegally, and the second of the persistent rumors had been verified. The actual charge against Lenker was the moving of cattle illegally while under quarantine. He was accused of contempt of court, since he had violated the injunction granted the state.

When questioned concerning the cattle, Lenker said:

> I've sold my cattle to a neighbor who has taken them to a feed lot. I would rather do that than let that crooked bunch get hold of them.
>
> I believe that Dan Turner sent the guard up here for an outing. I wouldn't believe anything he said anyway, for I don't think he knows what he is talking about, and then there is Hoover. He took prosperity away from us and hid it around the corner.[73]

There were others who objected to the tests just as violently as had Lenker. One person voicing an opinion concerning the general problem was C. L. McKinnon, who was vice-president of the Farmers' Protective Association:

> If the use of milk from reacting cows is harmful, the use of meat is equally objectionable, and yet 92 to 93% of the meat of reacting animals is sold for human consumption.
>
> We are opposed to the bovine tuberculin test as it is administered because we consider it unreliable, inaccurate, because it doesn't detect the worst reactors, because it ruins our cattle, because many of the tested cattle die while others abort and give milk unfit for human consumption.[74]

This view was shared by many farmers and their supporters, but no conclusive evidence had ever been brought to prove its validity. Enough people, however, believed abortions were the result of the test to cause many of them to hold the same opinion as McKinnon. Ed Scorpil of Route 1, near Tipton, maintained that the tests induced premature births among his cattle tested in 1930 and 1931. He claimed to have lost eleven of twenty-five calves born in 1931, and thirteen of sixteen calves born in 1930.[75] How he came to the conclusion that the tuberculin test caused the abortions was never explained by Mr. Scorpil, but his belief in the fallacy of the test was as effective in determining his course as if laboratory evidence had been submitted.

The arrival of troops aroused varying reactions in the populace of Tipton. The merchants felt that it aided business, and the farmers felt that it was a shabby, low trick, perpetrated by the governor. Regardless of the attitude of the various groups, the troops were in Tipton, and martial law was to prevail until such time as the governor recalled them and reestablished civilian courts.

The arrest of Lenker came as a definite shock to most of the farmers, for he had attained the position of leader. In a type of action lacking thorough organization, the loss of what little leadership existed was a staggering blow, but Lenker's release on bond was not long in coming. His bond was set at ten thousand dollars and he was given until October 1 to enter a plea.[76] The hearing was scheduled for Tipton, but it was changed later. Previous to his establishment of bond he had been removed from the National Guard encampment and taken to Anamosa Reformatory for the purpose of preventing violence in connection with his release.[77]

Governor Turner reiterated his previous statements concerning law and order and maintained that the Lenker case would be handled strictly according to law.[78]

Lenker's terms of release prevented his interference in the testing, and he returned to his farm to await trial. E. C. Mitchell, another of the original objectors, was arrested and released on five thousand dollars' bond after his lawyer, J. C. France, had obtained a writ of habeas corpus. This in itself posed a legal question, for the Iowa constitution definitely permitted the suspension of the writ of habeas corpus during time of martial law. Still the writ was issued and Mitchell was released on bond.[79]

Although the testing continued without opposition for the most part, not all farmers submitted quietly. Two men, Carl Rixe and R. P. Broders, were arrested for refusing to allow the test. On the Broders farm at least twenty-five farmers gathered and the veterinarians who attempted to test the cattle were allegedly attacked by Broders.[80]

This was the exception, however, and for the most part the testing proceeded without undue difficulty except from the mud and rain which befell Tipton upon the arrival of the troops. In two days at least twenty-seven herds were tested,[81] and for all practical purposes the war was over. Though the violence had ceased, the feeling of the populace had not appreciably changed. This was borne out by the fact that in Henry County a popular meeting sent the following ultimatum to the governor:

> We the undersigned, citizens of the state of Iowa, on this day, September 24, 1931, attending a mass meeting at Mount Pleasant in Henry county, go on record as asking Governor Turner to release J. W. Lenker and remove the soldiers from Cedar county immediately.
>
> We hereby bind ourselves not to pay unpaid taxes for 1931 and not to pay any in 1932 unless troops are withdrawn immediately from Cedar county.[82]

The petition had seven hundred signers. The receipt of it was the instigating factor in the governor's issuance of the statement concerning law and order in the handling of the Lenker case. Governor Turner was showered with telegrams and letters, all expressing the same general protest. The Farmers' Union and the Farmers' Protective Association joined in sending a petition asking that the testing be stopped until the merits of the test could be fully determined.[83]

Another shock suffered by the farmers was the rearrest of Jake Lenker and Paul Moore. This second arrest did not stem from their most recent actions, but was based on their original attempts to prevent the cattle from being tested. The two men were charged with conspiracy to violate the Iowa Tuberculin Law.[84]

The trial of Lenker and Moore began in the week of March 23, 1932, but not in Tipton. The state had asked for a change of venue to Jones County on the grounds that an impartial jury could not be obtained in Cedar County.[85] This fact had seemed obvious in the trials of other objectors, for of all the persons arrested by state agents and National Guardsmen, only Lenker and Moore received a sentence commensurate with their crime. A minor item in the *Des Moines Register* of March 10, 1933, pointed up this fact, by noticing that the "Cow War" cases against six farmers who had been indicted for conspiracy to incite rebellion against the Tuberculin Test Law were dismissed because the courts had been unable to draw an impartial jury. This was the settlement in the majority of cases. Others were dismissed with small fines or suspended sentences.

Finally the case against Jake Lenker and Paul Moore went to trial and the two men were convicted, which in view of public sentiment was an unexpected and somewhat startling turn of events. The Turner administration closed in January 1933, and Clyde E. Herring became governor. The state supreme court, in December 1933, upheld the conviction of Lenker and Moore,[86] and although they filed other appeals, by July 1934 they had exhausted all hope of obtaining releases from their sentences. And finally, on the sixth day of July 1934, Moore and Lenker were taken to the state penitentiary to begin serving the three-year term which had been given them for their part in the "Cow War."[87] On the fifteenth day of August, exactly forty days after their incarceration, the two men were released[88] on parole by the state board of parole.

The violent phases of the "Cow War" had ended long before the trials were held. The troops had been moved from Tipton on the second day of October 1931,[89] and within a week only a very small detachment remained to aid in the testing. The war had reached a conclusion, but it had not reached a solution. Now that the violence had been suppressed and the farmers had returned to their homes, it would seem that the state had won its case and that by noticing this fact the farmer would have come to the realization that violence, agitation, and unlawful action were out of place in a modern society. Yet if this were so, there would then have been no further disturbances elsewhere. J. S. Russell, the farm editor of the *Des Moines Register and Tribune,* in a personal letter to the author, gave this statement as his summary of the cause of the "Cow War":

> The Cow War had its roots in the same unrest that developed the Holiday movement. The protest against testing cows was, in my opinion, merely one form of expression of resentment against low prices and depression.

If Mr. Russell is correct in his thumbnail evaluation a complete solution to the farmers' grievances was not achieved. There was no increase in commodity prices, nor did the state provide any legislation to aid the farmer. . . . His market had not increased and, so far as the farmer was concerned, he felt that he had gained little through his efforts. The repeal of the Tuberculin Test Law would not have solved his problem. It might have saved him a cow or two, but that would not have raised the price of milk or beef. The "Cow War" did encourage the farmers to draw one general conclusion, however: that all farmers, not just a few, should be organized. This idea was later carried out by Milo Reno in the Farm Holiday Movement.

The "Cow War" had ended, but other outbreaks were to follow, born of the same circumstances, reacting in the same manner, and in some cases coming to the same conclusion. The final ending of the revolts may well have been speeded if the executive departments of the State of Iowa and the United States had realized that it was not a matter of suppressing a group of radicals but of aiding a group of citizens in time of need.

NOTES

1. *The Tipton Advertiser,* March 12, 1931.
2. George Mills, "Iowa Foreclosures and Farm Violence Hit Peak in '33," *Des Moines Register,* May 12, 1946, Sec. 4, p. 4.
3. U.S. Bureau of the Census, *Sixteenth Census of the United States, 1940, Agriculture,* I (Washington: Government Printing Office, 1942), 7.
4. *Ibid.*
5. U.S. Department of Agriculture, *Agricultural Statistics,* I (Washington: Government Printing Office, 1940), 45, 46, 9, 10, 344, 345. The prices quoted in this discussion are used primarily in relation to farmer reaction, rather than as a statistical study of agricultural prices.
6. Earle D. Ross, *Iowa Agriculture: An Historical Survey* (Iowa City: State Historical Society of Iowa, 1951), Chap. 11.
7. Jay N. Darling, "The Farmers' Holiday," *New Outlook,* CLXI (October 1932), 19.
8. Iowa State Department of Agriculture, *Iowa Year Book of Agricultures 1923,* I (Des Moines: State of Iowa, 1924), ix.
9. *Ibid.*
10. *Ibid.*
11. Iowa State Department of Agriculture, *Iowa Year Book of Agricultures 1930,* I (Des Moines: State of Iowa, 1931), 27.
12. *Ibid.*
13. *Iowa Revised Code* (1931), Ch. 165.2.
14. Iowa State Department of Agriculture (1930), p. 27.
15. *Fevold vs. Board of Supervisors of Webster County,* 202 Iowa 1019 (1926).
16. *Des Moines Register,* September 22, 1931, p. 1.
17. *Des Moines Sunday Register,* April 12, 1931, p. 1.
18. *The Tipton Advertiser,* March 12, 1931.
19. *Ibid.*
20. *Ibid.*
21. *Davenport Democrat,* March 10, 1931.
22. *Ibid.,* March 17, 1931.
23. *Des Moines Tribune-Capital,* March 19, 1931, p. 1.
24. *Ibid.*
25. *Ibid.*
26. *Ibid.*
27. *Ibid.*
28. *Ibid.*
29. *Des Moines Sunday Register,* April 12, 1931, p. 1.
30. *Des Moines Tribune-Capital,* April 11, 1931, p. 1.
31. *Ibid.*
32. *Des Moines Register,* April 11, 1931, p. 1.
33. *Des Moines Sunday Register,* April 12, 1931.
34. *Des Moines Register,* April 13, 1931, p. 1.
35. *Des Moines Tribune Capital,* April 13, 1931, p. 1
36. Milo Reno, *Farmers' Union Pioneer* (Iowa City: Athens Press, 1941), p. 10.
37. *Ibid.,* p. 19–22.

38. *Ibid.*, p 40.
39. *Des Moines Register,* April 13, 1931.
40. *Des Moines Sunday Register,* April 12, 1931.
41. *Ibid.*
42. *Des Moines Register,* April 13, 1931.
43. *Ibid.*
44. *Des Moines Tribune-Capital,* April 13, 1931, p. 8.
45. *Des Moines Register,* April 13, 1931.
46. *Des Moines Tribune-Capital,* April 13, 1931.
47. *Des Moines Register,* April 15, 1931, p. 1.
48. *Ibid.*
49. *Ibid.*
50. *Des Moines Tribune-Capital,* May 1, 1931, p. 1.
51. *Des Moines Tribune-Capital,* August 5, 1931, p. 1.
52. *Des Moines Tribune-Capital,* August 21, 1931, p. 1.
53. *Ibid.*
54. *Des Moines Register,* August 22, 1931, p. 1.
55. *Ibid.*
56. *Ibid.*
57. *Des Moines Tribune-Capital,* August 22, 1931, p. 1.
58. *Des Moines Tribune-Capital,* August 24, 1931, p. 1.
59. *Ibid.*
60. *Des Moines Tribune-Capital,* August 25, 1931, p. 1.
61. *Des Moines Tribune-Capital,* September 22, 1931, p. 1.
62. *Ibid.*
63. *Davenport Democrat,* September 22, 1931, p. 1.
64. *Ibid.*
65. *Davenport Democrat,* September 22, 1931, p. 1.
66. *Des Moines Register,* September 24, 1931, p. 1.
67. *Des Moines Register,* September 22, 1931, p. 1.
68. *Ibid.*
69. *Ibid.*
70. *Davenport Democrat,* September 24, 1931, p. 1.
71. *Ibid.*
72. *Ibid.*
73. *Des Moines Register,* September 24, 1931, p. 1.
74. *Ibid.*, p. 2.
75. *Ibid.*, p. 12A.
76. *Des Moines Register,* September 26, 1931, p. 1.
77. *Davenport Democrat,* September 25, 1931, p. 1.
78. *Ibid.*
79. *Ibid.*
80. *Des Moines Tribune-Capital,* October 5, 1931, p. 1.
81. *Des Moines Register,* September 26, 1931, p. 1.
82. *Davenport Democrat,* September 25, 1931, p. 1.
83. *Davenport Democrat,* September 27, 1931, p. 1.
84. *Des Moines Register,* October 2, 1931, p. 1.
85. *Tipton Advertiser,* March 24, 1932, p. 1.
86. *Marshalltown Times-Republican,* December 12, 1933, p. 1.
87. *Des Moines Register,* July 7, 1934, p. 1.
88. *Cedar Rapids Gazette,* August 16, 1934, p. 1, c.l. 8.
89. *Des Moines Tribune-Capital,* October 2, 1931, p. 5A.

The Farmers' Holiday Association Strike, August 1932

John L. Shover

The Farmers' Holiday Association strike of August 1932 took place at the same time as, and to some extent overlapped, the Sioux City milk strike. Actually there were two Farmers' Holiday Association strikes: an officially sponsored peaceful withholding of farm products from the market and a spontaneous movement involving picketing. That the milk producers, acting independently of the Farmers' Holiday Association, were the only strikers able to achieve immediate concrete results is instructive. Their relatively small number and their control of a restricted market comprising a handful of local distributors gave them tight organization and leverage. The nondairy farmers, on the other hand, could not, by blockading a single market, reduce the overall supply sufficiently to affect farm prices. The problem of the chronic surplus of farm products could be attacked effectively only on a national basis. The main accomplishment of the farm strike was that it publicized the farmers' plight.

An economic crisis without parallel gripped the American countryside in the summer of 1932. For a decade preceding it, farm markets had contracted and prices had dropped, but the depression of the twenties was only a prelude to the most disastrous collapse

[Reprinted from *Agricultural History*, XXXIX (October 1965), 196–203.]

in the history of American agriculture. Between 1929 and 1931 the price of wheat per bushel declined from $1.03 to 36¢; in 1932 the return for hogs fell from $11.36 to $6.14 per head, the sharpest drop ever recorded. The purchasing power of farm commodities was less than a third that of 1914. The only inheritance from the prosperous war years was a heavy and unchanging burden of debt. In Iowa, North Dakota, and South Dakota, nearly 6 per cent of farms changed ownership during 1932 through bankruptcy or foreclosure; in 1933 the ratio rose to 8 per cent. The emergency ensnared producers of all commodities, even corn-hog and dairy farmers, who had been spared the worst economic vicissitudes of the past.[1]

The American farmer has never been politically inarticulate or slow to rise in his own defense. The response to the depression of the thirties was neither so widespread nor so prolonged as such political movements as the Populist Party or the Nonpartisan League, but it reached peaks of intensity unequaled in earlier protests. The farm strike of 1932 was the first episode in a neglected little rebellion in the American cornbelt. Before it had run its course a year later, at least 140 foreclosure sales had been halted by direct farmer action,[2] a strike of milk producers had exploded into violence on the highways of Wisconsin,[3] and the Farmers' Holiday Association of Milo Reno had once threatened and once attempted a general strike of farmers to force legislative concessions from Congress and the new national administration.[4]

The farm strike manifested a spirit of frustration and resentment that the depression had set astir in the countryside. Only indirectly was it guided by leaders of the Farmers' Holiday Association or directed toward the goals of that organization. What was originally designed as a peaceable withholding of produce from market erupted at its very beginning into a direct-action movement of a magnitude seldom equaled in the history of farmer protests. At its climax it was a spontaneous grass-roots uprising seeking immediate redress of economic grievances. Except for a small core of participants, it was an irrational movement, too poorly organized and inchoate to achieve the remedies either leaders or participants sought. The effort achieved little, but it served to place the label "urgent" upon the necessity for some type of legislation to alleviate the economic plight of the American farmer.

The sequence of events that accelerated into the August farm strike was set in motion by the Farmers' Holiday Association, founded in Des Moines in May 1932. The Holiday Association was an offspring of the National Farmers' Union, produced by factional battles within that organization in the early thirties. Contending for control of the Farmers' Union were, first, a cooperative marketing group, consisting mainly of grain interests of the Northwest, friends and supporters of the Agricultural Marketing Act. In opposition was a political faction, largely representative of livestock areas where there was little to gain from the cooperative marketing features of the Hoover farm program. Led by Milo Reno of the Iowa Farmers' Union, the political group demanded of the National a vigorous program to win legislation guaranteeing cost of production prices for farmers. Reno had argued as early as 1927: "If we cannot obtain justice by legislation, the time will have arrived when no other course remains than organized refusal to deliver the products of the farm at less than production costs." [5] In the depression year of 1930 the political faction won control of the union with the election to the presidency of John Simpson of Oklahoma. The transfer of power was accompanied by acrimonious charges, by both sides, of corruption, mismanagement, and diversion of union funds for political projects.[6]

Milo Reno's proposal for a general withholding movement lay dormant for four years, but support reawakened as depression hardship pressed heavier in the cornbelt. Reno presented to the Farmers' Union convention of 1931 a resolution calling for a farm strike to begin January 1. Although Simpson was president and the political action wing in control, the resolution was defeated by a decisive majority.[7] This rejection should not be overemphasized. The Farmers' Union could *not* have sponsored a marketing strike. Given the strength of the minority cooperative faction, such a move could have permanently split the union or lost the political faction its control. Moreover, extensive investments in cooperative facilities could have been jeopardized by too bold political action. When Reno proceeded through his own affiliate, the Iowa Farmers' Union, to carry forward his withholding plans independently, he was sustained and advised by John Simpson and E. E. Kennedy, the national secretary of the Farmers' Union. In every particular the program of the Farmers' Holiday Association and that of the Farmers' Union were parallel. The most extreme of the political activists simply shifted their pressure tactics outside the bounds of the parent organization. The Farmers' Holiday Association was a strong-arm auxiliary of the Farmers' Union.

Within weeks after the Farmers' Union convention, Milo Reno and his state union chapter were mobilizing support for a withholding movement in Iowa. Glen Miller, president of the Iowa union,[8] coined a term when he declared that if banks could do it, why shouldn't farmers call a "holiday" when corn and meat and milk would be kept at home until legislators and the public alike learned the importance of the men who tilled the soil.[9] From February until May the pages of the *Iowa Union Farmer* contained little else but plans for the forthcoming withholding action. Farmers' Union leaders toured Iowa, often addressing two rural gatherings daily; Reno cultivated union associates in Wisconsin, South Dakota, and Minnesota.[10]

The organizing drive culminated when 2,000 farmers assembled in Des Moines on May 3 to launch the Farmers' Holiday Association as a national organization. Milo Reno, the inevitable choice, was named president. The convention resolved that a general withholding movement was to begin July 4 and continue for thirty days or until cost of production prices were realized.[11]

The objectives of the incipient farmers' movement were vague, the methods for achieving them ill-defined. There was a stress upon immediacy: implicit in the simple resolutions was the assumption that the goal of cost of production prices could be quickly achieved.[12] Nothing implied that the forthcoming withholding movement would be other than voluntary; there was no suggestion that coercion might be used against farmers who failed to cooperate. Neither was it clear how cost of production prices were to be achieved. Milo Reno, although sometimes ambivalent, seemed to insist they would be guaranteed by legislative action.[13] On the other hand, many local leaders as well as the press interpreted the farm strike as a self-help effort—farm produce would be held off the market until shortages forced prices up to the cost of production level.[14]

Cost of production, the principal demand of the union and the Holiday Association, was more a panacea than a concrete economic program. "Concede to the farmer production costs," Milo

Reno predicted, "and he will pay his grocer, the grocer will pay the wholesaler, the wholesaler will pay the manufacturer, and the manufacturer will be able to meet his obligations at the bank. Restore the farmers' purchasing power and you have reestablished an endless chain of prosperity and happiness in this country." [15] To compute cost of production, average expenses for producers of every commodity would be itemized and a price determined for products consumed domestically that would return to the average operator his costs, labor, and a reasonable profit. To have realized returns equal to cost of production in 1932 a farmer would have had to receive 92 cents per bushel for corn, 11 cents a pound for hogs, and 62 cents per pound of butterfat. Prevailing prices in June 1932 were 10 cents per bushel for corn, 3 cents per pound for hogs, and 18 cents per pound for butterfat.[16]

Throughout the summer months of 1932, evangelists of cost of production carried the message across the cornbelt. As momentum increased, state Farmers' Holiday Associations were launched in South Dakota, North Dakota, and Minnesota.[17] Organizers asked farmers to sign pledges to support the forthcoming withholding action. These enthusiasts had an inspired sense of numbers; they reported that half a million Midwestern farmers had signed by August.[18]

Original plans called for withholding to begin July 4, but the day passed without incident in the cornbelt. Organization plans were not complete and the declining price trend had momentarily reversed in June. A few hopeful observers prophesied that the high tide of depression had passed. A price slump on July 13 destroyed sanguine hopes, and the price index began a steady decline that was not arrested until December.[19] Indicating the confusion prevailing, the county Holiday chairmen in Iowa rescheduled the holding action for August 15, but then on August 10 the *Iowa Union Farmer* announced it had already commenced.[20]

The farm strike that began at Sioux City on August 12 was a different movement from that planned by the Farmers' Holiday Association. In all the preceding buildup there had been no mention of picketing; yet at the very inception of the withholding movement, farmers in Woodbury and Plymouth counties patrolled highways and threatened noncooperating farmers who tried to market their produce. Milo Reno conceded in a private letter: "I have not favored, at any time in our farm strike movement, picketing, because of the danger of loss of life and property, although I do feel that the action of the boys on the picket line has done more to focus the attention of the powers that be to the real facts of the situation than any other thing." [21] By this time it had become apparent that the Farmers' Holiday was two movements. One was the formal organization headed by Milo Reno that planned a peaceful holding action to bring pressure for enactment of cost of production legislation. The second was a spontaneous social movement triggered into action by the Holiday but looking to immediate remedies and seeking redress of local grievances.

The focal point in this unanticipated movement was a group of counties in northwest Iowa surrounding the terminal market at Sioux City. In the vanguard were 250 local milk producers for whom the strike was the culmination of grievances that had been accumulating for ten years.

Dairy farmers were the striking force of the depression farmers' protest. They were in the first echelon in Iowa in 1932 and they instigated both the Wisconsin dairy strike and a spirited movement in New York State in 1933. Milk producers had a legitimate economic grievance; in Sioux City, for example, the farmer's price for butter had declined from 40 to 19 cents between 1927 and 1932.[22] It was simpler to organize dairy farmers than other producers. Since milk was highly perishable, a "milk shed" area extended for no more than 20 or 30 miles around an urban center. Milk producers were relatively few in number and their total supply was sold to a handful of local distributors. It was reasoned, therefore, that price increases could be forced more surely by a withholding action.

The J. R. Roberts Dairy Company, the largest in Sioux City, had gradually extended its milk-shed area, assuring a constant surplus and permitting the company to dictate its own price. An adjustment in 1932 had raised prices so that the farmer received 2 cents and the consumer paid 8 cents for the same quart of milk. A Producers' Cooperative Association, organized in May 1932, had by August signed up 900 members, a sizable portion of those who shipped to the Sioux City market. The refusal of the J. R. Roberts

Dairy Company to negotiate and the boasts of the owner that he had broken cooperatives in the past forced the leaders to withhold as the only means for winning concessions.[23]

The campaign to form a milk producers' cooperative coincided with the organizing drive of the Farmers' Holiday; many were members of both groups. As the date for the beginning of the Holiday withholding movement approached, the milk producers voted to combine the two campaigns. On August 10 the organization presented to the distributors a demand for price increases, pledged to halt all shipments into Sioux City, and arranged for free milk distribution in order to avoid public inconvenience and embarrass the distributor's retail trade.[24]

On the night of August 11 fifteen trucks carrying milk were halted west of Sioux City and the milk of two of them was dumped on the pavement. By the next evening farmers had extended the vigil to all roads entering the city from the east and north. Trucks carrying livestock were also halted, and the drive of milk producers coalesced with a general attempt to seal the Sioux City market. On August 14, 1,500 farmers distributed over five highways virtually blocked all shipments. Pickets leaped on the running boards of farm trucks or threw such obstacles as hay bales, logs, and threshing-machine belts in the path of oncoming vehicles. There was little violence; most trucks simply turned back. One hundred deputies were recruited to keep the roads open, but no attempt was made to prevent the stopping of vehicles so long as the techniques remained persuasive only. The Producers' Cooperative claimed that 90 per cent of the city's milk supply had been stopped and on Thursday, August 18, hog receipts were just half those of the preceding Thursday.[25]

As the selling holiday spread, farmers in South Dakota and Nebraska blocked access from the north, and new picket lines sealed the southern route to Sioux City. "This movement," declared the mayor, "threatens to sweep the Midwest like wildfire."[26] Local strike leaders claimed that 90 per cent of farmers in the vicinity either joined picket lines or refused to sell produce. Had this been true there would have been no need for roadside blockades. Newspaper reports, although probably exaggerated, allow a better estimate. The number of pickets at any time or place was usually recorded as between 200 and 400. The largest number reported was the 1,500 who supposedly guarded the northern access to Sioux City on August 14. Allowing for exaggeration and the presence of non-farmers on the picket line, the maximum figure would constitute representatives from about one-fifth of the farm families in Woodbury and Plymouth counties.[27]

Few farmers out of the total rural population expressed their resentment by going to such extremes as picketing highways or defying sheriff's deputies. Those who did were a type of farmer largely immune to previous agrarian movements. Farm insurgency in the past had won principal Midwestern support in wheat-producing regions.[28] The unrest of the thirties was most evident in livestock- and milk-producing areas whose residents were considered more economically stable and less affected by vagrant price or weather fluctuations. The most enthusiastic support for the strike technique was in Iowa and Wisconsin; when it spread to Nebraska, South Dakota, and Minnesota, its greatest attraction was always in corn-hog and dairy regions.[29]

The farm strike centered on some of the most prosperous farming counties in the livestock and dairy belts. In Iowa, the state where activity was most intense, at least 300 incidents of protest were reported in August and September.[30] More than three-quarters of these occurred in seven counties in the Missouri River Valley at the western fringe of the state. In this, the leading meat-producing sector of the state, gross income per farm was well above the state average. By contrast, the single area in Iowa least affected by the farm strike was the so-called "southern pasture" area touching the Missouri border, where land values and gross income were the lowest in the state and home conveniences fewest.[31] Add to high gross income the fact that rate of foreclosure was apparently the highest in counties in northwest Iowa[32] and rainfall in 1931 and 1932 the least in the state,[33] and a pattern emerges. The farm strike was a response of individuals whose level of expectation had been conditioned by better times, and some immediate crisis—in this instance, foreclosure or drouth—threatened to deprive them of property or accustomed income. Bruce Bliven, a native Iowan reporting for the *New Republic,* concluded: "It's where the farmers had something a few years ago and have had it suddenly taken away, that the agitators find a responsive audience." [34]

The farmers' strike in Iowa might attract publicity to the farmers' plight; it could achieve little else. Two handicaps rendered success impossible: First, there was a lack of leadership and discipline. Second, the effort was ineffectively organized and support was too narrow to influence farm marketing or prices.

Any relationship of the spontaneous movement in northwest Iowa to the formal program or leadership of the Farmers' Holiday Association was incidental. Even local leaders, much less Milo Reno, were unable to govern the actions of pickets scattered over 100 miles of highway. Because of this, the farm strike rapidly deteriorated into chaos and violence.

The milk dispute was settled after ten days when the distributors agreed to a compromise price increase. The settlement put the discipline of the farm strike to a severe test. Many pickets still refused to allow milk trucks to pass.

Most explosive, however, was the situation 75 miles to the south at Council Bluffs, where shipments to Omaha were being blocked from the Iowa side of the Missouri River. County law-enforcement officials informed Clinton Savery, organizer of the blockade, that he would be personally responsible for any violence or property damage. When Savery attempted to call off the pickets, he was taunted with shouts of "Sell Out!" "I have washed my hands of the entire mess. The strikers are beyond my control," he protested. When 43 pickets were arrested on August 24, a mob of 500 farmers, unimpressed by the armed deputies hastily recruited by the Pottawattamie County sheriff, swarmed over the courthouse lawn at Council Bluffs. Throughout a tense day they negotiated with law-enforcement officials. A sympathetic farmer posted bail late in the afternoon and the release of the prisoners averted a situation perilously close to tragedy and bloodshed.[35]

A rapid succession of critical events in the last days of August broke the back of the farm strike. Deputies and pickets battled for three nights on the outskirts of Omaha; [36] in northeast Nebraska an interstate freight train was halted and livestock cars were uncoupled.[37] Woodbury County deputies arrested 87 pickets on August 26; four days later pickets at Cherokee were injured by shotgun blasts from a speeding auto. At Clinton, in eastern Iowa, another mob defied armed deputies by threatening to release jailed pickets.[38] Under duress of this sort, Reno and state Holiday leaders proclaimed on September 1 a "temporary truce," to begin immediately. Roland Jones, *New York Times* correspondent in Omaha, observed that the "national leadership blew up, frightened at the appearance of the ugly monster into which its innocent child had so unexpectedly grown." [39]

The second handicap was the ineffective organization and narrow support for both the strike action and the withholding movement. From a practical standpoint, a farmer could not long participate in a general embargo that deprived him of all income. To keep marketable hogs and cattle on the farm meant added costs and lower returns.[40] Even before the "temporary truce," Reno announced that the withholding action would be relaxed sufficiently to allow hardpressed farmers to market some of their products.[41]

The peaceful withholding movement, the major objective of the Farmers' Holiday Association, had been lost sight of in the flurry of dramatic activity around Sioux City. It had been a failure. Receipts of livestock had decreased only at Sioux City. There was an increase at neighboring markets. Indeed, prices for farm products dropped to the year's low while the farm strike was in progress.[42] Blockading a single market could not reduce the overall supply of agricultural products sufficiently to effect price changes. Even had a marketing boycott been successful, the accumulated produce released at its conclusion would have broken the bottom of the farm price structure. Only the milk producers, who operated independently of the Holiday Association, and were able to control a restricted market, could claim concrete benefits from the farm strike.[43]

Paradoxically, however, the strike achieved results better than the original organizers could have expected. The spontaneous movement in northwest Iowa publicized the farmers' plight and prompted political responses more effectively than could any ill-organized withholding movement. Elected political officials in the Middle West and national candidates could not ignore such dramatic evidence of rural discontent. Exemplifying the political prestige of the Farmers' Holiday Association was a meeting of four Midwestern governors in Sioux City in September in the wake of the farm strike. After listening to the declarations of Holiday leaders, they forwarded to President Hoover a suggested program to inflate the currency and restrict farm foreclosures.[44] Governor Roosevelt, campaigning in Sioux City, talked with Farmers' Union and Holiday leaders and promised that if elected he would devote more time to agriculture than to any other single problem.[45] Over the debates on a farm bill in 1933 and the implementing of the Agricultural Adjustment Act hung the threat of a renewed farm strike.[46] In the autumn of 1933 the Holiday Association was able to muster the support of five governors who bore to Washington a demand that the domestic allotment system be replaced by cost of production price guarantees.[47]

The political power of the Farmers' Holiday Association was illusory; the organization had won an unearned increment of importance, largely because of the farm strike. The strength of the association certainly was not in numbers. Membership statistics were never revealed, but the financial receipts of the national office in August 1933 indicate that returns equal to the dues payments of only 4494 members had been received.[48] What strength the association had was a tempestuous and little-organized force whose allegiance was tangential. The peaceful withholding movement planned by the organization in 1932 had been a failure. In October 1933, when Milo Reno, driven to extremism by his opposition to the New Deal agricultural program, attempted to mobilize farmers on the highways to compel the federal government to replace the Agricultural Adjustment Act with cost of production guarantees and currency inflation, the attempt perished in a flurry of rioting and violence.[49] The spontaneous support of discontented men was an insecure base for a permanent organization.

Generalizations drawn from one specific episode are obviously limited by the circumscribed scope of the data. Yet if made the basis for comparisons with other examples of similar phenomena and carefully tested for similarities and differences, such generalizations can form the bridge to broader and more useful concepts. The conclusions that follow are intended not only as summary but as reference points for possible comparison with other social movements in general and farmers' movements in particular.

First, the farm strike was not a movement from the social depths. Its highest incidence was in relatively prosperous areas where economic disaster threatened to deprive participants of status and livelihood. The fact that the movement centered in corn-hog and milk-producing areas calls into question those interpretations that establish an automatic equation between wheat farming and rural insurgency.

Second, although specific leaders may have set the protest in motion, the farm strike was a spontaneous effort pursuing immediate and sometimes irrational goals, different from those of the leaders. To view the Farmers' Holiday Association in terms of its formal program and through the perspective of the leadership would be misleading.

Third, ideology was of limited importance. Farmers who picketed highways and challenged legal authority did so in pursuit of immediate relief, not because they demanded such specific remedies as inflation or cost of production prices.[50] Attempts by Holiday leaders to perpetuate the battle for ideological goals after the adoption of the Agricultural Adjustment Act were futile. Milo Reno died in 1936, a disappointed and embittered man; the Farmers' Holiday disappeared in 1937, torn between followers of Popular Front liberalism and supporters of the Coughlin-Lemke Union party. The New Deal agricultural program brought farmers the immediate economic assistance they demanded and this was sufficient to quell the tempestuous spirit that nourished farm strikes and the Farmers' Holiday Association.

NOTES

1. U.S. Department of Agriculture, *Yearbook of Agriculture, 1928* (Washington, 1929), p. 670; *Yearbook of Agriculture, 1932* (Washington, 1932), p. 784; *Yearbook of Agriculture, 1935* (Washington, 1935), pp. 567–568, 681; *The Farm Real Estate Situation, 1933–34* (U.S. Department of Agriculture, Circular 354, Washington, 1935), p. 31; Horace C. Filley, "Effects of Inflation and Deflation upon Nebraska Agriculture" (Ph.D. dissertation, University of Minnesota, 1934), pp. 26–27.

2. This estimate of anti-foreclosure demonstrations is based upon a tabulation of incidents reported in six national and local newspapers, 1932 and 1933.

3. A. William Hoglund, "Wisconsin Dairy Farmers on Strike," *Agricultural History*, XXXV (January 1961), 24–34.

4. Theodore Saloutos and John D. Hicks, *Twentieth Century Populism: Agricultural Discontent in the Middle West, 1900–1939* (Lincoln, n.d. [Madison, 1951]), pp. 448–451; Van L. Perkins, "The Triple-A and the Politics of Agriculture" (unpublished paper delivered at the Seventy-Ninth Annual Meeting, American Historical Association, Washington, December 28, 1964); John L.

Shover, "The Farm Holiday Movement in Nebraska," *Nebraska History*, XLIII (March, 1962), 72–73.

5. W. P. Tucker, "Populism Up to Date: The Story of the Farmers' Union," *Agricultural History*, XXI (October 1947), 206–207; Milo Reno, undated ms, "For Miss Prescott," Milo Reno Papers, Library of University of Iowa, Iowa City.

6. *Iowa Union Farmer* (Columbus Junction, Iowa), July 29, August 23, 1931.

7. *Ibid.*, December 2, 1931.

8. Reno resigned the presidency of the Iowa Farmers' Union in 1930 to become head of the union's extensive insurance business, but he remained the *de facto* head of the organization.

9. *Iowa Union Farmer*, February 10 and 24, 1932.

10. *Ibid.*, March 9, 1932; Roland A. White, *Milo Reno: Farmers' Union Pioneer* (Iowa City, 1941), p. 74.

11. *Iowa Union Farmer*, May 4, 1932.

12. For a theoretical discussion of the characteristics of incipient protest movements, see Wendell King, *Social Movements in the United States* (New York, 1956), pp. 42–44.

13. Milo Reno, "Why the Farmers' Holiday?," radio address of July 20, 1932, in White, *Milo Reno*, p. 152.

14. John Chalmers, president of the Iowa Farmers' Holiday Association, still insisted 29 years later that this was the purpose of the Farmers' Holiday and further argued that had the attempt been better organized it would have succeeded. Personal interview with the writer, October 21, 1961.

15. Reno, "Why the Farmers' Holiday?," p. 151.

16. Howard W. Lawrence, "The Farmers' Holiday Association in Iowa, 1932–33" (M.A. thesis, University of Iowa, 1952), pp. 24–26; Saloutos and Hicks, *Twentieth Century Populism*, p. 443.

17. *Willmar* (Minnesota) *Tribune*, August 1, 1932; *Sioux City Tribune*, July 20, 1932.

18. *Willmar Tribune*, August 2, 1932.

19. Julius Korgan, "Farmers Picket the Depression" (Ph.D. disseration, American University, 1961), pp. 31–32; Lauren K. Soth, *Agricultural Economic Facts Basebook of Iowa* (Iowa Agricultural Experiment and Extension Service, Special Report No. 1, Ames, 1936), p. 22.

20. *Sioux City Tribune*, July 30, 1932.

21. Letter to Ben McCormack, November 8, 1933, Reno Papers.

22. Frank D. DiLeva, "Iowa Farm Price Revolt," *Annals of Iowa*, third series, XXXII (January 1954), 172; Korgan, 34 *et passim*.

23. I. W. Reck, president and founder, Sioux City Milk Producers' Cooperative Association, personal interview with the writer, March 12, 1962; Sioux City Milk Producers' Cooperative Association, *Record of Progress* (Sioux City, n.d.); *Unionist and Public Forum* (Sioux City), March 3, July 28, 1932.

24. *Sioux City Journal*, August 10, 1932; I. W. Reck, personal interview.

25. *Sioux City Journal*, August 12–15, August 19, 1932; *Sioux City Tribune*, August 15, 1932.

26. *Sioux City Journal*, August 22, 1932.

27. U.S. Bureau of the Census, *15th Census of the U.S., Population*, VI (Washington, 1933), 451–452. If this figure is even a fair approximation, this percentage of local participation is remarkably high, particularly when contrasted with the sitdown strikes or such modern social movements as the 1963 March on Washington or the Free Speech Movement at the University of

California. It would seem even more so given the obstacles to communication and organization in rural areas.

28. This point is particularly stressed in Benton H. Wilcox, "An Historical Definition of North-Western Radicalism," *Mississippi Valley Historical Review,* XXVI (December 1939), 384–386; Richard Hofstadter, *The Age of Reform* (New York, 1955), 99–100; Seymour M. Lipset, *Agrarian Socialism* (Berkeley, 1950), 10–11.

29. This can be explained, I believe, by three factors: (1) The depression of the 1930's was more severe in corn-hog and dairy areas than any preceding crisis; (2) the only existing federal remedy, the Agricultural Marketing Act, was geared to the needs of producers of nonperishables such as wheat and cotton, and the funds of the farm board had already been absorbed in heavy purchases of these commodities when the worst crisis struck dairy and corn-hog regions; (3) perishable products such as meat and milk were more easily made the objects of withholding actions.

30. This figure was computed on the basis of a tabulation of reports of protest activities from two leading area newspapers, the *Des Moines Register* and the *Sioux City Journal,* August and September 1932. Each occurrence was classified by county; an event reported in both newspapers was recorded twice, avoiding purely local reporting and giving double weight to an incident important enough to have reached both. The actual total was 335. The nine counties that scored highest were, in order: Woodbury, Plymouth, Pottawattamie, Polk, Harrison, Monona, Cherokee, Clay, and Black Hawk. Only Polk and Black Hawk are outside the northwestern meat-producing area.

31. Soth, *Agricultural Economic Facts Basebook of Iowa,* pp. 139, 10, 117, 114, 104–105, 160.

32. Reliable data on foreclosures are difficult to obtain. Authority for my statement is a listing of foreclosure suits pending, by counties, published in the *Des Moines Register,* July 15, 1934, showing that in 1933 Woodbury County, the county with most strike activity, had three times more foreclosure suits pending (485) than any other Iowa county.

33. U.S. Weather Bureau, *Climatological Data, Iowa Section,* XLII (August 1931), 99–100; XLIII (July 1932), 54; XLIII (August 1932), 66.

34. Bruce Bliven, "Milo Reno and His Farmers," *New Republic,* LXXVII (November 29, 1933), 64. For a theoretical discussion of this type of interpretation, see James C. Davies, "Toward a Theory of Revolution," *American Sociological Review,* XXVII (February 1962), 5–19.

35. *Sioux City Journal,* August 26, 1932; *New York Times,* August 26, 1932.

36. *Omaha World-Herald,* August 30 and 31, September 1, 1932.

37. *New York Times,* August 24, 1932.

38. *Sioux City Journal,* August 26 and 31, 1932; *Des Moines Register,* September 1, 1932.

39. *New York Times,* September 4, 1932.

40. Dan W. Turner, governor of Iowa in 1932, reports he received "hundreds of telephone calls, letters and personal calls from farmers all over [the] western half of Iowa to open up the roads." He notes as an example of the problem that hogs between 190 and 230 pounds were priced as bacon hogs; as they grew heavier they became lard hogs, and the demand for lard was diminishing. Dan W. Turner to the writer, October 15, 1961; *Sioux City Journal,* August 25, 1932.

41. *Ibid.,* August 31, 1932.

42. The number of hogs marketed in Iowa was 750,525 in July, 804,335 in August, 787,353 in September, 806,035 in October. Computed on the 1910–1914

base, the index numbers for Iowa hog prices were July, 58; August, 53; September, 49; October, 41; November, 38; December, 33. Soth, *Agricultural Economic Facts Basebook of Iowa*, pp. 22, 41.

43. The original demand of the Milk Producers' Cooperative was for an increase in the price of milk containing 3.5 per cent butterfat from the prevailing $1.00 per cwt. to $2.50. The settlement set the price at $1.80.

44. *Sioux City Journal*, September 10, 11, 1932. Present were Governors Turner of Iowa, Green of South Dakota, Shafer of North Dakota, and Olson of Minnesota.

45. *Iowa Union Farmer*, October 5, 1932. The farm leaders attending the conference, probably overly optimistic, also alleged that Roosevelt agreed to press for legislation refinancing farm loans at a low rate of interest and guaranteeing cost of production prices to farmers.

46. John L. Shover, "Populism in the Nineteen Thirties: The Battle for the AAA," *Agricultural History*, XXXIX (January 1965), 17–24.

47. Henry A. Wallace, *New Frontiers* (New York, 1934), pp. 56–58.

48. Reno, "For Miss Prescott," Reno Papers.

49. *New York Times*, November 5 and 7, 1933.

50. Angus Campbell, *et al.*, *The American Voter* (New York, 1960), pp. 402–440.

The Economic Effects of Drouth and Depression upon Custer County, 1929–1942

Maurice C. Latta

This selection presents the economic and demographic history of a predominantly agricultural community for a period of time sufficiently long to enable us to see the impact of the Great Depression (and, in this instance, drouth) and to view New Deal agricultural policies in the context of long-run developments. As Carl Degler points out: "Certainly there is much in the New Deal that bespeaks the urban society in which it operated. . . . Yet there is also a strong preference for country life running through the activities and interests of the New Deal." (Carl N. Degler, ed., The New Deal *[Chicago: Quadrangle Books, 1970], p. 7.)*

Nationwide there was a slight migration from city to farm in 1931 and 1932, but in 1933 and 1934 there was a slight net movement from farm to city (in Custer County, farm population remained constant from 1920 to 1934, but from 1935 to 1940 it declined 15 per cent). It was not as easy to grow one's own food as many people thought it would be, and back-to-the-land as a solution for the nation's economic ills was a flight from reality. The overriding trend in farm population is clear: in 1900 farmers, farm managers, and farm laborers accounted for 37.6 per cent of the labor force; in 1960, 6.8 per cent. Custer County reflected the nationwide trend, which, as this selection shows, is closely related to long-run changes in crops and land use, technology, and farm ownership.

[Reprinted from *Nebraska History*, XXXIII (December 1952), 220–236.]

In 1970 the support measures the farmers obtained in 1933 apply to a vastly changed American agricultural scene. As in Custer County, the number of farmers has decreased and the average size of farms has increased. The farm population has dropped from 20 million in 1950 to 10 million. Most of the Department of Agriculture's budget is spent on 3 million farmers, largely on the one million "serious commercial producers," and 4 per cent of these 3 million receive more than a third of the subsidies (New York Times, *April 5, 1970).*

In 1929 there began a decade in which it appeared as though "the Fates" had undertaken, "after great deliberation, to shake the confidence of the American people in their economy." [1] National income fell by more than one-half in four years and remained depressed for six more; not until 1941 did it exceed the 1929 figures.[2] For the first time a decade passed without significant additions to the stock of our national wealth.[3]

For the agricultural sector the situation was worse than for the nation as a whole,[4] while for the farmers of the Great Plains there was added the ordeal by drouth, as though to make men doubt the very land which was their home. But "Great Plains" is a collective term which names a most varied area; within its limits there are great differences, both in experience and in response. We need to know not only the overall experience of the nation and of the large region but also the detailed experience of the locality. To provide this detailed information was the task to which Loyd Glover set himself in his master's thesis, upon which this article is based.[5] In this article, as in its predecessor,[6] most of the facts will be drawn from the student thesis, with acknowledgment both general and specific; the interpretation may be regarded as my own, unless there is specific attribution. It is proper to note here that some of the difference of opinion from Mr. Glover, which will appear later, is due to research findings subsequent to the completion of his thesis. Some, however, is due to differences of opinion which should be recorded and made clear. Mr. Glover, for example, accepts the principle, stated in the first article, of the essential instability of the Custer County economy in 1929, but regards that

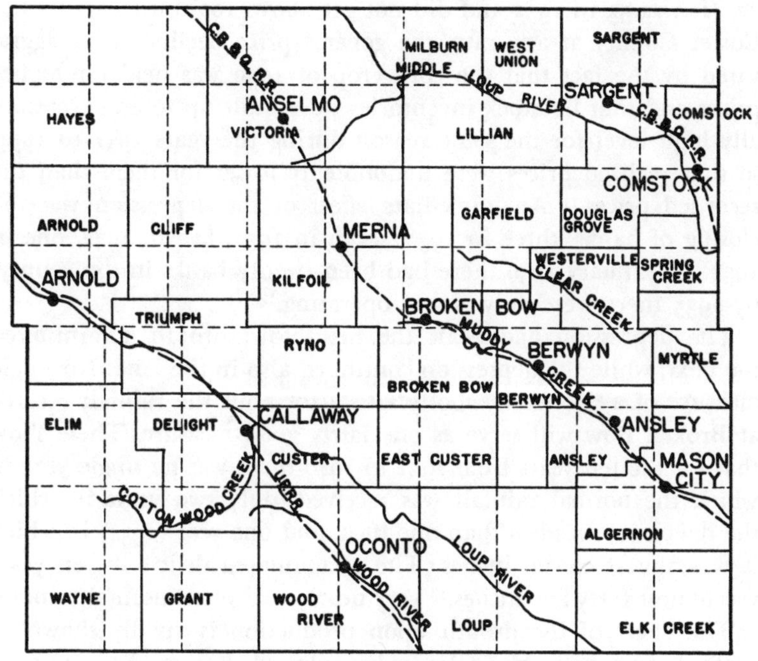

MAP OF CUSTER COUNTY

primarily as the result of an historic mistake in land policy: the attempt to apply the 160-acre family-farm pattern of settlement to an area where it did not "fit." Beyond this, however, as a result of my own recent studies in Iowa farm adjustment [7] as well as those of Wayne M. Smith and of Clinton Warne,[8] I pointed to the financial pressures upon the farmers consequent upon the great land boom, the adoption of the automobile, and the parallel rise in the level of living evidenced by better schools, good roads, and new housing facilities such as running water, electricity, and radios.

For the farmers of the nation as a whole the depression was initiated by a dismaying drop in income, in three years, to a level that was only 40 per cent of the 1929 level.[9] Even the 1929 level had not been a favorable one, for the parity figure for that year—the ratio, that is, between prices received by farmers and prices paid, interest, and taxes (1910–1914 being 100)—had been only

87. (It was 53 in 1932 and did not get above 100 until 1942.)[10] For Custer County at any rate, the general price declines were aggravated by the fact that the corn crop of 1930 was held for higher prices and that livestock inventories were built up to an exceptionally high level for the same reason during the years 1931 to 1934, so that realized prices were undoubtedly lower for them than the recorded prices.[11] An immediate effect of the depression was the closing of banks, three in 1930, seven in 1931, five in 1932, one in 1934. In January 1930 there had been twenty banks in the county; by 1935 there were only eleven operating.[12]

The depression had dealt the first blow; drouth administered the next, while the depression continued also in the land. No single measure of a drouth is wholly satisfactory but the rainfall records at Broken Bow will serve as one fairly good measure. These show that for the ten years from 1931 to 1940 there was no single year in which the normal rainfall was received, only two years in which the deficiency was less than one inch, and one year (1934) in which it was almost eleven inches. The accumulated deficit in ten years was almost forty-five inches,[13] very nearly two years' normal rainfall.

The effect of the drouth upon production is vividly shown in Plate I, in which Mr. Glover has plotted Broken Bow rainfall against the production figures for corn and spring grain for the county. The showing in this plate would appear even more drastic had he chosen a year earlier than 1932 for the base, while the plate itself reveals another measure of drouth than rainfall alone. The graph shows that corn production began its precipitous decline in 1931, a year in which the rainfall deficit was only moderate but in which there was a protracted period of intensely hot weather during July and August.[14]

Another measure of the crushing impact of the drouth is afforded by the figures for aggregate corn production in the county for three successive four-year periods. Of these the first, 1930 to 1933, was marked by fairly good growing conditions and an aggregate yield of twenty-five million bushels of corn, valued at something over ten million dollars. The next four years, 1934 to 1937, however, saw a total production of less than five million bushels of corn, valued at less than four million dollars, while the somewhat better quartet, 1938 through 1941, still saw less corn produced in the four years (seven million bushels) than had been grown in the single year 1933.[15]

The first year of the drouth, 1934, was the worst, and its effect upon Custer County agriculture was the more telling because the number of cattle and hogs in the county was exceptionally large. One hundred and forty-six thousand cattle, estimated as on farms in the county on January 1, 1934, made a number larger than for any other year of the period 1920–1942, and there were, besides the cattle, over 156,000 hogs reported as well. The nearly complete failure of crops forced a rapid contraction, so that one year later, at the beginning of 1935, three-quarters of the hogs and 45 per cent of the cattle had disappeared.[16] Government emergency purchases had accounted for 45,166 head of cattle; [17] many more of course were marketed through ordinary channels. For the maintenance of the remainder some were driven to Sandhills pastures outside the county, while quantities of feed were shipped in for sale. In addition to the sums received on this forced sale of livestock, compliance payments under the original AAA brought in over a million dollars in 1934 and nearly eight hundred and fifty thousand the following year. Nearly normal sales were enjoyed by a Broken Bow clothing store whose proprietor supplied Mr. Glover with information as to his volume during the depression years.[18]

But the drouth continued. There were to be no more good corn crops in the thirties; stands of alfalfa were lost and could not be reestablished; small grains were almost as poor as the corn. Radical readjustment in farming methods appeared to be called for. The introduction of Spartan, an early-maturing, drouth-resistant variety of barley, encouraged a shift to barley from oats. Corn acreage shrank by nearly a third, oats acreage by more than half, but barley acreage tripled. Sorghum rose spectacularly. This crop, favored for its ability to produce forage under the most adverse conditions, had been sown on some eight thousand acres each year in the first quadrennium of our study, 1930–1933, producing a total of fifty-seven thousand tons of forage in the four years. In the next four years, those of the most severe drouth, acreage was nearly doubled, although the increase in total output of forage was not much more than a third. Then, for the less adverse years, 1938 through 1941, an average of over 67,000 acres was devoted to sorghum, with forage output zooming up to more than three hundred thousand tons.[19] A greater acreage, although a less impressive percentage change, is represented by the shift to permanent pasture. Here, however, there was only the continuance of a trend which had set in as early as 1925 and which had by 1945 added over a quarter of a million acres to the pasture lands of the county.[20]

Drouth, with these changes in cropping practice, meant relatively more forage and less grain, and this in turn meant fewer hogs in relation to cattle. Through the 1920's swine numbers had run generally above cattle numbers. Even in 1928 they outnumbered cattle by more than two to one, and in no year from 1920 to 1934 had there been fewer than one hundred thousand hogs on Custer County farms.[21] But the drouth brought an immediate and sweeping change. For the eight years from 1935 through 1942 swine never numbered over sixty thousand, while cattle numbers recovered promptly from their low of eighty thousand in 1935 to remain steadily above one hundred thousand head throughout the period.[22]

The drouth challenged the wisdom and effectiveness of the farmers' adjustment to Custer County soils and climate. Was the Corn Belt complex the best system for this region? The shift to sorghum, the acquisition of sandhill pastures, the slashing of the hog enterprise all represented tentative readjustments. That the federal government stood ready to subsidize such shifts was a fortunate circumstance and undoubtedly made it easier for the farmers to try out the new arrangements. Nonetheless many farmer owners could not or would not hold on. The number of farms actually increased from 1930 to 1935, while the average size rose by only 2 per cent,[23] but the percentage of tenancy increased by over four points.[24] In the next five years, however, over four hundred farms disappeared, average size jumped by more than seventy acres (an increase of 17 per cent),[25] and the percentage of tenancy climbed another four points to crest at 55.9.[26]

The farm population had remained nearly constant for fifteen years, through the New Era and the first phase of the depression, but in the first years from 1935 to 1940 it declined by 15 per cent.[27] For the drouth and depression decade as a whole, the loss of the entire county was only 14 per cent (3,598 persons), but of this total the ten-year decline in farm population accounted for all but 453 persons.[28] We noted that, at the end of the twenties, the evidence indicated that the farms of Custer County were being hard-driven to meet the cash demands of motorization and of higher living standards.[29] Under the pressures of drouth and depression combined, the farms could no longer yield an income sufficient to hold their people, even though migration was into the forbidding society of the great depression. Across the nation the depression decade saw very little change in the number employed in agriculture,[30] but in the nation as a whole the depression was not reinforced by a protracted drouth as was the case generally in the Great Plains region and its borders.

The simple difference in population totals does not, however, measure the county's full loss. The nature of this loss will be more evident with a little study of Table I, prepared by Mr. Glover. In this table a comparison is made of the age groups of the 1930 population with the corresponding, ten-year-older age groups of the 1940 population. The assumption is made that if the estimated deaths are added to the 1940 population and this total subtracted from the corresponding group in 1930, the differences will show the amount of migration either into or out of the county. A very hasty glance at the table will show that three-quarters of the migrants were under twenty-five in 1930. Of the upper-teen-age group in 1930, 40 per cent left the county. Of the survivors of the 1930 population as a whole, 23 per cent migrated, the percentage of the farm population which joined the trek standing even higher.[31]

The population of the county naturally showed a higher proportion of aged and a lower proportion of children and young people as a result of these shifts. If we can for a moment consider the county as a social unit, a terrific capital loss was suffered in the departure of so many young people whose birth and early rearing had been charges upon county income and who now departed just as they were entering upon the productive years of life. In the 1940 population alignment children and young adolescents under fifteen years of age comprised only 28 per cent of the total as against 32 per cent for the same age group in 1930. Those sixty-five and over were half again as prominent in 1940 as they had been in 1930, having increased percentage-wise from 6 to 9. In spite of these changes, and the heavy losses of young people, the working potential of the county population was slightly increased, since those from fifteen to sixty-five, who had been only 61.5 per cent

PLATE I

Rainfall and Cereal Production, Custer County, 1928–1942

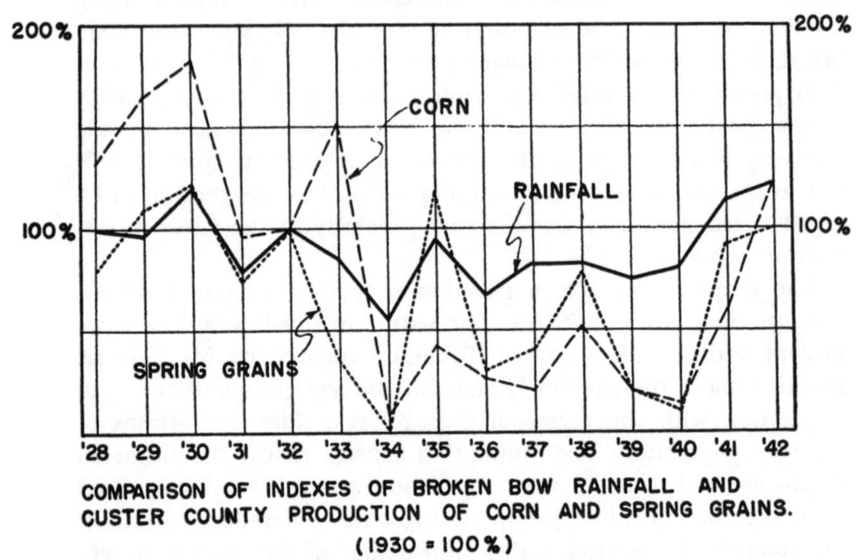

COMPARISON OF INDEXES OF BROKEN BOW RAINFALL AND CUSTER COUNTY PRODUCTION OF CORN AND SPRING GRAINS. (1930 = 100%)

PLATE II

Age Composition of Custer County Population, 1930 and 1940

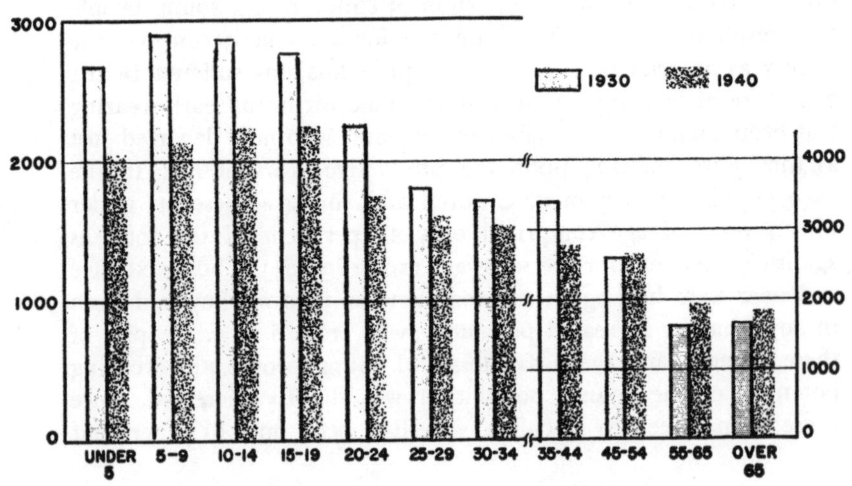

PLATE III

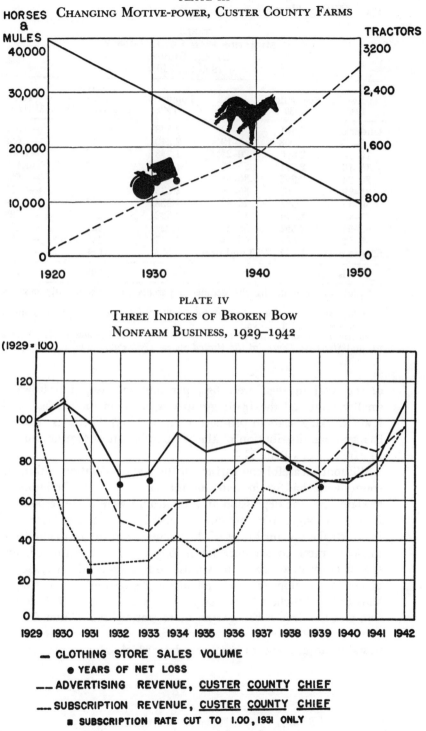

CHANGING MOTIVE-POWER, CUSTER COUNTY FARMS

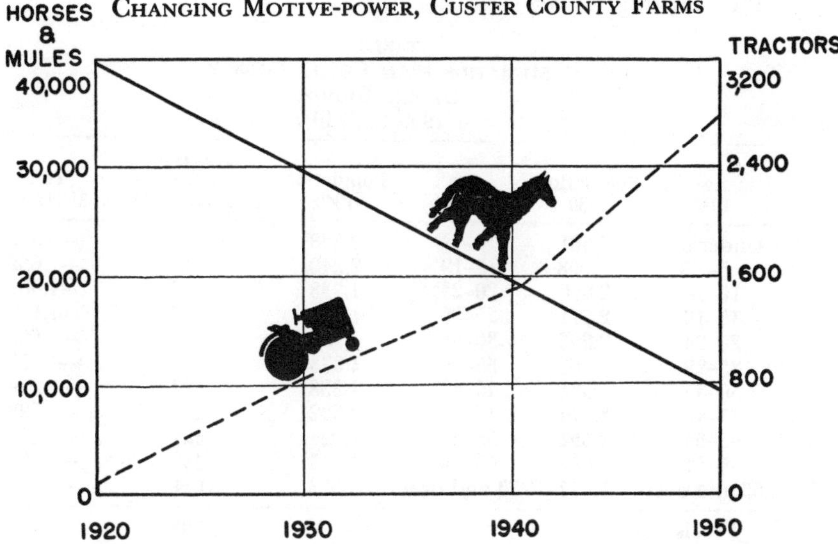

PLATE IV

THREE INDICES OF BROKEN BOW NONFARM BUSINESS, 1929–1942

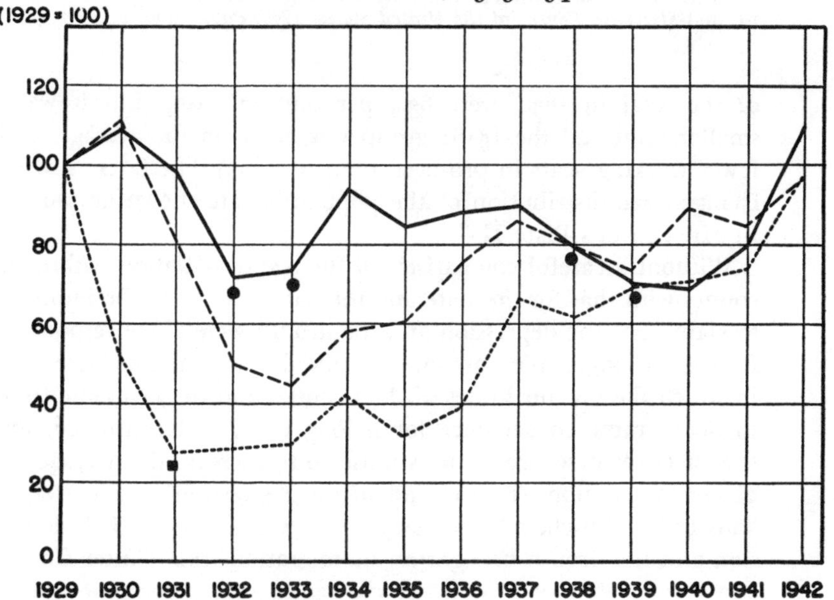

TABLE I
MIGRATION FROM CUSTER COUNTY
By Age Groups
1930 to 1940

Age 1930	Population 1930	Age 1940	Population 1940	Deaths to 1930 Population **	Total Migration
Under 5	2,681	10–14	2,238	67	– 376
5– 9	2,908	15–19	2,240	36	– 632
10–14	2,850	20–24	1,738	50	–1,062
15–19	2,771	25–29	1,604	65	–1,102
20–24	2,263	30–34	1,523	74	– 666
25–29	1,803	35–39	1,373	71	– 359
30–35	1,694	40–44	1,338	77	– 279
35–44	3,379	45–54	2,622	237	– 520
45–54	2,552	55–64	1,924	324	– 304
55–64	1,626	65–74	1,145	453	– 28
65 and over	1,647	75 and over	673	1,154	+ 180
Totals				2,608	–5,148

* Children born during the decade to parents who subsequently migrated are not included.

** Mortality rates approximated from tables in *Length of Life,* by Louis I. Dublin and Alfred J. Lotka.

Source: *Fifteenth Census of the United States: 1930, Population,* III, Part 2, 64; and *Sixteenth Census of the United States: 1940, Population,* II, Part 4, 618.

of the total in 1930, were 63.4 per cent in 1940. (But it was a smaller total and the 15–64 group was older on the average, with fewer working years in prospect, than in 1930.) The facts as to the changed age distribution of the population are shown graphically in Mr. Glover's Plate II.[32]

Without a careful comparison of the age distribution within the county with that for the state and the nation, it would be improper to claim that the depression and the drouth were alone responsible for these changes. We do know that the depression years were years in which the low birthrates of the twenties and the favorable trend in death rates, in evidence for a long time, had continued, and the effect of these two changes must be to increase the average age of any population. (By the end of the depression decade Nebraskans had the highest life expectancy in the nation.)[33] The depression and the drouth brought an outmigration from Custer County and from Nebraska as well, which was in part a correction of an unstable adjustment to resources but which also reinforced the demographic forces mentioned above in promoting that "general, gradual and unspectacular" process of aging of the population which had been going on for a long time.[34]

Custer County people had had a briefer, less severe bout with drouth and depression combined in the 1890's, but with the return of good times and good weather after 1900 the trends existing prior to the drouth resumed. Not so in the 1940's. From 1940 to 1950 the number of farms in the county fell by more than 20 per cent, the average size went up another 120 acres, and the farm population went down by another 24 per cent.[35] The corn acreage recovered somewhat—in 1949 it was only 236,900 acres, almost exactly that of 1919. With the larger acreage in farms, however, this meant that the 1949 corn intensity (percentage of land in farms which was planted to corn) was only 13.9 per cent as compared with 23.9 per cent in 1924.[36] This is almost the same as that for the lowest Iowa county in 1949,[37] and, if the Custer County figure is corrected for the excess land in farms credited to Custer but actually lying outside of the county in the Sandhills, the corn intensity figure for the county would be nearer 15 than 14. Custer County is still, then, to be counted as a corn-belt area, although a transitional type.

But it is a corn-belt landscape that is radically different from that of the 1920's. Outstanding is the size of farm, which in 1950 was 611 acres, an increase of two hundred acres in twenty years.[38] This increase does not represent the spread of landlordism and rural poverty as it would were drouth and depression the only factors operative. But the depression should be viewed as a purgative experience, of which the very violence was in some degree the measure of the readjustments which had been delayed too long.[39] On the margin of the Great Plains there was an initial error in land use and farm size. Attempts were made to spread tillage agriculture over lands that were so rough, so dry, or otherwise so ill-adapted that their use for crop production exposed the land to destruction by erosion and the farmers to poverty and insecurity. Then the steep rise in the level of living in the tens and twenties led to more intensive cropping, but on farms that were too small—in the marginal zone of twenty-two to twenty-four inches of annual rainfall[40]—for efficient use of labor.

A new technological element not only provided pressure for change but also supplied means for beneficial readjustment. This was the internal combustion engine in its varied mountings—automobile, motor truck, tractor, and the like. We noted the appearance of the automobile as an element in the level of living and a cost item to the farms in the twenties.[41] The automobile raised family costs without greatly influencing farm productivity, but the tractor and motor truck, especially when supplemented by the new race of implements designed for tractor power—combine, hay-baler, corn-picker, etc.—increased productivity per worker, making possible the income required to support the increased level of living *if* the worker could have access to the greater acreage of land which he could tend with motor power.

The inter-censual period from 1930 to 1950 included two radically different decades. In the first, the dominant influences appear to be those of drouth and depression; in the second, good weather and boom (war and postwar) conditions are uppermost. Yet the trends developed in the first decade persist in the second. The shift in ratio between cattle and hogs or the number of horses in relation to automobiles, tractors, and motor trucks will serve as an example. In 1930 there were more hogs than cattle on farms in the county, with only eighty-nine cattle for every hundred hogs. In 1940, after ten years of drouth, the ratio was sweepingly reversed, with four cattle to every hog. Better corn crops after 1940 brought only a very limited recovery on the part of the swine enterprise, with thirty-seven cattle in 1950 for every ten hogs. Hogs require corn and labor; cattle, if beef cattle, use forage and proportionately less labor. In 1930 one-sixth of the cattle in the county were classified as milk cows; in 1940 the proportion had risen to one-fifth; in 1950 milk cows were only one-eleventh of the cattle population.[42] The figures are not wholly comparable but they point the direction of evolution, away from the intensive corn-belt type of farming with heavy emphasis upon corn, hogs, milk cows, and human labor, toward a more extensive type involving beef cattle, forage crops, and scanty human population.

In this transition the tractor was a vital element, for it placed the man in control of more horsepower than he could handle when the horsepower was provided by real horses. Horse numbers in Custer County for the period 1920 to 1950 provide a statistical freak in the form of a "curve" that forms a straight line in a simple arithmetical plotting (cf. Plate III). A glance at the curve will show that the horse and mule population of the county fell at the rate of ten thousand every ten years. The corresponding rise in tractor numbers does not make as smooth a line; for the depression made difficult the acquisition of so costly a capital item, while the persistence of the drouth reduced power needs and purses alike. But the tractor, especially when equipped with rubber tires and a high-speed road gear, not only made it possible for one man to till more acres but also made it easier for him to increase the size of his "farm," since it was no longer as important as it had once been to make his holdings compact and contiguous.[43] Mr. Glover gave detailed attention to one tract in the county known as the Dry Valley community. This area of Holdrege-Colby soils is fairly median in the county, being neither as rich and level as some of the bottom land nor as rough, eroded, and poor as some of the rougher hill land. Of the twenty sections in the area he found that in 1930 only one half-section was farmed by operators residing outside the area, but that in 1942 the equivalent of three sections were so farmed.[44]

The economic trend of the county for the past twenty years has, then, been toward larger farms, beef cattle, motor power, and fewer people. That this trend has meant misery and loss for many is demonstrated by the depression-decade trends in land ownership. At the end of the New Era, 1,209 Custer County farms were operated by their owners, 707 farms were operated by men who owned a portion of the land they farmed, and the remainder, approximately 48 per cent of the total, were operated by tenants. Of the owner-operated farms of both classes, over 60 per cent were mortgaged, with the ratio of debt to estimated value for the mortgaged farms very nearly 42 per cent.[45] The position of the owners was precarious, but detailed study by Mr. Glover of land transfers for the Dry Valley community showed that land transfers for the preceding decade (including the tail end of the great land boom), although affecting nearly 30 per cent of the area, included transfers by foreclosure for only 2.7 per cent of the total area.[46]

The depression decade showed a drastic difference. For the twenty square miles of the Dry Valley community, 4,000 acres (34.7 per cent) were transferred in the ten years, of which nearly one-half was by foreclosure. (Foreclosures continued at a high rate for the first four years of the next decade, with 960 acres foreclosed in the period 1940 through 1943, with which year Mr. Glover ended his study.) Comparable data for the entire county are not available, but the Census report of 1940 showed that farms operated by full owners had lost over a quarter of their number in ten years, there being only 877 of them in 1940, compared with 602 part owners and 1,907 tenants. True, the percentage of owner-operated farms which were mortgaged had declined slightly to 56.9, but the ratio of mortgage debt to estimated value of the farms mortgaged had risen sharply, to 65.9 per cent.[47] Farmers will need no diagnosis of these figures. They indicate that for many the mortgage on owner-operated farms had been eliminated by eliminating the ownership and that for the remainder who still preserved their deeds "ownership" was a term implying little security.

Happily for the farmers and for the "American" nature of the county society, the war and postwar boom, with its bumper crops, brought a reversal of this trend. By the end of the war, 1945, the number of owners and part owners had increased by fifty while the number of farms operated by tenants had fallen by 464, bringing the percentage of tenancy down to 48.5, almost that of 1930. By 1950 the census enumerated 1,095 farms operated by full owners and 699 by part owners, with tenants operating 980 to give a percentage of tenancy of only 35.2, the same proportion as in 1910.[48] If one were to make a snap judgment it might well be this: that what the automobile had imperiled the tractor had restored, at any rate, so far as farm equities were concerned.

But farm and village societies were not so easily restored as were farm finances and operating conditions. If we look at the non-farm component of the Custer County society we find a different picture. In the absence of adequate income figures for the county unit, the best indicator of status and achievement is that of population. In Table II population totals and subtotals for the county, the county seat, the villages, and the farms are given for the Census years 1920, 1930, 1940, and 1950. In 1920 the population of the county was at its maximum, so that trends can be readily shown by recording beneath the absolute figure for each year as an index the percentage which that figure is for the same item in 1920.[49]

We have neither the space nor the information for an extensive discussion of the non-farm sector of the county, but the data above and some very interesting figures gathered by Mr. Glover on two

Broken Bow enterprises may be utilized for some very general comments. The figures, plotted on a simple time-quantity graph in Plate IV, are indices of volume of sales for a clothing store and of advertising revenues and subscription revenues, respectively, of the *Custer County Chief.* Crosses, marking the years in which the clothing store experienced net loss, indicate the importance of volume,

TABLE II
POPULATION TRENDS IN CUSTER COUNTY, 1920–1950
WITH INDEX NUMBER, 1920 : : 100

	1920	1930	1940	1950
Custer County	26,407	26,189	22,591	19,207
Index	100	99	85	73
Broken Bow	2,567	2,715	2,968	3,415
Index	100	105	115	133
10 villages	6,043	5,630	5,280	4,919
Index	100	93	88	82
Farm population	17,500 *	17,468	14,343	10,874
Index	100	100	82	62

* Estimate

but the proprietor reported that volume of sales alone was not the sole criterion, since adverse price trends experienced within each year were at least as important.[50]

Railroads and public services aside, the non-farm sector of the county economy was composed almost wholly of mercantile and service agencies whose fixed capital investment was not heavy and for which the proportion of fixed costs was not as high as it was for the farm sector. It was thus possible for these firms to adjust their volume of operations more easily and promptly than the farmers were able to do. The relatively smooth trend of population totals for Broken Bow and the ten villages in the county indicate this smooth readjustment. The farms were slower and experienced drastically hurried changes with the onset of the depression. These changes were almost all in one direction—a direction which represented an apparently sounder adjustment to the soil *under the conditions of current technology.* The boom of the forties made it possible to salvage the family-unit, owner-operated farm as the dominant type, but this was effected through such a thinning out of the rural population as to disrupt established community life patterns[51] and to confront the people of the county with a new series of problems, essentially those of mastering space in the development of adequate social organization.[52] There is still pioneering to be done in Custer County.

NOTES

1. John K. Galbraith, *American Capitalism* (Boston, 1952), p. 68.

2. U.S. Department of Commerce, *National Income: A Supplement to the Survey of Current Business*, 1951 ed. (Washington, 1951), pp. 158–159.

3. Simon S. Kuznets, *National Income: A Summary of Findings* (New York, National Bureau of Economic Research, 1946), p. 53; quoted in Arthur D. Gayer, C. Lowell Harriss, and Milton H. Spencer, *Basic Economics* (New York, 1951), p. 396.

4. *National Income*, 1951 ed., pp. 158–159.

5. Loyd Glover, Jr., "The Economic Effects of Drouth and Depression on Custer County" (M.A. Thesis, University of Nebraska, 1950).

6. Maurice C. Latta, "The Economic Effect of World War I and the New Era upon Custer County, 1914–1929," *Nebraska History*, XXXIII (September 1952), 139–153.

7. Maurice C. Latta, "Some Aspects of the Adjustment of Iowa Agriculture to the Soil," *Land Economics*, XXVIII (May 1952), 171–177.

8. Ph.D. Thesis in progress, University of Nebraska.

9. Computed from Table 13, p. 158, of *National Income*, 1951 ed.

10. Glover, p. 7, citing *The Agricultural Situation*, Bureau of Agricultural Economics, U.S. Department of Agriculture, February 1942, p. 24.

11. Glover, pp. 8, 46.

12. *Ibid.*, p. 10.

13. Figures from Glover's Supplementary Table 2, p. 86, a compilation from *Climatological Data*, 1920–1944, a publication of the Nebraska Section, United States Weather Bureau.

14. Personal recollections. I spent the summer at Wayne.

15. Computed from Glover's Supplementary Table No. 3, p. 87.

16. January 1 livestock estimates, *Nebraska Agricultural Statistics*, compiled in Glover, p. 47.

17. Glover, p. 48.

18. County Extension Service, Custer County, *Reports*, in *ibid.*, p. 73, also p. 57.

19. See Glover's Supplementary Tables, pp. 87–91.

20. This had the apparent nonsense result of showing "land in farms" as an acreage in excess of the county area. The Bureau of the Census reckons a farm location as its headquarters and credits the entire acreage of the farm to the civil subdivision in which the headquarters is located. Since many Custer County farms included Sandhills pasture land in adjacent counties, this land was counted as "land in farms" for Custer County. See Glover, p. 45, where data are drawn from the Census reports.

21. Wayne M. Smith, "The Effects of World War I and the New Era on

Custer County, Nebraska" (M.A. Thesis, University of Nebraska, 1951), p. 42. Based upon *Nebraska Agricultural Statistics.*

22. Glover, p. 47.

23. *Fifteenth Census of the U.S., 1930, Agriculture,* II, Part 1, 1201; *Sixteenth Census, 1940, Agriculture,* I, Part 2, 578.

24. The percentage of tenancy, as reported by the Census for the respective years, was as follows: 1910, 35.7 per cent; 1920, 40.2 per cent; 1930, 48.2 per cent; 1935, 52.6 per cent.

25. *Sixteenth Census, 1940, Agriculture,* I, Part 2, 578.

26. *U.S. Census of Agriculture, 1945,* I, Part 12, 142.

27. Glover, p. 25. Data from respective Census reports.

28. *Ibid.,* pp. 23, 25.

29. Maurice C. Latta, "World War I and the New Era," *Nebraska History,* XXXIII (September 1952), 129.

30. U.S. Department of Agriculture, *Agricultural Statistics* (1946), p. 533, in W. Nelson Peach and Walter Krause, *Basic Data of the American Economy* (Chicago, 1948), p. 30.

31. Glover, pp. 27–29.

32. *Ibid.,* p. 21.

33. John P. Johansen, "The People of Nebraska: A Mid-Century Summary," mimeograph, Department of Agricultural Economics, College of Agriculture, Lincoln, Nebraska, pp. 5–6, citing Federal Security Agency, *State and Regional Life Tables, 1939–1941.*

34. *Ibid.,* p. 5.

35. *Seventeenth Census, 1950, Agriculture,* I, Part 12, 41; 1950 farm population in a preliminary report from *Custer County Chief* (Broken Bow), June 12, 1950.

36. My own computations, from Census data.

37. My computations, from *Seventeenth Census, Agriculture, 1950,* I, Part 9, 38–81.

38. *Fifteenth Census, 1930, Agriculture,* II, Part 1, p. 1201; *Seventeenth Census, 1950, Agriculture,* I, Part 12, p. 41.

39. Joseph A. Schumpeter, *Business Cycles* (New York, 1939), II, 801–803.

40. "Normal" rainfall at Broken Bow is about twenty-four inches. Cf. Glover, p. 86, and *Climatological Data.*

41. Latta, "World War I and the New Era," p. 129.

42. My own computations from Census data. Glover and Smith worked from assessors' reports, which are not strictly comparable.

43. "Farm" is used here in the Census meaning—that area of land operated as a unit under one management. It has now become commonplace in many farm communities, both inside and outside Custer County, for farmers to go miles with their tractors to tend crops on isolated tracts, which are, from the Census point of view, portions of their "farms." Such scattered tracts, however much they may form portions of an economic unit, are very far indeed from the American traditional concept of a farm as a contiguous tract of land which is at once the field of work and the home of a family.

44. Glover, pp. 39–43.

45. *Fifteenth Census, 1930, Agriculture,* I, Part 1, 1274.

46. Glover, pp. 51–53.

47. *Sixteenth Census, 1940, Agriculture,* I, Part 2, 632.

48. *Seventeenth Census, 1950, Agriculture,* I, Part 12, 53.

49. Compiled from Glover, p. 23. Census figures are drawn from population

volumes for the respective years, except 1950, which are preliminary figures from *Custer County Chief,* June 12, 1950.

50. Glover, pp. 56–60.

51. *Ibid.*, pp. 75–79. As one illustration, Dry Valley had a 13-grade school in 1930, with 35 high school pupils; in 1950 it had an 8-grade school with 15 pupils.

52. Cf. A. H. Anderson, "Space as a Social Cost," *Farm Economics,* XXII (August 1950), 411–430.

The Harlan County Coal Strike of 1931

Tony Bubka

This selection is a particular illustration of the general theme of the Communist party's failure to recruit the American proletariat to its revolutionary cause. The miners of Harlan County are "workers," a group ordinarily associated with urban centers, but the Kentucky coal fields are located in isolated rural areas. The circumstance of the miners in Harlan County, however, resembled that of workers across the nation in a number of ways, especially in the weakness of the organized labor movement in the mining area during the 1920's: the percentage of soft coal production mined under union contracts declined from 70 in 1919 to 20 in 1930. The total output, moreover, had been declining, so that the Great Depression struck an already ailing industry (the leather, textile, shipbuilding, and railroad equipment industries were also sick well before the Great Crash).

The themes of the immobility of the unemployed, bitter labor-management relations, indiscriminate hanging of the "Red" label —as in the case of the charges of radicalism hurled at the men on trial in connection with the "Battle of Evarts," a conflict that took place before the Communist National Miners Union made an appearance in the county—and brutal repression of radical activity were far from unique to Harlan County. Yet the background and

[Reprinted from *Labor History*, XI (Winter 1970), 41–57.]

character of the Kentucky miners, "essentially mountaineers," imparted a special quality to their attitudes and conduct.

Harlan County was still a primitive, backwoods region in 1910. Until the advent of the railroad in 1911, travel was either by horseback or buggy, and hard-surfaced roads were unknown.[1] For two decades thereafter the county's coal industry expanded. In 1911, for example, there were only six mines operating. But by the end of 1931, with new mines continually opening, seventy-one had begun operation.[2] How Harlan County became coal-conscious is reflected in these figures: in 1911 there were 169 miners digging in the pits of Harlan County; by 1923, 9,260 miners were employed, and this number kept increasing until it reached a peak in 1930.[3]

The World War I years created a limitless need for coal, and consequently huge profits awaited those who undertook to exploit coal developments. Coal output in 1918 surpassed all previous levels of production when 346,540,000 tons were mined. Production figures for the years between 1913 and 1918 are equally impressive. In that brief five-year span, 2,960,938 tons of coal poured out of the pits; this was equivalent to approximately 33 per cent of all the coal mined in the United States since 1807.[4] Much of it came from new mines in the southern coal fields which were opened to supply the needs of expanding industry.[5]

Overexpansion of the coal industry was stimulated by factors other than the market created by World War I. At first the wartime Fuel Administration set a ceiling price of $2.58 a ton for bituminous coal. The maximum limit brought about a temporary stability in the coal industry and also provided a tidy profit for the coal producers. But in 1920 Italy and France were in dire need of coal. The Fuel Administration canceled its wartime limitation on prices, and the profits on coal shipped to European countries reached their peak, while coal shipped to the Great Lakes brought $10.00 a ton. The operators rushed into the field to grab up these profits.[6] Kentucky's coal output was temporarily stimulated by the 1926 general strike in England.[7] This general strike lasted a few days, but the coal mine stoppages began in May, varying in intensity in different localities, and the disputes were not finally terminated till November and December.

Still other factors stimulated coal expansion in the South. Wage discrepancies between the union and the non-union mines tended to encourage new operations in the southern coal fields where there was no unionization. Coal operator Howard N. Eavenson, testifying before a Senate committee, asserted that periodic strikes in the northern fields, which grew out of the miners' struggle for greater bargaining power, was one of the chief reasons for the development of Harlan's coal fields.[8] An investigator for the La Follette Civil Liberties Committee made this point more emphatic by declaring that the sole reason for opening Harlan's coal pits was to supply coal that would be mined by non-union labor and thus, by selling coal cheaper, to compete favorably with the union production price scale of the northern fields. In short, the tapping of Harlan coal veins by non-unionized labor was to serve as a cudgel; it would force union labor's submission to the operators' terms.[9]

The Harlan County operators' attitude toward labor is explained by Howard N. Eavenson. From the beginning of the county's coal history, he asserted, operations were non-union, and during the World War I years Harlan's owners negotiated contracts with the United Mine Workers of America (U.M.W.) only because of the coercive tactics of the Fuel Administration. These contracts were terminated after the war ended.[10] But before they were, because of Fuel Administration pressure, 70 per cent of the soft coal output was mined by 1919 according to union-wage contracts. During the postwar years, however, union organization dwindled, so much so that by 1930 the soft coal production by non-union mines amounted to 80 per cent of the total.[11]

The crippling effects of a hastily expanded industry became noticeable a decade after World War I. An overgrown industry had stagnated owing to many factors—notable among them several modern mining innovations which increased the rate of production, the digging of countless new pits which tended to oversupply the market with coal, improvements in technology by which more energy was derived from a ton of coal, and the relentless competition coming from other energy-producing markets.

The depression was still another disturbing factor which affected the coal industry. Its consequences for the coal fields are illustrated by the national production figures for this period. The total coal production in the bituminous mines for 1930 was 467,000,000 tons, but in 1931 tonnage declined to 360,943,000, a drop to the low production record set in 1909.[12]

Because of these various figures, contributing to a dysfunctional coal industry, unemployment increased in the fields. The soft coal operators employed 704,793 wage earners in 1924; this number was reduced to 294,000 nine years later.[13] The depression and declining production notwithstanding, the soft coal operators did not unite among themselves to foster fair prices, to limit expansion, or to set up a framework of codes which would govern regulation of the industry. If the entire coal industry was disorganized, these operators seemed particularly so.

As new mines had opened in Harlan County during the 1915–1918 coal boom, a corresponding increase in population had occurred. To recruit labor for these mines, a group of labor agents was sent out to scout the surrounding counties. They offered seemingly incredible inducements, in particular a high-wage appeal that guaranteed more earnings for one month of work than a mountaineer could possibly earn in a year's labor in the hills. They also offered to assume the transportation cost to the mines, and held out the lure of decent living quarters: homes with electric lights and running water.[14] High wages, however, were the greatest appeal. Before the advent of the railroad in the mountain counties (and the Louisville and Nashville began to extend its operations in 1911), there was scarcely a farmer who earned $100 a year.[15] The mountaineer entered a machine-dominated world when the railroad came and when World War I sent coal prices soaring. He tasted a new way of life, and when the boom passed there was nothing to go home to.

The data from Homer L. Morris' field investigations in 1932, based on interviews with unemployed miners, reveal that their lack of vocational training and their educational shortcomings handicapped them in seeking employment in other industries. Of the miners questioned, 78.2 per cent had never completed any education beyond the primary-school level.[16] The Committee for Kentucky report notes that, in the national scale of illiteracy, Kentucky was ranked forty-seventh.[17]

Kentucky's coal fields are situated in rural areas, so that the miners were detached from industrial centers. Moreover, the only major source of employment in eastern Kentucky, other than coal mining, was farming and small-scale lumbering.[18] Therefore, when the Harlan disorders occurred, geography, depression, and limited occupational opportunities made it impossible for unemployed miners to transfer to other industries.[19]

Nor did Kentucky's limitations on public relief help the situation. Indeed, when unemployment became widespread in the Harlan region after 1929, Harlan's unemployed miners suffered more than did their northern counterparts. Many communities simply lacked tax resources to support a public welfare program.[20] They did their best in assisting the destitute miners. And the majority of coal operators also helped, at least to the extent of providing the unemployed miner a dollar-a-day credit for food.[21]

The significance of inadequate relief, and its relationship to the Harlan strike, cannot be overemphasized. Being impoverished, the miners gradually became willing to follow the leadership of any organization that would help them in their plight. The promise of food and relief was a principal factor in encouraging membership in the left-wing unions that entered the Harlan region to capitalize on this unrest.

THE "EVARTS BATTLE"

With the depression in full swing, Harlan County operators decided to minimize their production costs in order to remain in business. In February 1931 the Black Mountain Coal Corporation issued notice of a 10 per cent wage reduction to all of its employees. Rather than accept these terms, the miners chose to walk out of the pits.[22] Their action was the first in a series of events that helped to precipitate the "Battle of Evarts." The walkout was not, it must be noted, prompted by outside agitation. Indeed, the U.M.W. did not endorse, or act in any way to stimulate, the strike.[23]

Some of the older miners who had previously belonged to the United Mine Workers began to have visions of the good old U.M.W.A. days when wages were high. The unorganized miners, happy to better their conditions, talked of unionization and held meetings toward this end in various sections of the county. The miners had resorted to this 1931 strike to dramatize their plight;

and now they staged marches, made speeches, and voiced their grievances in militant, unyielding terms.

The restlessness of Harlan County miners was conveyed to the U.M.W., whose first official action occurred on February 15, when William Turnblazer, U.M.W.A. president of District #19, circulated thousands of leaflets urging the miners to join the union. This literature outlined the miners' grievances, denounced the industrial overseers, and pointed out that the solution to the miners' problems lay in union organization.[24]

Turnblazer scheduled a general mass union meeting at the Gaines Theatre in Pineville, Kentucky, on Sunday, March 1, 1931. More than 2,000 miners attended, filling the theater to capacity, and many more, unable to get in, gathered outside. Philip Murray, vice-president of the U.M.W.A., addressed the crowd assembled there, and appealed for unionization as the key to better conditions. When the meeting was concluded, union agents began to recruit miners into the union.[25]

U.M.W.A. policy at this time was to organize, and not to sanction or to engage in strikes. Its unwillingness to do either was bitterly opposed by radical groups who claimed that the U.M.W.A. had betrayed the miners. But the union seemed to have good cause, for its membership strength suggests U.M.W.A. impotence. For instance, of the nation's total coal output in 1930, only 20 per cent was mined under union contracts.

Following this Pineville meeting, the miners flocked to the union. The U.M.W.A. drive developed into a threatening movement, and operators retaliated by dismissing union organizers and those sympathetic to union demands. The Black Mountain Coal Corporation, for example, discharged a number of U.M.W.A. agitators, and other mines in the county followed suit. Before long, about 500 of the most militant miners were without work.[26]

Miner-operator relations continued to be unsatisfactory, with ill feeling aggravated by the operators' policy of forcibly evicting the discharged miners from company-owned homes. Justifying such evictions, one operator explained: "It is a nasty business and I hate to do it—but I can see no other way of dealing with the problem. I must have these houses for other employees who will work under my conditions, accept my wage scales and pay their rent." [27]

The miners evicted by the Black Mountain Company began to gather at the independent town of Evarts. Picket lines were formed there, and the road leading to Black Mountain Camp was patrolled. On April 1 a miner named Carpenter, who continued to work at the Black Mountain Camp in spite of several warnings, came to Evarts. Several unemployed miners seized him, took him out to a town lot, forced him into a kneeling position, and then lashed him unmercifully.[28]

Violence increased as the strike progressed. A dynamite explosion wrecked the mine-shaft structure of the Bergen Coal Company (located at Shields) on April 20.[29] The month ended with a series of store robberies. Seven shops were burglarized and some of them were completely looted of their stock.[30]

The strike situation became further aggravated when the operators decided to bring in strikebreakers. On April 27 the Black Mountain Company issued a lockout order designed to evict the striking miners, so that the company-owned houses would be made available for those willing to work under its terms. Many of the families were ordered to vacate.[31]

The influx of strikebreakers inflamed the situation. And on April 28 gunfire broke out and shots were fired upon Black Mountain Company deputies from the hills, when these deputies attempted to bring miners in to work the pits.[32] Further trouble occurred the next day when sixteen unoccupied company dwellings at the Ellis Knob Coal town were consumed by fire.[33] Taking notice of the inceasing acts of violence, Judge D. C. Jones of Harlan declared on May 4 that "a state of lawlessless" now prevailed in the county, and requested a special grand jury to assess the state of unrest.[34]

On the night of May 4, while preparations for a grand jury inquiry were taking shape, between 300 and 400 striking miners (non-union miners were excluded) gathered at the Evarts Theatre to form a plan of action.[35] Incendiary speeches characterized the meeting. William Hightower, Evarts local U.M.W.A. president, exhorted the group: "Come to Evarts with your rifles and shotguns and bring a good head. We'll win out if we have to wade in blood up to our necks. We won't have those Black Mountain thugs to contend with much longer." [36]

On the morning of May 5 a procession of miners—100 to 200

men, townsfolk judged—poured into Evarts. This group carried assorted firearms, including shotguns, rifles, and pistols. They scattered along the highway and concealed themselves behind any object which provided protection. Numerous and contradictory stories relate what happened then. It was reported that Jim Daniels, a deputy sheriff employed at the Black Mountain Camp, relayed a message to the miners "that he was coming down to clean up the whole damn town." [37] We do know that three cars conveying a force of ten deputies arrived in Evarts and that gunfire broke out all around the cars when they crossed the railroad junction.[38]

George Dawn, another of the deputies in the squad, declared that when the miners began shooting, Daniels replied with machine-gunfire, and that when he, Daniels, reached the road bank a shotgun discharge tore his head from his body. Thousands of shots were exchanged and when the fury of the skirmish subsided four persons lay dead.[39] The brief encounter brought other repercussions to strike-torn Evarts. Schools suspended classes, and all mining operations were halted.

THE "REIGN OF TERROR"

The "Battle of Evarts" was the climax of those disorders growing out of the miners' desire to organize. It helped catalyze an emotional response of such proportions that county officials were unable to restrain the insurrectionary mood, and troops were ordered to the strike area. Coal operator R. W. Creech of the Wallins Creek Company plainly summed up the employer attitude: "They'll bring a union in here over my dead body. I would rather close this mine forever than work with a union." [40]

Such intransigence meant that operators and union miners were on a collision course. Only chaotic and ineffectual unionization drives deterred a head-on crash. The initial drive was carried out by the U.M.W.A. But the union's strength had waned to the point where it was unable to make any progress. Consequently, rival, more radical, union groups entered Kentucky.

At about this time, the Industrial Workers of the World dispatched representatives, who began to set up locals in Harlan County. Believing that "the working class and the employing class have nothing in common," the Wobblies had the destruction of capitalism as their ultimate goal.[41] Their activities, as could be predicted, were suppressed by county authorities. Moreover, the Wobblies were handicapped by lack of funds, and could not compete with Communist organizers.[42]

Shortly after the "Battle of Evarts," the National Miners Union (N.M.U.), an organization directed by the Communists, sent agents into Harlan County to discredit the U.M.W.A. and to capitalize on its failure to organize the miners. The N.M.U.'s organizing drive was supported by other radical groups, especially by the International Labor Defense (I.L.D.), a left-wing agency set up in Chicago in 1925 in order to fight sedition and criminal syndicalism statutes. The guiding spirit of the I.L.D. was J. Louis Englahl, a Communist party member and former *Daily Worker* editor.[43] The Federated Press, a party wire service, also helped by sending special correspondents into the strike zone. Established in 1918, its purpose was to supply news that supported the Communist viewpoint.[44]

The N.M.U. was the largest affiliate of the Trade Union Unity League (T.U.U.L.), the central agency of all Communist unions in the United States. The league had as its objective (according to the central council of the Red International of Labor Unions at a Moscow convention held on February 15, 1930) the mobilization of "the masses of workers in order to smash the offensive of the capitalists." [45] Its salient aim was trade-union control, which was essential because the expected revolution was considered possible only with working-class support.[46] T.U.U.L. subsidiaries, according to the House Report on Communist Propaganda, assumed organizational titles similar to those of legitimate unions in order to conceal their identity.[47]

In July 1931 the N.M.U. held a national convention in Pittsburgh. Its purpose was to adopt strike action tactics to be carried on throughout the national coal fields. Twenty-eight miners who represented the various coal camps in Harlan County attended the conference.[48] The delegates adopted the following resolution: ". . . Our answer . . . is the organization of the . . . miners, together with all workers toward the breaking of the rule of the capitalist class, the confiscation of the coal mines, and all factories, . . . which can only be achieved through the establishment of the rule of the workers, along the path of the workers in the Soviet Union. . . ." [49]

Supporting the N.M.U., the Communist party, on July 29, affirmed: "In those sections [of Kentucky] where the Party is now being built for the first time the Politbureau must give direct attention. In the mine fields of Kentucky . . . we must aim to develop the strike movement as rapidly as possible. . . ."[50]

N.M.U. agitation continued throughout 1931, and the union movement encountered bitter resistance from the operators, who resorted to extra-legal devices to subdue it. The months following the "Evarts Battle" were characterized by violence so intense that writers who reported upon events in the strike area declared "a reign of terror" existed in Harlan County. A small-scale war was waged against unionism, in which shootings were an almost daily occurrence. The tactics used against the miners and their sympathizers included evictions, black-listing, raids on miners' homes, and arrests of miners on charges of criminal syndicalism. Intimidation and wholesale arrests were the mildest aspect; dynamiting, beatings, the shooting of reporters, the deportation of undesirable visitors, and the closing down of miners' relief kitchens were the more tangible ways in which the union drive was thwarted.

On November 6 a group of writers led by Theodore Dreiser entered Harlan County to conduct a self-appointed inquiry into the situation. The basic purpose of the Dreiser Commission was to investigate, and to learn whether civil rights and liberties were being denied in the strike area. But its importance lay in the commission's effect on events in Kentucky. Major Chescheir, a National Guard officer who was sent to the strike zone, testified that commission activities gave the N.M.U. a new lease on life, for these tended to stimulate and encourage the N.M.U. organization drive.[51] Some credence may be given to his testimony, for we learn that George Maurer, an I.L.D. representative, spoke at a public meeting sponsored by the commission, where he declared:

> We are for the working class and against all enemies of the working class, the coal operators, the county officials, the State officials that are the tools of the bosses. . . .
>
> We will try to have, I hope, something in America like they have in the Soviet Union. . . .[52]

THE EVARTS BATTLE CONSPIRACY TRIALS

On May 6 the special grand jury called by Judge Jones began its inquiry. The grand jury was kept busy turning out indictments, and 335 criminal cases were listed for trial when the fall court session convened, a number setting a new record in Harlan County judicial history.[53]

Charges of communism were rife throughout the Evarts conspiracy trial proceedings. But there is no evidence that the Communists were responsible for the disorders which culminated in the battle of Evarts. According to Daniel M. Carrell, a Kentucky National Guard colonel who entered Harlan County with troops immediately after the battle, no trace of the radical element (which included the I.W.W. and the Communists) was noticeable. Radical groups did not begin their operations until it became evident that the U.M.W.A. efforts to unionize the mines were futile.[54] Some of the miners on trial were U.M.W.A. officials. Yet the Congressional report on *Communist Propaganda* concluded that the A.F.L., including the U.M.W.A., had ". . . patriotically borne the greater brunt of the communist attack in this country, and still constitutes our one great bulwark of defense against potential dangers of communism." [55]

Harlan County officials, however, accused radicals and Communists of being responsible for the lawlessness. What is important is whether such accusations influenced the outcome of the Evarts murder trials, and whether in fact they were so designed. That is, were those on trial identified in the minds of the jury and the public with "communism"? The miners on trial were the key figures in the union drive; to associate them with radicalism would tend to discredit any attempt at labor organization. The Communist issue and its relevance to the trials can be demonstrated by a study of the August 1931 *Harlan Daily Enterprise.* Throughout the conspiracy proceedings, this organ of the coal operators barraged its readers with anti-Communist articles. Significantly, all of these articles were long, which is unusual for a country newspaper. The Harlan trials, on a prosecution motion, were transferred to other counties on August 24. The Mt. Sterling Court took jurisdiction of the Evarts cases. Other cases were to be tried at Winchester, Kentucky. After this date the *Harlan Daily Enterprise* abruptly discontinued its publication of anti-Red articles, or at least did so for the time being.

The atmosphere at the Mt. Sterling trials is best revealed in a *Mt. Sterling Gazette* editorial shortly before the court opened: "It is useless to send men and women of the stripe of the Harlan agitators to the penitentiary. They would be safer in a pine box six feet under ground."[56]

On December 10 the first of these trials ended; W. B. Jones was convicted of murder, and the punishment fixed by the jury was life imprisonment.[57] Court sentiments during his trial are reflected in prosecuting attorney W. C. Hamilton's closing address to the jury: "In Russia they will read the fate of this man . . . and if you turn him loose there will be celebrations in thousands of places and in Moscow the red flag will be raised higher."[58] The *Knoxville News-Sentinel,* which covered the trials, pointed out that a good proportion of Hamilton's address was devoted to denouncing radicals and that no evidence was introduced to indicate that Jones was affiliated with any radical organization.[59] William Hightower, the next miner to be tried, also was found guilty of the charge of conspiracy to murder and, like Jones, was sentenced to life imprisonment.[60]

Lacking funds to pay the expenses of its witnesses, the defense introduced a motion to have the remaining Evarts cases returned to Harlan County. On January 14, 1932, Judge Prewitt, in spite of protests from the prosecution, ordered the remaining twenty-eight cases to be sent back to the Harlan circuit court.[61]

Fifteen trials were ultimately held; seven ended in convictions and life sentences and three in acquittals. There were five hung juries. Herbert Mahler, secretary-treasurer of the Kentucky Miners Defense and defense strategist of the I.W.W., worked unceasingly on the cases from the beginning, and his efforts resulted in the release, in 1935, of three of the seven who were imprisoned. Mahler continued to fight until the last man was pardoned in 1941.[62]

The Jones-Hightower cases were reviewed by Kentucky's highest judicial body, the Court of Appeals. In its opinion the court declared that Jones and Hightower did unlawfully and intentionally conspire to murder Jim Daniels and that the miners gathered at Evarts to prevent the law officers from fulfilling their duty. Many defense witnesses testified that the deputies fired the first shot, but the prosecution's evidence indicated that the miners opened fire. For the court, however, the question about which side fired first had no real bearing on the issue, since "The man who seeks his adversary for the purpose of shooting him cannot be acquitted on the grounds of self-defense, if, when he finds his adversary, the adversary is quicker than he and makes the first shot."[63]

The obstacles which the miners faced in the Evarts trials are indicated by Daniel B. Smith, who had served as defense counsel for six of the defendants. In a letter to Governor Ruby Laffoon, dated February 5, 1934, Smith, who was now state attorney for Harlan County, reminisced:

> In the cases that I practiced, and those that were tried in Harlan County, I can safely say that the defendants never had a fair chance in any of the trials.
>
> Handicapped by some court officials who were in my opinion overzealous, and by lack of financial help, under the disapproval of powerful interests, these men were at a great disadvantage.[64]

THE NATIONAL MINERS UNION STRIKE

The N.M.U. had a short life, one marked by militant attempts to gain recognition as a bona fide labor union. It had been conceived on April 1, 1928, at a Pittsburgh National Mine Conference sponsored by the Communists and designed to displace the U.M.W.A.[65]

Benjamin Gitlow, an important Communist official who renounced the party, claimed that the World Congress of the Profintern ordered a change of strategy. Communists were instructed to cease "cooperating" ("boring from within") with legitimate trade unions and to start a drive for dual unionism. Destruction of the U.M.W.A., it was hoped, would prompt the miners to enlist in the Communist trade union. To finance this new movement, $29,329.46 was given to Gitlow and connections established with Moscow for further financial aid.[66]

With these funds, an organizing drive was mounted. For Communists, the miners seemed a perfect choice, a typical example of the exploited classes. Apparently the N.M.U., with its obviously revolutionary nature and demands, appealed to some of the Kentucky miners. For by December the zealous union organizers were convinced that they had sufficient adherents to strike every mine in that territory. They called a district convention which met at Pineville on December 13, 1931, and some 250 delegates in attendance voted to strike the southeastern Kentucky and Tennessee coal mines on January 1.[67]

This N.M.U.-sponsored "strike against starvation wages" initially met with a disappointing response, and only a few mines in Kentucky were closed down. Thirty-five Harlan County pits continued working, while seven were idle. In Bell County the response was even less encouraging for the union; only two mines were closed with approximately 120 miners going out on strike. Lack of coal orders caused a few Knox County mines to be idle, and their owners expressed their intent to continue operations under non-union wage contracts when the pits were re-opened.[68]

Arrests of the principal N.M.U. leaders became an important method of stemming the strike, and a number were jailed on the charge of violating Kentucky's criminal syndicalist law. On January 6, county officials also arrested on the same charge Allan Taub, an International Labor Defense lawyer sent down to Pineville as defense counsel.

The N.M.U. continued to agitate for broadening the strike movement, and scheduled a rally for January 16 at Harlan town. This demonstration never materialized because precautions were taken to prevent it by sheriff's deputies, who kept a sharp lookout for union organizers seeking to work in the county. A more positive effort to check the new strike offensive occurred the following day when Joe Weber and Bill Duncan, active N.M.U. members, were apprehended in Tennessee, placed in custody of Harlan deputies, deported from the county, and then beaten.[69]

A New York relief group—the "Independent Miners' Committee," composed predominantly of writers—sought admission to Pineville. One of their objectives was "to defend the rights of the Workers International Relief to distribute relief"; another was to circulate subversive literature and to make a lecture circuit of the coal towns. A few hours after their arrival in Pineville, the entire committee was placed under arrest on grounds of being public nuisances. The misdemeanor warrants against them were canceled and, instructed that their presence was not desirable, they were convoyed out of the state. Their expulsion was carried out in the best Harlan manner, including the usual beatings—given to Allan Taub and Waldo Frank, chairman of the committee, both of whom were dragged from their car at the state line.[70]

The ejection of the writers' committee had a deeper significance than according brutal treatment to two "undesirable" visitors. Their automobile escort was composed of many prominent Pineville citizens. It symbolized the mass participation of the respectable element in the community who, believing their labor problems local in nature, had combined with county authorities against outside interference.

The strike agitation extended to neighboring counties. About the time of the ejection of the writers' committee, youthful Harry Simms, a key N.M.U. organizer, entered Knox County to speak at a miners' demonstration there. But he was intercepted and shot to death by a deputy sheriff.[71] Charging that it was a case of deliberate murder, New York City's Communists attempted to make a martyr of Simms, a kind of John Reed of the great American class struggle.[72] The *Daily Worker* printed a thumbnail sketch of the nineteen-year-old hero: "He was sent to the South by the Young Communist League as District Organizer . . . arrested there repeatedly . . . released by the Young Communist League at the request of National Miners Union to organize youth sections in Kentucky and Tennessee." [73] Simms's body was shipped to New York City, in time for a mass demonstration there amid calls for revenge for the fallen comrade. His coffin became the centerpiece for a mute, rain-drenched procession, dotted with red flags and the glittering scarlet neckerchiefs of uniformed teen-age Communists, that marched to the Lower East Side.[74] When Simms's body was transferred to the Bronx Coliseum, an estimated 10,000 people gathered there for what the *Daily Worker* termed "one of the most impressive working class demonstrations ever held in New York City." Vindictive oratory and fists clenched in salute marked the occasion. Simms's father declared: "He died on the battlefield of the class struggle." William Z. Foster, the principal speaker, proclaimed: "One thing we must do is to make the capitalist class pay dearly for the murder of Simms . . . it will not be long before they will face workers' courts in America." Party functionary Israel Amter concluded: "His body goes to the soil, but his spirit goes to the masses." [75]

In March 1932, the N.M.U., aware of its shortcomings and mistakes, formally declared the strike a failure and retreated from the Kentucky coal fields. Party leader Jack Stachel, in reviewing the debacle, offered a long list of reasons why the venture failed. What did the strike accomplish, he asked? Communists, according to him, "succeeded in recruiting dozens of miners into the Party and for the first time establish[ed] our organization among the miners in Kentucky." [76]

In retrospect, one of the greatest blunders was not the N.M.U.'s failure to educate the miners in the importance of the historic class struggle, but rather the Communists' failure to understand the background, nature, and character of the Kentucky miners. Essentially mountaineers, they were people who preferred to be left alone. Their character had been molded by endless years of seclusion, continual conflict with the "law," generations of family feuding and moonshining—all of which combined to produce the psychology of the Kentucky miner. From a religious and behavioral viewpoint, the mountaineer miners formed a homogeneous class. The N.M.U. leaders ignored their deep-rooted religious inheritance. They had selected several promising local miners and sent them north to be briefed and instructed in revolutionary practices. But these novitiates learned that the N.M.U. was Communist-inspired; and, given their view of communism, they believed they now belonged to a union embracing atheism and treason to their country. The would-be converts, upon return, became the strongest anti-N.M.U. propagandists in the strike area. They were encouraged by county authorities to reveal what they had learned about the N.M.U. while in the north, and their penitent revelations were printed in newspapers and in broadsheets entitled "Miners Expose Reds," which were widely distributed.

The anti-religious sentiments unwisely expressed by some N.M.U. representatives confirmed their opinion and helped undermine the union. Trial testimony of Doris Parks, W.I.R. secretary, serves as an illustration. She was arrested in February and jailed on a criminal syndicalism charge. During a court trial she replied to Attorney Smith's queries as follows:

> "Do you believe in any form of religion?"
> "I believe in the religion of workers. . . ."
> "Does your party propose to take over private property for their own use?"
> "They intend to take over everything for their own use. . . ."
> "Do you believe the Bible and that Christ was crucified?"

"I affirmed, didn't I, that I believe only in the working class and their right to organize and to teach them they can be led out of this oppression by the Communist Party."[77]

Nor did prison silence her. "When that day comes," she boasted, "we will not be satisfied with the crumbs—with beans and potatoes. . . . Our victory will be brighter than the sun in the sky."[78]

The N.M.U. withdrew from the Kentucky fields, and for the remainder of its history the union's activities centered in the tri-state area of Pennsylvania, Ohio, and West Virginia. But it made no advances in these northern coal fields, and along with the entire family of T.U.U.L. party-line locals, the N.M.U. was dissolved in 1935. The dissolution was ordered by a New York T.U.U.L. convention directive: "In line with this policy of a unification of its unions with the A.F. of L., the Trade Union Unity League . . . had no further need of continuing in its present organizational form. . . ."[79] The T.U.U.L. now reverted to its original position of "boring from within."

The Harlan County coal strike of 1931 had its foundation in a combination of many factors: a wildcat walkout, a lockout, unemployment, undesirable working conditions, and a disorganized coal industry. The union struggle developed into a local war when the Communists invaded the area to exploit the miserable conditions that prevailed. The miners, in the long run, were adversely affected, since their struggle delayed the coming of unionism. Hence the coal operators had successfully defeated all attempts to unionize the mines, and industrial peace prevailed in Harlan County until 1933. With the passage of the National Industrial Recovery Act in that year, the U.M.W.A. once again launched an organizing drive; but not until about 1939 did it achieve recognition in Harlan County.

NOTES

1. *Harlan Daily Enterprise* (Kentucky), April 25, 1932, p. 1.

2. U.S. Congress, Senate, Committee on Manufactures, Hearings on S. Res. 178, *Investigation of Conditions in the Coal Fields of Harlan and Bell Counties, Kentucky,* 72nd Cong., 1st sess. (Washington: Government Printing Office, 1932), Chart, p. 287.

3. Homer L. Morris, *The Plight of the Bituminous Coal Miner* (Philadelphia, 1934), p. 21.

4. David J. McDonald and Edward A. Lynch, *Coal and Unionism* (Maryland, 1939), p. 136.
5. *Ibid.*, p. 181.
6. Malcolm Ross, *Machine Age in the Hills* (New York, 1933), p. 51.
7. *Ibid.*, p. 54.
8. U.S. Congress, Senate, Committee on Mines and Mining, Hearings on S. 2935, *To Create a Bituminous Coal Commission and for Other Purposes*, 72nd Cong., 1st sess. (Washington: Government Printing Office, 1932), p. 497.
9. U.S. National Archives, Hearings on S. Res. 266, *Violations of Free Speech and Rights of Labor*, 74th Cong., 1st sess., Harlan County, Miscellaneous notes folder #4.
10. Hearings on S. Res. 178, p. 203.
11. Morris, pp. 13–14.
12. U.S. Congress, Senate, Committee on Manufactures, Hearings on S. 174 and S. 162, *Unemployment Relief*, 72nd Cong., 1st sess. (Washington: Government Printing Office, 1932), p. 225.
13. Norman M. Thomas, *Human Exploitation in the United States* (New York, 1934), p. 97.
14. Morris, pp. 60–61.
15. Hearings on S. Res. 178, p. 152.
16. Morris, pp. 76–77.
17. John Gunther, *Inside U.S.A.* (New York, 1947), pp. 640–641.
18. Hearings on S. Res. 178, p. 187.
19. Morris, p. 22.
20. Grace Abbott, "Improvement in Rural Public Relief: The Lesson of the Coal-Mining Communities," *Social Service Review*, VI (June 1932), 205.
21. Hearings on S. Res. 178, p. 183.
22. Louis Stark, "Harlan War Traced to Pay-Cut Revolt," *New York Times*, September 29, 1931.
23. "Fine Bedfellows," *United Mine Workers Journal*, XLII (June 1, 1931), 7.
24. "Appeal Made to Kentucky and Tennessee Miners To Join United Mine Workers of America at Once," *United Mine Workers Journal*, XLII (February 15, 1931), 8–9.
25. "Union Is Reborn in Two Kentucky Counties After Big Meeting at Pineville; Philip Murray Talks," *ibid.*, XLII (March 15, 1931), 12.
26. Hearings on S. 2935, p. 142.
27. Morris, p. 124.
28. *New York Times*, November 27, 1931, p. 6.
29. *Harlan Daily Enterprise*, April 20, 1931.
30. *Ibid.*
31. American Civil Liberties Union, "The Kentucky Miners Struggle," p. 6.
32. *Harlan Daily Enterprise*, April 28, 1931.
33. *Ibid.*, May 1, 1931.
34. *Ibid.*, May 4, 1931.
35. *Kentucky Reports—Reports of Civil and Criminal Cases Decided by Courts of Appeals of Kentucky: Jones* v. *Commonwealth*, vol. 249 (Frankfurt, April 12, 1933), 505–506.
36. John F. Day, *Bloody Ground* (New York: 1941), p. 300.
37. American Civil Liberties Union, p. 6.
38. *Jones* v. *Commonwealth*, *Hightower* v. *Commonwealth*, Vol. 249, Kentucky, 506.
39. *Harlan Daily Enterprise*, May 5, 1931.

40. J. C. Byars, Jr., "Harlan County: Act of God?" *The Nation,* CXXIV (June 15, 1932), 673.

41. *Industrial Worker* (Chicago), January 19, 1932.

42. Selig Perlman and Philip Taft, *History of Labor in the United States* (New York, 1935), IV, 610–611.

43. U.S. Congress, House, Special Committee to Investigate Communist Activities in the United States, House Report 2290 on H. Res. 220, *Investigation of Communist Propaganda,* 71st Cong., 3d sess. (Washington: Government Printing Office, 1931), p. 57.

44. *Ibid.,* p. 58.

45. *Ibid.,* p. 24.

46. According to the House Report, the T.U.U.L. was a branch of the Red International Labor Unions. *Ibid.,* p. 82.

47. *Ibid.,* pp. 16, 23.

48. Sterling D. Spero and Jacob Aronoff, "War in the Kentucky Mountains," *American Mercury,* XXV (February 1932), 231.

49. *Daily Worker* (New York), July 25, 1931.

50. *Ibid.,* August 3, 1931.

51. Hearings on S. Res. 178, p. 151.

52. *Ibid.,* pp. 142–144.

53. *Harlan Daily Enterprise,* August 10, 1931.

54. Hearings on S. Res. 178, p. 121.

55. House Report 2290 on H. Res. 220, p. 82.

56. American Civil Liberties Union, p. 14.

57. *New York Times,* December 11, 1931.

58. American Civil Liberties Union, p. 15.

59. *Ibid.*

60. *New York Times,* January 15, 1932.

61. *Mt. Sterling Advocate* (Kentucky), January 14, 1932.

62. Loyal Compton, "He Won a Fight for the Right. Now What To Do?" *Louisville Courier-Journal,* February 12, 1941, magazine section.

63. Jones *v.* Commonwealth, Hightower *v.* Commonwealth, 249 Ky., 505–511.

64. Hearings on S. Res. 266, pp. 4309–4310.

65. Hearings on S. Res. 178, p. 28.

66. Benjamin Gitlow, *I Confess* (New York, 1940), pp. 387–388.

67. *New York Times,* December 14, 1931.

68. *Ibid.,* January 2, 1932. See also Hearings on S. Res. 178, pp. 37–42.

69. American Civil Liberties Union, p. 19.

70. *New York Times,* February 11, 1932.

71. American Civil Liberties Union, p. 20.

72. Ross, pp. 180–181.

73. *Daily Worker* (New York), February 13, 1932.

74. *New York Times,* February 18, 1932.

75. *Daily Worker* (New York), February 19, 1932.

76. Jack Stachel, "Lesson of Two Recent Strikes," *The Communist,* XI (June 1932), 529–535.

77. Morris, pp. 134–137.

78. Ross, p. 183.

79. William Z. Foster, *From Bryan to Stalin* (New York, 1937), p. 274.

Oklahoma Tribes, the Great Depression, and the Indian Bureau

B. T. Quinten

*The studies of bureaucracy published in the last decade would fill a very long shelf. A central concern of much of this literature is the emergence of a vested bureaucratic interest. This interest sometimes results in the bureaucracy's contributing to the development of a situation quite the opposite of what, according to its original assignment, it was supposed to create. This selection shows the bureaucratic phenomenon at work in a special context, involving the question of the place of the original Americans in American life. New Deal policy toward the Indian, embodied in the Wheeler-Howard Act of 1934, substituted for efforts to absorb the Indians into white society the policy of rehabilitating them as vigorous minority groups by granting them significant rights of self-government and self-determination. Yet in 1969 one reads that at a conference of an Indian study group in Denver the main emphasis was on the need for self-determination: "Indians making decisions for Indians" (*New York Times, *August 24); and that at a National American Indian Conference in Minneapolis one of the major educational needs stressed was the restoration of Indian culture (*New York Times, *November 23). In 1969 one also learns, from the Association of American Indian Affairs, that for Indians the average period of schooling is five years, the average family income is $1,500, the rate of unemployment is 45 per cent, and the average*

[Reprinted from *Mid-America,* XLIX (January 1967), 29–43.]

life span is forty-three years. For them the Great Depression began early and has yet to end.

American leaders only slowly recognized the grave effects of the Great Depression years of 1929–1933 on the nation's Indians, most of whom were hardly wealthy even in times of national prosperity. Not until the autumn of 1931, nearly two years after the numbing stock-market crash, did the federal Indian Bureau organize a relief program and call for support by Congress. Even this help, consisting mostly of surplus food, did not completely suffice, and like most needy Americans impoverished redmen had to await the New Deal for satisfactory economic assistance. Since more than 100,000 Indians resided in Oklahoma during this period, an analysis of their experience clearly reveals the causes and consequences of this prolonged aid delay.[1]

Loosely divided into two large groups, the Indians of Oklahoma represented twenty-nine former tribes. The Five Civilized Tribes—the Choctaw, Chickasaw, Cherokee, Seminole, and Creek—were the most assimilated. Scattered over more than forty counties in southern and eastern Oklahoma, they constituted nearly four-fifths of the state's tribesmen.[2] Living as neighbors to whites in some communities, they occasionally participated in community affairs and often sent their children to public schools. Integration was quickened by intermarriage, adoption of the English language, and acceptance of white habits and customs.[3] The other tribes, largely located in the central and western portions of the state, had only limited contact with the whites and retained much more of their original culture. Since all were small in number, the government grouped them together at six agencies for administrative purposes.[4]

Many of these tribesmen for a variety of reasons had taken up farming. According to a 1931 report there were then 45,629 Indian agrarians in sixty-seven Oklahoma counties.[5] Some thought farming would make them independent and prosperous; others hoped to acquire social prestige.[6] Still others, who neither understood nor desired a new agricultural economy, yielded to the pressure of ambitious Indian Bureau agents.[7]

But much of their land was infertile, and few Indians were first-class farmers. After whites purchased a large portion of the productive acreage, the southeastern Oklahoma tribes were left largely with rocky, badly eroded, weed-covered land in the hills. From some of the land, skilled white agrarians could not have produced a living, and some tribesmen seemed incapable of cultivating the acreage which was suitable for agriculture.[8] Hence, though the Cheyenne and Arapaho tribes cultivated 85,000 acres, only forty members of these tribes were completely self-supporting. They grew about all they consumed, which, as one county agent explained, "isn't much."[9] Only the Kiowas were truly successful farmers, producing goods worth $40,000 in 1928, which provided an income of nearly $1,200 for each forty-acre farmer. The Kiowas took full advantage of the fertile Washita Valley soil, an agricultural advantage which the other tribes lacked.[10]

Prior to the Great Depression many Indians had derived income from land leasing, made legal by an 1891 act. Indian acreage rentals required approval by agency superintendents, but the Indian Bureau generally encouraged the practice.[11] Some of the less productive land could be used more effectively in large units, and leased property was far more easily administered. Besides, leasing freed the field agents from the obligation to teach the Indians agriculture.[12] Even the Indians who leased extensive acreage generally received unjust compensation, however, and low drouth-year yields virtually eliminated this source of revenue. Remaining close to their homestead, most Indians infrequently visited their surplus acreage, though it was sometimes more valuable land. Potential white tenants exploited this lack of knowledge, and thus saved themselves the best portion of a realistic rent.[13] Moreover, as the economic crisis intensified, Indian landlords could not so much as collect the specified amount.[14] Sometimes the white tenants paid half the rent, stalled on the balance while harvesting another crop, and then quietly departed.[15] Nor were the Indians able to force delinquent renters to move, for these men sought government aid with favorable results. Pressure from Congress prompted the Indian Bureau to block many proposed cancellations, and even when allowed to terminate a lease, Indian owners could rarely afford the required patent fee to switch renters.[16]

Timber, which had once given the hill land value, provided a living for some tribesmen, but the depression also curtailed this income. The best sale was for one to two dollars per acre to lumber companies, though a few Indians sold or traded ties, hickory sticks, and stave bolts. In the wake of the general financial crisis, however, the selling price of ties ceased to be worth a good woodsman's efforts. Nevertheless, Indian Bureau officials soon began preparations to sell the remaining timber at a time when the market value had slumped to a twenty-year low.[17]

Despite Choctaw and Chickasaw efforts to reverse the trend, Indian income from coal and asphalt also dropped during the economic crisis. These tribes owned 376,000 acres of coal and 3,000 acres of asphalt, estimated by the United States government to be worth more than ten million dollars.[18] Leased to private coal mining companies, these minerals had steadily enriched tribal treasuries. However, the Great Depression coincided with an unrelated decline in coal values. The flood of fuel oil in Oklahoma and the discovery of additional western coal fields had greatly decreased the demand for the Indian deposits. Furthermore, railroads in Arkansas, Kansas, Texas, and Oklahoma had substituted oil for coal in their engines.[19]

Many of the suffering Indians were already without property, having dispensed with their share of the tribal acreage, and removed themselves from government supervision. Interior Department efforts to alleviate their difficulties were largely unsuccessful. The first such attempt, initiated in 1922, was a five-year industrial program aimed at training landless tribesmen for urban trades. When the inadequacy of this approach became apparent, the Department established Indian labor bureaus to help Indians without income to locate gainful work. This service accomplished some positive results in California, yet not a single bureau was even created in Oklahoma. Vocational schools for Indians were more effective than either of these programs, but even the graduates of these institutions had small chance of locating profitable work in the cities and towns of Oklahoma.[20]

Long before the Great Depression, therefore, these tribesmen had limited employment opportunities, and the typical family's earned income was extremely low. Wage-paying jobs were few in reservation areas, and most Indians had no urban contacts. In addition, many were unable to speak proper English and thus were regarded as unintelligent. In spite of all these obstacles, a fortunate few were able to secure roles as unskilled laborers, but these they lost in the first layoffs of the general financial crisis. Some seasonal employment of an agricultural character was usually available, but the returns were relatively small. Indian cotton-pickers, for example, though highly regarded by white farmers, seldom made more than seventy-five cents per day. Furthermore, the severe drouth which accompanied the depression virtually ended this type of employment. A large number of the landless returned to live with friends and kin, where they intermittently picked cotton, fished, hunted, trapped, and perhaps cut timber.[21]

With almost no individual income, the Indians tried to draw on tribal funds, but the Indian Bureau proved to be extremely reluctant to make such per-capita payments. The Bureau contended that Congress had frequently made mass distributions of this type when only a few tribesmen were actually in need. Bureau officials also believed that the expectation of unearned dividends hindered Indian economic progress by encouraging indolence and thriftlessness.[22] Yet though the Bureau continually reiterated this policy, the Choctaws and Chickasaws asked for a $200 payment to each tribesman. This award would have required slightly more than $5,000,000, but the total assets of these tribes was over $23,000,000, and they won the powerful support of Oklahoma mercantile interests.[23] Local merchants hoped the income involved would enable Indians to "buy the things they need and pay the obligations they have made," and thus bring relief both to "the Indians and the communities in which they reside." [24] Nevertheless, the Indian Bureau notified the Choctaws and Chickasaws that their treasury balance would not justify the payment, and until 1933 the proposals of other tribes met the same fate.

Indian Bureau policies contributed heavily to growing friction between the tribesmen and Oklahoma merchants as the Great Depression continued. During the nineteen-twenties, partially because of the oil boom, the Indian trade had vastly increased. Members of the tribes found their buying power much multiplied, and local businessmen accepted the situation as permanent. Tribesmen were therefore often furnished credit without the technically required prior approval of a field clerk. As the business cycle began its rapid downturn, however, merchants soon began complaining that they were unable to collect sizable accounts.[25] An audit of one firm disclosed that Indians had defaulted on bills totaling more than $20,000.[26]

Though the tribesmen seemed willing to meet their financial obligations they needed the approval of the Indian Bureau, and officials of this agency often refused to pay claims authorized by individuals with funds on deposit. Business firms increasingly protested this policy, particularly when the rejection of their claims seemed to be the product of corruption and graft among Bureau officials. Field clerks were accused of favoring certain firms, even of accepting bribes to approve unfair accounts. Yet the Bureau adhered persistently to its controversial policy, as is evidenced by the case of a Miami, Oklahoma, lawyer. He assembled a battery of lawyers to testify on the value of his services and was given judgment. Nonetheless, the department still refused to pay.[27]

Concurrent with these debates, the average Oklahoma Indian's economic position was steadily deteriorating. Improper nourishment and lack of food promoted disease, especially pellagra and tuberculosis, and even starvation. Some tribesmen were found to be so weak from hunger that they were unable to arise from bed. In Delaware County the entire Indian population once was expected to starve if aid was not provided. Thirty per cent of the Wheelock Indian Academy children enrolled were at least thirty pounds underweight, and, so at least one estimate contended, three-fourths of all Oklahoma Indian children were undernourished.[28]

The food shortage was most critical among the Choctaws, Chickasaws, and Seminoles, many of whom were living on what others would share. Majorities of these tribes were subsisting on a daily fare of dry-salt meat, beans, and bread, and some of their more needy fellow tribesmen lived on two portions of cornbread and water per day. When a prominent Choctaw died at Antlers his family was unable even to provide food for the funeral attendants as was the tribal custom.[29] But the problem of food was not restricted to the southeastern Oklahoma tribes. Some of the Cheyenne began skinning diseased horses.[30]

Unable to purchase food, the Indians tried gardening, fishing, and hunting, but even these sometimes failed. Seed for vegetable farming was not always available, and gardens frequently wilted in the drouth. Fishing produced some food, though the element of chance restricted the amount. Successful hunting families consumed squirrel and rabbit, but many lacked funds for hunting licenses, and although game was plentiful most of the land was fenced and posted. The limited number of Indian-owned chickens were being rapidly stolen by white men in passing cars.[31]

Inadequate clothing and shelter undoubtedly contributed to the rapid decline of health in the tribes. Tuberculosis, long a dreaded enemy of the Indians, drastically increased during the depression. The clothing shortage was most critical among the Chickasaws and Seminoles, many of whose children were without shoes.[32] A large group of Cheyenne and Arapaho families went back to creek-bank tents, while considerable numbers of Seminoles resided in crude log houses, neither of which provided much protection against inclement weather.[33]

Overwhelmed by these economic and social problems, each directly produced or at least made worse by the Great Depression, Oklahoma's Indians desperately sought assistance. But for almost twenty-four months imposing obstacles smothered their pleas for relief. Of these, three Indian Bureau weaknesses were perhaps the most formidable: ineffective inspection procedures, inefficient and corrupt agents in important field positions, and the basic Bureau approach to the Indian problem.

Numerous Indians, particularly the southeastern Oklahoma tribes, were isolated and immobile. The Cherokees showed a decided preference for remote living, but not all tribes lived apart by choice. In depression or prosperity Indians could exist only where they were. At best, consequently, this difficult problem of geography made agency services hard to obtain.[34] Yet many Indian Bureau field clerks seldom visited the homes of tribal members, and some seemed unaware of the growing poverty. Preoccupied with the affairs of a few oil-rich Indians they neglected the bulk of the tribes. Supervisors from Washington periodically toured the reservations, but traveled without any systematic inspection arrangement. One tribe's affairs were reviewed by fifteen visiting officials within a three-week period; other tribes were almost never inspected. Members of the Five Civilized Tribes complained, moreover, that their superintendent never saw the various groups he controlled.[35]

In view of the increasingly heavy Bureau expenditures for the wages of supervisory personnel, this lack of observation seems inexcusable. Between 1929 and 1933, the Bureau's employee force was increased by nearly 300 per cent.[36] In 1931, when a desperate effort was being made to balance the national budget, the Bureau successfully requested an appropriation of $27,000,000. Its ability to obtain a $12,000,000 increase over 1928 resulted from a Congressional desire to aid destitute Indians. Instead, however, 2,200 new employees were hired and salaries were raised 25 per cent. With the addition of these workers, the Bureau had a supervisor for every thirty-six Indians.[37]

In some cases the field clerks were morally, physically, and intellectually inferior to the Indians they served. At least one agent forced an Indian woman to "take a ride with him" before he gave her a rent check. Some favored certain Indians and still others pressured tribesmen to patronize particular business firms. Agents constantly diverted funds in illegal ways, and at one point in the depression Indian suits against agents totaled $19,000,000. The probate attorney at Hugo was deaf, and the field clerk at Idabel was a tubercular.[38] Revelations of this kind encouraged one newspaper editor to characterize Indian Bureau policy as "a scheme to accomplish robbery and destruction under a pseudo-legal system." [39]

The Bureau seemed to base all its actions on a basic premise of Indian ignorance. As proof of this notion's validity, agents pointed to the ease with which whites had stripped away Indian property since allotment. Consequently, Indian finances were closely managed, and when a tribesman wanted something he went to his agent. The agent, arbitrarily making all decisions, approved or rejected the request. Furthermore, when an Indian requested an article which required purchase he was not trusted with the money but was issued a store order. Indeed, it was even difficult for a tribesman to lend money to a member of his family.[40] All this, of course, was keenly irritating to the Indian. In addition, some friends of the tribes correctly argued that such an approach tended to decrease responsibility and build up a pauper attitude.[41]

Of all its procedures the Bureau's health policies undoubtedly provoked the most intensive discontent. Although its medical staff was too small to care adequately for all, especially in the face of abnormal demands during the Great Depression, the Indian Bureau demanded the right to determine when a tribesman was ill, the nature of the treatment needed, and the person or facility to provide this help. Faced by this regimentation and their own poverty, the Indians could rarely obtain medical and hospital services of their own choosing. Private doctors usually served willingly, but the average tribesman—unless graced with Bureau approval—had no way to compensate. Thus the seriously ill sometimes had to settle for a field clerk's patent medicine order.[42] Yet drugstores regularly complained that they had provided medication for Indians in pain, only to have their claims disallowed by agency officials. Hospitals chosen by field clerks generally received their due, but others were often less fortunate.[43]

These rigid controls attracted scathing criticism. Indeed, a Shawnee hospital manager blamed the deaths of three tribesmen on the Bureau's medical policy. Asserting that these individuals would have survived with a physician and the facilities of their choice, he demanded that the field clerks involved be prosecuted for murder.[44] Another aroused critic of the agents maintained that "narrow-minded" officials assumed that the Indian "did not have enough sense to know he was sick . . . without looking up a field clerk to find out." [45] But long delays in decision-making were perhaps the most distasteful feature of the Bureau's approach to health problems. To one Indian it seemed that, "If our people are sick, they may be dead before they get any relief." [46] And, in fact, tuberculosis did kill at least three children in one tribe before treatment was provided. In sharp contrast, government supervisors sold the land of certain deceased tribesmen before burying them, thus making the Bureau appear even more inhuman to the Indians.[47]

Internal attempts to expose the shortcomings of this system were quickly stifled. White fieldworkers who endeavored to reveal the alarming condition of the Indians were sometimes forced to resign for causing the Bureau to be publicly criticized. Dissident tribesmen also feared retribution. The wisdom of silent endurance seemed clear, for example, when a Senate committee's Indian witness against a Bureau physician was later denied medical care. The right of appeal to the Interior Department offered little solace, for the Secretary almost always sustained field official actions.[48]

Yet, while generally refraining from detailed criticisms of specific practices, some Oklahoma tribesmen worked to staff the Bureau with better qualified personnel. Though field agents were charged with aiding the Indians with each of their problems, especially those of an economic nature, many had no farming or livestock-raising experience. They were therefore scarcely able to give sound practical advice. Worse still, agency officials seemed unnecessarily cold and aloof, as when old tribesmen with a few dollars on deposit were denied tobacco, or when others were deprived of blankets because they referred to them as bedclothing, or when survivors of deceased persons were forced to wait more than two weeks to hold funerals.[49]

The placement of their own people in Indian Service positions seemed to be the most nearly perfect solution. The Five Civilized Tribes went even further, talking of an Indian superintendent, one who would, except for an annual report, be entirely independent of the Indian Bureau.[50] But while Secretary of the Interior Ray Lyman Wilbur indirectly and perhaps unintentionally encouraged the advocates of these reforms, vigorous opposition soon materialized. The Oklahoma Congressional delegation was brought under intense pressure from influential friends of the incumbent white field officials. These critics stressed one deadly effective argument: since whites paid the taxes supporting the federal Indian program, the removal of like-colored administrators, especially during depressed times, was completely unjust. In the end, the reformer tribesmen failed even to secure a compromise, since the Bureau was urged, not ordered, to employ more Indians as positions became vacant.[51]

Another equally effective hindrance to Indian aid was a too widely accepted viewpoint which opposed helping any Indian. Several groups for very different reasons adhered to this position. Possibly repulsed by the strange consumption habits of a few tribesmen, one group blamed liquor drinking for Indian poverty. The most curious liquid consumed was prepared by pouring water on canned heat and straining it through a rag, a practice which some claimed reduced several "strong men" to "skin and bones" and rendered others "crazy as bats." Likewise, a man feeling its effects was once judged insane, although he was later released.[52] Other unusual and notorious Indian beverages included rubbing alcohol and vanilla extract.[53] While these practices were rare they were accepted by many as typical. One newspaper editor was thus favored with considerable agreement when he declared that "All the reformers in Christendom cannot keep the drinking Indian from his cups." [54]

Grounding its views on an interpretation of history, a more sophisticated group asserted that relief would merely further pauperize the Indians. They pointed out that the Indian Office had been compelled temporarily to feed and clothe the Indians while relocating them on reservations. Unfortunately this experience suppressed Indian ambition and initiative, and they henceforth desired and expected permanent care by the United States government. Somehow, although this explanation's exponents never showed exactly why, the traditional communalism of the tribes made them willing to accept dependency. Even in a Great Depression, therefore, the only solution to tribal economic problems was not charity but a more vigorous individualism and competition.[55]

A third group sincerely doubted that the tribes needed aid. In the prosperous years of the nineteen-twenties, a considerable number of Americans had developed a dangerously false Indian image. This stereotype had derived nourishment from gaudy photographs of fancy-costumed Indians and from stories of wealth and improvidence among the tribes. Since individual tribesmen, as the trust estate hearings revealed, could invest thousands of dollars in transportation alone, they saw no need for concern over the general economic status of Indians. Any remaining doubt may have been eliminated by Indian Bureau propaganda which repeatedly asserted that the tribesmen were being civilized, educated, and protected. Small wonder, then, that these worried Americans of Great Depression days only slowly realized that the redman faced perhaps his greatest crisis.[56]

Yet another impediment to Indian relief was the variety and multiplicity of laws relating to the tribes, which even bewildered some legal experts. Many of these statutes were inconsistent with modern conditions and some prevented effective administration. Secretary of the Interior Wilbur described the general condition of Indian laws as a "legislative maze." [57]

Finally, federal Indian aid was delayed by the conflicting views of government leaders. President Herbert Hoover consistently blocked relief bills. Toward the close of 1930, for example, Senate Democrats proposed a $15,000,000 Indian food loan, but Hoover's aides threatened a veto, and the plan was dropped.[58] Frustrated in this approach, Congress tried to arrange for Oklahoma to assume the responsibility for aiding its tribes, but, as it might have expected, the state's legislature proved to be even less cooperative.[59] Furthermore, the Indian Bureau was consistently unwilling to accept advice by members of the Congressional Committees on Indian Affairs. Prompted by appeals from the Apache, Kiowa, and Comanche tribes, for instance, Senator Thomas requested an earlier than scheduled 1930 payment to these tribes. Maintaining that the money would be more useful later, the Bureau flatly refused.[60]

For two years after the great stock-market crash, therefore, requests for help by the Indians of Oklahoma were to no avail. Somehow most of them managed to survive. A fortunate few had benevolent and resourceful supervisors; they helped each other and they were sometimes permitted to share in state and local programs. Benefits from all these sources were distressingly lean. Field clerks generally could not aid individuals without personal funds on deposit, though the most impoverished were occasionally employed on various agency jobs.[61] Only the Shawnees had an emergency fund for indigents and it was insufficient. The Seminoles divided food, blankets, furniture, and implements from the old tribal missions. Some members of all tribes with pensions or lease money were "dividing their eats." [62] A few Indian farmers qualified for help by the Oklahoma State Drought Relief Committee—help which generally constituted from two to five dollars per week.[63]

At last, in October 1931, the Indian Bureau reluctantly acknowledged mass destitution among the Oklahoma tribes. The state's Indians then received extensive benefits from a large national relief program, which included surplus wheat and flour from the Federal Farm Board and used clothing from the United States Army. Agricultural extension agents met with groups of Indians, provided them with seed loans from the Department of Agriculture, and urged the planting of gardens. Meeting in December, Congress immediately provided an emergency appropriation of $1,000,000 for destitute tribesmen.[64] Moreover, the Red Cross organization provided food for around 3,000 Indian families weekly throughout the winter.[65]

Yet this hastily fabricated program completely ignored Indians without property, a shortcoming which the most energetic efforts could not soon correct. In 1929 the Comptroller General had ruled that landless tribesmen could not qualify for federal aid.[66] Furthermore, since these Indians were no longer a national legal responsibility, the Indian Bureau did not request an appropriation for them. Congress, apparently unaware of the legal ruling, believed the benefits provided were being distributed to all tribesmen regardless of status, and most members did not completely realize their error until vigorously criticized by John Collier of the American Indian Defense Association.[67] Oklahoma Congressman Wilburn Cartwright was a notable exception. Alarmed by reports of dramatic deprivation among this group, he telegraphed requests for help to Red Cross leaders in his southeastern Oklahoma district. But only one of thirteen city chairmen was able to announce the ability of his chapter to assist. Contending that these Indians were still a national moral, if not legal, responsibility, some members of Congress proposed a partial refund of local expenditures in their behalf. Nevertheless, this bill and a 1932 House bill for the direct relief of non-wards were defeated.[68]

Meantime the agency Indian relief program began to falter. The subsistence-garden program had at first looked promising, for by April 1931 the Indians had planted 95 per cent of their free seed. Choctaw Chief Ben Dwight reported the planting of two thousand gardens by his people.[69] Anticipating the success of this project and another large Congressional appropriation, the Indian Bureau instructed the Red Cross to give no more aid to Indian wards.[70] The charity organization, since the number of unemployed whites was constantly growing, happily agreed and subsequently rejected agency Indian applications. In the months that ensued, the number of destitute tribesmen steadily increased; many of the subsistence gardens were lost to the drouth, and the second Congressional appropriation proved to be less than half the size of the first. More Red Cross aid was needed badly, but that organization's ability to provide it was now questionable. In addition, many Indians refused to apply, believing their previous denial had been racial discrimination. As one tribesman explained, "If it's Indian money, we go; if it's white man's money, we no want." [71]

The Oklahoma Indians had very little hope for a more intensive program from either the Indian Bureau or the Hoover administration. Convinced that the source of their problems was politics, many decided that political action was the only way to solve them. To this end tribal leaders determined to unite the votes of Oklahoma's Indians. These would be cast for the party that would promise to deliver them the best service. Accordingly, on May 15, 1932, delegates from the various tribes assembled at the famous 101 Ranch to organize for this purpose.[72] A Potawatomi perhaps best stated their decision: "Because Republicans believe in depression, the Indians are praying for a Democratic administration."[73] Ninety per cent of the state's Indians voted for Roosevelt in the presidential election of the following November.[74] Hence, while further weakening the already unhealthy economy of Oklahoma's tribesmen, the Great Depression called attention to serious policy flaws and thus set the stage for fundamental reforms in Indian administration.

NOTES

1. U.S. House of Representatives, 71st Cong., 1st sess., Committee on Indian Affairs, *Hearings . . . Tax-Exempt Indian Lands,* Washington, 1930, p. 24; hereafter cited as *Tax-Exempt Indian Lands;* U.S. Department of the Interior, *Annual Report of the Commissioner of Indian Affairs, 1929,* Washington, 1929, pp. 25–26.

2. Muriel H. Wright, *A Guide to the Indian Tribes of Oklahoma,* Norman, 1951, p. 25.

3. D. P. Trent, *Extension Work Among the Indians of Oklahoma, 1929–1930,* Stillwater, 1931, p. 3.

4. *Tax-Exempt Indian Lands,* p. 8.

5. Trent, *Extension Work,* p. 3.

6. U.S. House of Representatives, 73rd Cong., 2nd sess., Committee on Indian Affairs, *Hearings . . . Readjustment of Indian Affairs,* Washington, 1935, p. 463; hereafter cited as *Readjustment of Indian Affairs.*

7. Lewis Meriam, *et al., The Problem of Indian Administration: A Summary of Findings and Recommendations,* Washington, 1928, p. 7; U.S. Senate, 71st Cong., 2nd sess., Committee on Indian Affairs, *Hearings . . . Survey of Conditions of Indians in the United States,* Washington, 1931, XIV, 5395, 6305, hereafter cited as *Survey of Indian Conditions.*

8. *Survey of Indian Conditions,* XIV, 5333, 5514, 5618, 5713, 6259, 6273.

9. U.S. Department of the Interior, *Annual Report of the Board of Indian Commissioners, 1928,* Washington, 1928, p. 33.

10. *Ibid.,* p. 32.

11. U.S. Department of the Interior, *Annual Report of the Board of Indian Commissioners, 1929,* Washington, 1929, p. 13.

12. Meriam, *Problem of Indian Administration,* p. 44.

13. *Survey of Indian Conditions,* XIV, 5391, 6317; *The Daily Oklahoman,*

(Oklahoma City), April 18, 1931; U.S. Senate, 70th Cong., 2nd sess., *Indian Funds . . . Letter from the Comptroller General of the United States Treasury Department*, Washington, 1929, p. 89, hereafter cited as *Indian Funds.*

14. U.S. Department of the Interior, *Annual Report of the Board of Indian Commissioners, 1931*, Washington, 1931, p. 5. Will Justice to Elmer Thomas, June 15, 1932, in Senator Elmer Thomas Papers, Division of Manuscripts, University of Oklahoma Library. All communications hereafter cited as either to or from Thomas are in this collection.

15. George Hunt to Thomas, December 16, 1930.

16. Isabell Sturn to Thomas, January 20, 1932; Folder III, Indians, 1930.

17. *Survey of Indian Conditions*, XIV, 5690, 6249, 6293, 6318.

23. C. J. Rhoads to Thomas, November 29, 1930; Folder II, Indians, 1930.

19. *Survey of Indian Conditions*, XIV, 5298; Wilburn Cartwright to Ben Dwight, March 1, 1929, Wilburn Cartwright Papers, Division of Manuscripts, University of Oklahoma Library. All communications hereafter cited as either to or from Cartwright are in this collection.

20. Folder I, Indians, 1930, Thomas Papers; *Annual Report of the Board of Indian Commissioners, 1929*, p. 20.

21. Meriam, *Problem of Indian Administration*, pp. 4–5; *Survey of Indian Conditions*, XIV, 6275; *Annual Report of the Board of Indian Commissioners, 1928*, pp. 5–6, 32.

22. Meriam, *Problem of Indian Administration*, p. 8; *Annual Report of the Board of Indian Commissioners, 1928*, p. 14.

23. C. J. Rhoads to Thomas, November 29, 1930; Folder II, Indians, 1930.

24. *The Valliant Tribune* (Oklahoma), December 19, 1930.

25. Rank P. Marlowe to Thomas, November 23, 1931; W. S. Key to Thomas, February 12, 1932; Mrs. R. B. Stevens to Thomas, January 19, 1931; C. J. Rhoads to Thomas, February 10, 1931; W. S. Key to Commissioner of Indian Affairs, February 8, 1932, Thomas Papers.

26. W. S. Key to Thomas, February 10, 1932.

27. S. C. Fitzgerald to Thomas, January 13, 1931; C. J. Ayers to Ray Lyman Wilbur, January 14, 1931; G. H. Hale to C. J. Rhoads, November 20, 1930; Folder III, Indians, 1930, Thomas Papers.

28. *Survey of Indian Conditions*, XIV, 5393, 5599, 6289, 6305.

29. J. N. Harber to Thomas, February 9, 1931; *Survey of Indian Conditions*, XIV, 5698, 5700, 5702, 5704, 5714, 5515, 5323, 5351.

30. Folder III, Indians, 1930, Thomas Papers.

31. *Survey of Indian Conditions*, XIV, 5394, 5599, 5868, 6272.

32. *Ibid.*, XIV, 5350.

33. *Annual Report of the Board of Indian Commissioners, 1928*, p. 33; *Survey of Indian Conditions*, XIV, 5714.

34. Trent, *Extension Work*, p. 7; *Survey of Indian Conditions*, XIV, 6228–6229, 6283; Folder I, Indians, 1930, Thomas Papers.

35. U.S. House of Representatives, 71st Cong., 2nd sess., Committee on Indian Affairs, *Hearings . . . Creation of Trust Estates*, Washington, 1931, p. 48, hereafter cited as *Creation of Trust Estates; Annual Report of the Board of Indian Commissioners, 1928*, p. 9; *Survey of Indian Conditions*, XIV, 5919, 6320; Agnes M. Farris to Thomas, June 11, 1932; Lillie McKinney to Thomas, February 9, 1933.

36. *Washington Evening Star*, April 22, 1932.

37. *American Indian*, IV (February, 1930), 8.

38. *Survey of Indian Conditions,* XIV, 5331; Franklin Stewart to C. J. Rhoads, February 15, 1930, in Cartwright Papers.

39. *McAlester News-Capital* (Oklahoma), February 1, 1933.

40. Max Frizzlehead to Thomas, January 23, 1931.

41. Meriam, *Problem of Indian Administration,* p. 8.

42. R. V. Dunlap to Thomas, December 22, 1930.

43. *Survey of Indian Conditions,* XIV, 5499, 5874, 5876, 6322.

44. Folder III, Indians, 1930, Thomas Papers.

45. *Survey of Indian Conditions,* XIV, 5392.

46. E. W. Hailey to Cartwright, January 16, 1930; *Survey of Indian Conditions,* XIV, 5320, 5328, 5693.

47. *Ibid.;* J. A. Nolan to G. W. Sickles, June 30, 1932, Thomas Papers.

48. Charles J. Smith to Thomas, February 7, 1931; Agnes M. Farris to Thomas, June 11, 1932; *Readjustment of Indian Affairs,* p. 316; U.S. Senate, 71st Cong., 1st sess., Committee on Indian Affairs, *Hearings . . . Revision and Codification of Statutes Affecting American Indians,* Washington, 1930, p. 33, hereafter cited as *Revision and Codification of Statutes.*

49. *Survey of Indian Conditions,* XIV, 5326, 5333, 5389, 5691; Folder I, Indians, 1930, Thomas Papers.

50. *Survey of Indian Conditions,* XIV, 5328–5329.

51. L. Simmons to Thomas, January 29, 1933; *Revision and Codification of Statutes,* p. 21.

52. *Survey of Indian Conditions,* XIV, 5261, 5338.

53. *Ibid.,* XIV, 5561; *Tulsa Tribune,* July 10, 1931.

54. *The Daily Ardmorette* (Ardmore, Oklahoma), April 24, 1931.

55. Meriam, *Problem of Indian Administration,* p. 7; *Annual Report of the Board of Indian Commissioners, 1928,* pp. 6–9; U.S. House of Representatives, 71st Cong., 3rd sess., Committee on Indian Affairs, *Hearings . . . Emancipated Citizenship for American Indians,* Washington, 1931, p. 13.

56. *Extension of Restrictions,* p. 6; *Creation of Trust Estates,* pp. 3–10.

57. *Revision and Codification of Statutes,* p. 41.

58. *The Daily Oklahoman,* January 14, 1931.

59. *Congressional Record,* 72nd Cong., 1st sess., p. 9405; *Readjustment of Indian Affairs,* p. 325.

60. H. B. Jolley to Thomas, January 12, 1931; *Survey of Indian Conditions,* XIV, 6253, 6708.

61. U.S. Department of the Interior, *Annual Report of the Commissioner of Indian Affairs, 1931,* Washington, 1931, p 28; *Extension of Restrictions,* pp. 46–47.

62. Frank C. Griffin to Thomas, February 10, 1931.

63. J. C. Puterbaugh to Thomas, January 29, 1931.

64. U.S. Department of the Interior, *Annual Report of the Board of Indian Commissioners, 1932,* Washington, 1932, p. 5.

65. *Annual Report of the Board of Indian Commissioners, 1931,* p. 25.

66. *Readjustment of Indian Affairs,* p. 40; *Tax-Exempt Indian Lands,* p. 19.

67. Ida Wauhucha to Thomas, December 6, 1930; *Readjustment of Indian Affairs,* p. 65.

68. Cartwright to American Red Cross chairmen, January 7, 1931; L. T. Burton to Cartwright, January 7, 1931; M. C. Moon, J. E. Guymon, R. E. Gates, Mrs. J. M. Harrison, Grover Flanagan, Charles B. Caldwell, J. M. Craig, J. W. Sturges, and R. M. Lacy to Cartwright, January 8, 1931; J. J. Enole to

Cartwright, January 9, 1931; *Congressional Record,* 72nd Cong., 2nd sess., pp. 2852, 5152; *Annual Report of the Commissioner of Indian Affairs,* 1931, p. 28.

69. *Annual Report of the Board of Indian Commissioners, 1931,* p. 6.
70. *The Daily Oklahoman,* April 18, 1931.
71. *Ibid.; Annual Report of the Board of Indian Commissioners, 1931,* p. 6.
72. S. U. Hacker to Thomas, April 10, 1932.
73. Frank Davis to Thomas, February 9, 1932.
74. Lillie McKinney to Thomas, February 9, 1933.

Town and Country III

When the Banks Closed: Arizona's Bank Holiday of 1933

William H. Jervey, Jr.

Some of President Hoover's admirers later claimed that he had carried on a vigorous campaign for bank reform for three years before he issued a call for action in this field in his annual message to Congress in 1933. H. Parker Willis, technical adviser to the Senate Banking Committee, has refuted this claim (see Raymond Moley, After Seven Years *[New York: Harper, 1939], p. 142). Political partisans and historians have differed on the question of the effect of the poor relations between Hoover and President-elect Roosevelt during the lame-duck interlude on the banking situation, which underwent its final crisis in February 1933. The striking feature of the historical literature that emphasizes the events of early 1933 is its neglect of previous developments and Hoover's failure to respond to them efficaciously. As gold exports were mounting in February 1933, Hoover wrote his successor, "We are confronted with precisely the same phenomena we experienced in late 1931 and again in the spring of 1932" (quoted in Rexford G. Tugwell, "The Protagonists: Roosevelt and Hoover,"* Antioch Review, *XLI [December 1953], p. 420). Bank failures in the United States, moreover, had grown from 659 in 1929, to 1,352 in 1930, to 2,294 in 1931.*

This selection shows that Arizona tried to respond to weaknesses

[Reprinted from *Arizona and the West,* X (Summer 1968), 127–152.]

in banking: "On a broad front, Arizona bank legislation was progressive in the decade before the banking moratorium." There was nevertheless at least one bank failure in Arizona in every year except two from 1922 through 1932 (and two more after Roosevelt took office), and "for the decade as a whole, the bank mortality rate for Arizona was greater than for the nation at large." From December 31, 1929, to June 1933, the number of banks in Arizona fell from forty-three to nineteen, a decline of 55.5 per cent. (In Custer County, Nebraska, the subject of a previous selection, from January 1930 to 1935 the number of banks fell from twenty to eleven, a decline of 45 per cent.) Governor Moeur's declaration of a bank holiday in Arizona on March 2, 1933, occasioned little panic in Phoenix, and Tucson reacted "in something of a gay spirit."

Although the Great Depression hit Arizona hard, recovery was evident there well before it was enjoyed in leading industrial states: Massachusetts, New Jersey, New York, Pennsylvania, Illinois, Ohio, and California together accounted for half the nation's unemployed. This selection shows the impact of developments in California on her neighbor, Arizona. Perhaps the relatively early recovery of Arizona had something to do with an Arizonan presidential candidate's stating in 1964 that the eastern seaboard should be sawed off and allowed to float out to sea.

In the darkness before dawn on March 2, 1933, Walter R. Bimson, president of Arizona's Valley Bank and Trust Company, was awakened by a telephone ringing in his suite at the Westward Ho Hotel in Phoenix. Over the wire came word that California Governor James Rolph had acted earlier in the night, closing every bank in that state. To an Arizona banker, this spelled impending calamity, for the banking systems of California and Arizona were inextricably linked. With California banks closed, Arizona financial institutions would be unable to draw on their deposit balances in the sister state. Potentially even more dangerous, Arizona banks, by remaining open, would encourage California institutions to withdraw their Arizona bank balances. With liquidity of the state's banks already squeezed by the depression to the danger point, any sudden withdrawals might spell insolvency for even the best managed Arizona banking institutions. To Walter Bimson, the news meant just one thing—Arizona's banks could not be allowed to open that morning.[1]

By March 1933 the United States was in the fourth year of a paralyzing economic depression. As if the break on Wall Street, the general prostration of trade and markets, and the constant erosion of prices had not been enough of a conflagration, the nation's entire banking structure was on the verge of complete collapse. In the three years since 1930, more than 6,000 banks with $3.5 billion in deposits had disappeared from the scene. Statewide bank holidays were becoming common, the first one having been declared by Nevada in October 1932. On February 4, 1933, Louisiana declared a holiday to aid a large bank in New Orleans which found itself in difficulty. A week later, Michigan, symbol of American industrial might, closed every bank following the collapse of Detroit's Union Guardian Trust Company. The Michigan moratorium was "the opening signal of alarm which rapidly extended from one state to another." Maryland was forced to suspend banking activity ten days later because of difficulties in Baltimore. Seven additional states fell in line by March 1. Included in the number of "holiday banks" were two in Washington, D.C., only a short walk from the United States Treasury.[2]

At the outset of the Depression decade, Arizona was still basically a frontier region. Although population had jumped by more than 100,000 in the 1920's (a 30.3 per cent gain), the rural population was still almost twice as great as the urban. Indeed, the percentage of the total state population accounted for by the rural sector had actually grown from 64.8 per cent in 1920 to 65.6 per cent in 1930. The populations of the two largest cities, however, indicated a contrary trend, with the growth of more than 60 per cent in the populations of Tucson and Phoenix.[3]

Arizona had suffered a postwar depression in 1920–1922 which in some respects was more severe than that of the 1930's. A raw-commodity producer of cattle, copper, and cotton, the state felt the full impact of the postwar crash of raw-commodity prices. For the decade as a whole, the bank mortality rate for Arizona was greater than for the nation at large. On December 31, 1929, the state had twenty-nine state banks with twenty-five branches, and fourteen national banks. Thirty-one state banks had collapsed since 1920, a reduction of 51.6 per cent. National banks had lost seven units for a reduction of 33.3 per cent.[4]

Seventeen, more than half, of the state banks had capitalizations of less than $100,000 in 1929. Six of the national banks had capitalizations of less than $100,000. Although both figures indicated an improvement over 1920, Arizona banking in 1929 tended to be relatively undercapitalized. Despite this fact, concentration in banking assets was already under way, having begun in the 1920's when the Valley Bank and Trust Company and the Gila Valley Bank and Trust Company forged ahead of their competitors. The period of the 1930's kept alive this trend toward concentration. The desire to merge reflected basic economic considerations such as loan diversification, greater lending potential, and lower production costs. This trend toward concentration also reflected efforts to prevent bank failures.[5]

During the 1920's, when dealing with banks, Arizona legislators had been concerned primarily with the issue of bank solvency. Under 1922 legislation, the minimum capitalization of a state bank was $25,000, with a gradually rising scale to $200,000 for cities of more than 50,000 population. Officers and directors could not borrow more than 20 per cent of paid-in capital and surplus (lowered to 10 per cent in 1927), a regulation which antedated similar federal legislation by eleven years. A state banking department was established under the direction of a superintendent of banks, who would examine state-chartered banks at least twice each year. In 1925 the Seventh Legislature authorized the state treasurer, in the event of bank failure, to purchase securities pledged to the support of funds deposited by the state in the banks involved, so as to protect public deposits. Various deposit guarantee plans were introduced in the 1920's, but none was enacted into law. On a broad front, Arizona bank legislation was progressive in the decade before the banking moratorium.[6]

Conditions went from bad to worse in Arizona after 1930, and banking moved accordingly. Commodity prices for cattle, cotton, and copper continued to fall. Indeed, the cotton sector had been suffering since the postwar depression of the early 1920's. The dollar value of general farm production between 1929 and 1932 declined by more than two-thirds. Unemployment figures steadily mounted as they did nationwide. The opening of rich copper mines in southern Africa, coupled with curtailed American demand, resulted in the price of the red metal plummeting to only 4 cents a pound, the lowest price in history. This was less than one-half the cost of production in Arizona, and compared with an average 18.1 cents per pound price in 1929. Not surprisingly, Arizona copper production, a mainstay of the state's economy, declined 95 per cent over a three-year period. The dismal economic picture also was reflected in the state's per-capita income, which fell to $263 on the eve of the bank holiday.[7]

Arizona's banks were a prime casualty in the debacle. The undercapitalized nature of the banking system made it particularly vulnerable to the impending economic collapse. With uncollectable loans and large deposit withdrawals, often only for hoarding purposes, proceeding at an unprecedented rate, many banks found themselves nearing a technical state of insolvency. On April 30, 1930, the Glendale Bank of Commerce was closed. Two months later, the Yuma Valley Bank went the same way, and in July the Citizens State Bank of Phoenix passed out of existence.[8]

By 1933 several of the smaller banks, such as the Traders Bank of Wickenburg, were closing voluntarily without loss to their depositors, while larger institutions, such as the Arizona Bank (with five branches), were being forced to close with losses of 50 per cent or more to their customers. Others went the merger route, the First National Bank of Prescott, for example, being absorbed by the Valley Bank. The number of state-chartered banks stood at only eleven in June 1933, in contrast to twenty-nine at the end of 1929, while the nationally chartered banks had declined from fourteen to eight in the same period.[9]

The decline in overall bank deposits was less spectacular, but still severe. Of the $72,833,828 in the bank coffers in 1929, only $41,035,840 remained by 1932. Commercial bank loans outstanding declined by almost two-thirds, from $34,471,394 to $12,903,455 over a similar period. The situation at the Valley Bank, the state's largest, illustrated the severity of the deposit and loan contraction: [10]

VALLEY BANK AND TRUST COMPANY (in millions of dollars)	Deposits	Loans
December 31, 1929	$17.7	$7.1
June 30, 1930	14.9	7.7
December 31, 1930	14.1	6.7
June 30, 1931	11.9	4.7
December 31, 1931	10.3	3.8
June 30, 1932	7.4	3.3
December 31, 1932	6.7	2.9

By late 1932, the Valley Bank had slipped out of first place in Arizona, and the Consolidated National Bank of Tucson emerged temporarily as the state's largest in terms of deposits. Half the Valley Bank's personnel had been laid off, and the total staff of the Phoenix headquarters and nine branches was down to eighty-seven. The situation was far from optimistic when forty-one-year-old Walter R. Bimson, formerly with the Harris Trust and Savings Bank in Chicago, became president of the Valley Bank.[11]

From the first, Bimson exuded confidence. On New Year's Day 1933 he declared: "We enter the new year with a sounder basis for hopefulness than we have known during the three years of Depression. . . . Instead of wishing for a prosperous New Year, you and I are henceforth working for a prosperous New Year." Bimson moved fast. He ordered a temporary 10 per cent salary cut, and, as one employee later remarked, "he made us like it." He thought of the Valley Bank "as a financial department store vigorously selling money and credit in packages of all sizes to trustworthy customers on a mass-production basis." As he stated: "This bank's credit capacity isn't what it will be, but we have some capacity, and I want it used." Thus, in the middle of the depression the cry went out to "make loans!" The way out of depression, Bimson believed, was to return money to circulation and increase effective demand. This display of confidence bred handsome dividends for the bank in the form of new deposits. Indeed, during the first ten days of Bimson's presidency, the bank's deposits increased by $200,000.[12]

Although comparatively new to the Arizona scene, Walter Bimson appreciated the historical ties that bound the banks of Arizona and California together. For many years California bankers had displayed great interest in the economic development of Arizona.

Bank Failures
December 30, 1922—April 14, 1933

Name	Date Closed
Stockmans State Bank	12–30–22
Pinal Bank and Trust Company	4–11–23
Bank of Northern Arizona	12–28–23
Bank of Winslow	10– 4–24
Merchants and Miners Bank	10–31–24
Bank of Jerome	11–25–25
Prescott State Bank	11–25–25
Commercial Trust and Savings Bank	11–25–25
Bank of Duncan	3–23–26
Gadsden State Bank	3–31–27
Glendale Bank of Commerce	4–30–30
Yuma Valley Bank	6–20–30
Citizens State Bank	7–31–30
Farmers Commercial State Bank	10–17–30
Arizona Southwest Bank	6–22–31
Cochise County State Bank	9– 4–31
Security Trust and Savings Bank	9–19–31
Sonora Bank and Trust Company	11–19–31
Old Dominion Bank	4–15–32
Payson Commercial and Trust Company	4–18–32
Bank of Safford	5–27–32
The Arizona Bank	6–24–32
Casa Grande Valley Bank	6–27–32
United Bank and Trust Company	11–16–32
Farmers State Bank	3–21–33
Round Valley Bank	4–14–33

As early as 1921, they looked upon Arizona "as part of their territory," and began focusing as much interest on the Salt River Valley as they had on the Imperial Valley. In terms of personnel, direct links also had been established between the states. In 1920, for example, William Brophy, president of the Bank of Douglas, had been elected to the board of directors of the Los Angeles Trust and Savings Bank. The First National Bank of Los Angeles shortly after gained control of the Arizona Central Bank of Flagstaff. Arizona banks, including the Valley Bank, maintained significant balances in California institutions, and the latter reciprocated, holding a large portion of the loans on livestock in Arizona. This close relationship made it inconceivable that one state could close its banks while the other kept them open. The main question on the night of March 2, 1933, was how quickly Arizona could declare a banking moratorium.[13]

As the state legislature was in session, Governor Benjamin B.

Moeur [14] was in Phoenix, staying at the Westward Ho Hotel, as was Bimson. With the news of the California moratorium, Bimson rushed to Moeur's suite and, after much pleading, gained an audience with the pajama-clad, sleepy chief executive. Moeur, unfortunately, was not a financial man, and Bimson had to repeat the details several times before the magnitude of the impending crisis became clear. By then, it was nearly dawn. Moeur did not feel he had the authority to close the state's banks and announced he would have to check with the attorney general. It was agreed that the three would meet at eight o'clock in the governor's office. In the meantime, Bimson would draft a tentative bank holiday proclamation.

Bimson hurried back to his room and phoned John L. Gust, the Valley Bank's attorney, arranging to meet him immediately at the bank's headquarters. After running the half-dozen blocks in the crisp 38-degree night air, the bedraggled bank president was admitted by a guard, who must have been somewhat suspicious of Bimson's sanity. While the rest of Arizona slept, Gust and Bimson got down to the task of writing a proclamation, which proved difficult for they had nothing to use as a model. The final draft explained the necessity for a holiday by noting the closing of California banks and the fact that many Arizona banking institutions had a considerable portion of their funds and credit tied up with these institutions. With this in hand, Bimson rushed to the governor's office, arriving shortly before eight. The matter had to be argued all over again for the attorney general's benefit, but by 8:30 the point was won.

Early that morning, March 2, the governor proclaimed a three-day moratorium. It was too late to send the word out to the small-town banks, which opened at nine, but the radio carried the news and most banks took a chance and suspended payments. In the larger cities, the following was received during the morning and posted on bank doors: "The governor has proclaimed a three-day holiday. You are authorized to close for this period. Possibly additional regulations later. Treat as any other holiday. The dates are March 2, 3 and 4." The situation had been saved. A possible epidemic of runs and failures had been prevented.[15]

The next step was to allay panic now that bank doors were to be closed. Young C. White, state superintendent of banks, helped ease the tension by declaring in the public press that the state banks were "in good shape and the move was not necessarily because of any local conditions but was taken to protect the Arizona banks affiliated with the California banks." He added that it was hoped the banks could reopen in three days without any restrictions. The press generally supported the bank holiday and discouraged panic. The Tucson *Arizona Daily Star,* for example, expressed the view that Arizona finances "are, perhaps, in better shape than almost any other similar district in the United States." The state was sound, but it was "a small community" and could not finance the entire nation. Most bankers joined the chorus of approval, although many agreed with Gordon Sawyer, vice-president of the Southern Arizona Bank and Trust Company, who stated that his bank had prepared to meet such a situation as the California closure and did not particularly favor the holiday.[16]

The governor's action was "legalized" on March 2 in an unprecedented fifty-five minutes by the state legislature. Speaker Stephen A. Spear (D., Prescott) introduced House Bill 247 almost as soon as the ink was dry. Under suspension of the rules, the bill was passed quickly by the House and carried by the speaker himself to the Senate. President Harry W. Hill (D., Greenlee) of the upper chamber asked for suspension of the rules, and similar swift action was taken. As an emergency measure, the bill became law at once. The act provided that the governor might by proclamation not only authorize the superintendent of banks to suspend banking business but allow him, "whenever in his judgment he deems it necessary for the safety and protection of deposits," to regulate and limit the withdrawal of deposits from any Arizona banking institution. In a public statement, Moeur reminded Arizonans that this was only a precautionary measure, and did not indicate that any of the banks in Maricopa County (Phoenix) or in the state were in bad shape. "In fact many of them are in better condition than they were six months ago," he said.[17]

Shortly after issuing his order closing the banks, Moeur addressed a banking conference in the office of the superintendent of banks. Twenty-four prominent Arizona bankers attended the meeting, and plans for reopening the state's financial institutions were tentatively drawn. Even before the meeting, Gordon Sawyer of the Southern Arizona Bank commented optimistically that if "the Coast banks open Monday [March 6], our banks will follow suit. Tucson's banks are as strong as any in the United States, I believe, but they must be protected from out-of-state irregularities." [18]

Despite the fact that thirty-nine other states had taken similar action, there remained some doubt as to the strict legality of a governor's declaring a bank holiday. The attorney general of Minnesota had ruled against such action, as had the auditor of Illinois. Governor Moeur, in issuing his proclamation, had taken emergency action for which no definite authority was bestowed by Arizona statute. Some banks in California were refusing to accept the legality of Governor Rolph's pronouncement, and it was feared that a similar situation would occur in Arizona. The fear was well grounded. A handful of banks remained open on March 2, having failed to receive the news prior to nine o'clock. Others refused to close, questioning the governor's prerogative in the matter. There was an impression that Moeur's proclamation was only advisory. This notion the chief executive attempted to dispel on March 3 by stating that the holiday was mandatory and that all banks must heed his proclamation.[19]

Several banks remained firm in their conviction that the order was illegal and refused to close. Three banks in particular—the Bank of Bisbee, the Bank of Douglas, and the Bank of Clemenceau —all controlled by James S. Douglas, stayed open, challenging the sufficiency of legislation for gubernatorial action. Douglas maintained that he would close his banks only if the legislature put adequate laws on the books. "I challenge the right of the governor to close solvent banks under the law as it now stands," he asserted, adding: "I have so advised him by telegram." Bisbee's other bank, the Miners and Merchants, likewise remained open for business. Lemuel C. Shattuck, the president, issued a joint statement with Michael J. Cunningham, president of the Douglas-controlled Bank of Bisbee. They announced that they had been "preparing for such a situation for many months and . . . now have and always will have sufficient cash to care for any demand that may be made on us." [20]

Governor Moeur ordered that copies of his proclamation be

posted on the doors of the Bank of Douglas, the Bank of Bisbee, and the Miners and Merchants Bank. He "suggested" that if the proclamations were removed, either the National Guard or Cochise County law-enforcement officers would be called out to enforce the order. This threat did not worry Cunningham and Shattuck. They declared that conditions in Bisbee were "more or less isolated," and that there was no reason "for discommoding patrons of the banks." Furthermore, Bisbee banks were not accepting deposits "from other sections" of the state. The sole desire of Bisbee bankers was "to accommodate regular patrons of the bank and to prevent, if possible, any inconvenience to the citizens of the district." Finally, on March 4, the Miners and Merchants Bank decided to comply, and the next day the Bank of Douglas reluctantly closed its doors. The latter institution, before doing so, sent out substantial bundles of money to loyal customers who would need the cash to get through the emergency. As late as 1950, the Bank of Douglas advertised that it had not yet found it necessary "to ask anybody (including the Federal Government) to bail us out with insurance or so-called bank holidays." [21]

National banks, under the supervision of the Comptroller of the Currency in Washington, could not be compelled to close. The First National Bank of Nogales announced that it would remain open and "transact business in the usual manner and will not take advantage of the banking holiday." Otto H. Herold, president, elaborated by stating: "The bank is liquid. We have a large available cash reserve and besides we do not consider the governor's order mandatory, although he may consider it such himself. We feel that it is our duty to protect our depositors and we cannot perform that important function by closing our doors or restricting withdrawals." Wirt G. Bowman, Democratic national committeeman from Arizona and board chairman of the First National of Nogales, wired the bank officials congratulating them for keeping the bank open despite the holiday proclamation. Another institution not complying with the governor's order initially was Yuma's lone bank, a branch of the Miners and Merchants, which did not close until March 6, when the national moratorium went into effect. Also remaining open during the first three days of the state holiday were the First National Bank of Winslow and the

First National Bank of Holbrook. The reasons given by these two institutions were much the same as the others. Thus, closing of Arizona banks was by no means a unanimous act.[22]

In the meantime, Governor Rolph on March 4 had extended California's bank holiday to March 9. Little could be done in Arizona but to follow suit. Superintendent White stated in Phoenix on March 4 that at Governor Moeur's request he had issued a supplementary proclamation prolonging the holiday in Arizona until March 13. "It was necessary to extend Arizona's banking holiday," White said, "due to the holidays in California and New York." [23]

Working under suspension of the rules with little debate, the House of Representatives approved a bill which would extend the holiday, authorize the issuance of scrip through clearing house associations, and impose severe penalties for failure to keep banks closed. The scrip would be legal tender and would be backed by bank deposits. Under the penalty clause, the superintendent of banks could apply in Superior Court for a mandatory injunction against bankers refusing to close their institutions. Such a refusal would be a felony, each day of refusal being a separate offense, punishable by a fine of up to $5,000, six months imprisonment, or both. Superintendent White wired President Franklin D. Roosevelt and Secretary of the Treasury William H. Woodin on March 6 the text of the bill, with a request that Arizona banks be permitted to open on a scrip basis on March 7. The national moratorium made this impossible.[24]

On Monday, March 6, President Roosevelt declared a national banking moratorium. The national holiday was, in fact, an anticlimax, for forty-seven states had already declared statewide banking moratoria by March 4, the date of the Inauguration. Roosevelt's order, however, went considerably beyond most state actions. All banking transactions were suspended except those authorized by the Secretary of the Treasury with the approval of the President. An embargo was placed on gold exports, and clearing house certificates of scrip were authorized for the conducting of business. The Emergency Banking Act of March 9 confirmed the President's proclamation issued three days earlier. It required the Treasurer's approval for the reopening of banks, authorized the Comptroller of the Currency to appoint conservators for national banks whose condition did not permit them to open, and liberalized the powers of the Federal Reserve to issue circulating notes.[25]

On March 10 President Roosevelt issued another proclamation, extending the moratorium for an indefinite period. The Phoenix Clearing House Association and representatives of its member banks went into conference at 8:00 that night in an effort to determine their status under the new proclamation. Little came of the meeting. As Walter Bimson commented in a personal letter: "For days we have been under a strain that is now beginning to show on the faces and in the temper of the officers. I feel weary—very weary. . . . For days we have been marking time, anxiously waiting for permission to reopen the bank." On March 11 Governor Moeur acted in line with Roosevelt's second proclamation, issuing a supplementary proclamation extending until further notice the bank holiday in Arizona.[26]

Most Arizonans welcomed President Roosevelt's nationwide bank holiday. Governor Moeur expressed the thought that it would "instill courage and confidence in the hearts" of the people. T. N. McCauley, president of the Consolidated National Bank of Tucson, suggested that the prompt actions by the President would "bring about a restoration of confidence to the public not only in banking but in employment of several hundred thousand people within a comparatively short time." [27]

With the bank holiday, the feeling was that the bottom of the depression had finally been reached—and the only way to go was up. But what was to be done about the immediate money shortage which accompanied the closing of the banks? Although much of the shortage was due to hoarding rather than to an actual lack of currency, the fact remained that money seemed scarcer than it had been heretofore. The situation was similar to that in the Panic of 1907, when Arizonans faced a lack of sufficient money for several days. At that time scrip, as a substitute for money, was issued by merchants. Pressure was mounting for a similar recourse in March 1933.[28]

The use of scrip as a medium of exchange had been authorized in Arizona by a special act of the state legislature on March 6, and arrangements for the printing of $1, $5, $10, and $20 denominations were completed on March 7. It was estimated in Tucson that several million dollars of the money substitute would have to be printed for that city alone. The Phoenix Clearing House Association contracted with a California firm for the lithographing of three million dollars' worth.[29]

By March 9, however, the planned use of scrip had been abandoned, pending the outcome of action then being taken by the national government to substitute currency for that method of exchange. Several consignments of scrip were, by that time, reported to be reposing in Phoenix bank vaults. There remained some question as to whether Secretary Woodin's action forbidding the use of scrip pertained only to a national issue or to local issues as well. "We are ready with clearing house scrip if that is to be used, and we are ready to retire that in favor of a national issue if such is decided upon," stated Carl W. Gibson of the Phoenix Clearing House Association.[30]

Meanwhile, private businesses throughout Arizona began issuing their own scrip, usually backing it with bank or postal savings balances. Tucson's *Arizona Daily Star,* for example, met its payroll with scrip printed in one-dollar denominations. The *Star* scrip became acceptable at all but a few Tucson stores, and was eagerly sought as a new medium of exchange. In Phoenix the Republic and Gazette Publishing Company issued "certificates of indebtedness" which were accepted by several main stores in the capital city. The Nogales *Herald* issued scrip of one-dollar denomination which became rapidly acceptable in the border town's stores. In Nogales money became so short in supply that the Mexican peso was soon circulating at a significant premium over its official rate of exchange. Cochise County's clearing house association organized itself for the issuance of the medium, and such companies as Piggly Wiggly produced scrip backed by postal savings. The Buckeye Valley Bank issued the money substitute in denominations from 5 to 50 cents. The total of such private issues was probably small, but in some areas it did help to alleviate the critical money shortage.[31]

With the banks closed, America's entire financial system had to be modified. It was impossible to deal on the stock and commodity exchanges, and they were closed. In some parts of the country, moratoria were declared on insurance policy payments, court fines, utility bills, and other forms of personal debt.

Arizona reacted similarly. To protect the shippers of the state, Governor Moeur proclaimed the suspension of all demurrage charges on goods carried by transport systems in Arizona. A real estate mortgage foreclosure moratorium was passed by the state legislature. It was ruled that attorneys without access to their bank accounts could still file legal instruments in Superior Court. Every effort was made to conduct business as usual, but without the banks this usually proved a herculean task.[32]

In Phoenix, Arizonans accepted the bank holiday with little panic. News of the closing of Phoenix's financial institutions on March 2 had spread rapidly through the city of 50,000, and crowds collected that day in front of bank entrances, reading and rereading the formal phrases of Governor Moeur's proclamation. The city banks were allowed to open to make change and to permit customers access to safety deposit boxes. Nevertheless, business in the capital city was somewhat curtailed, being conducted primarily on a cash basis. The initial tendency was for housewives and businessmen to conserve cash. Grocery stores reported business almost up to normal, but they discerned a decided tendency for shoppers to select necessities and pass up luxuries.[33]

By March 4, cash was beginning to circulate and business in many stores returned to normal. A majority of the downtown Phoenix merchants honored charge accounts, and checks with proper identification were accepted up to the amount of purchase. With business being conducted primarily on a cash basis, the probability of burglary was enlarged. Police Chief N. W. Matlock assigned extra patrolmen to the business district. They were instructed to pay particular attention to theaters, markets, gas stations, stores, hotels, drugstores—places of business where protection might be needed. With police protection, many downtown merchants transferred surplus funds to local banks having night depository facilities.

The manager of a large New York newspaper passed through Phoenix at the time and commented on the situation. He reported that hotels were accepting checks from letter-of-credit holders, but cashing none. Messenger boys were handing out telegrams and not even waiting for a tip. "The American Airways line," he added, "gave me credit for a plane ride to El Paso, and there the officials of the Texas and Pacific Railroad told me they'd accept a check for the fare to New York." [34]

Western Union and postal telegraph agencies in Phoenix limited the amount of money orders sent or received to $100. Payment of money orders was partly in cash and partly by check. The Veterans Administration made arrangements with the Treasury Department to permit Federal Reserve Banks and their branches to cash government checks received by veterans. By the advice of Maricopa County attorney Renz L. Jennings, all county offices declined to accept checks. Suits could not be filed with the county clerk during the holiday, nor could business be transacted with the county recorder, treasurer, or tax assessor except by payment of cash. City and county jails accepted cash only for the payment of fines and bonds. Nevertheless, neither city nor county offices observed the closing of the banks as a legal holiday for their personnel, remaining open to conduct minor routine business. Marriage licenses were still being issued, but for cash only, and business was reported at a standstill.[35]

Tucson ushered in the bankless period in much the same spirit. After an initial stunned moment on the morning of March 2, when the report stalked the streets that "both banks have closed," a more accurate picture became known and smiles replaced stricken faces. Indeed, Tucson took the bank holiday in something of a gay spirit. The lighthearted feeling was due to such men as the Southern Arizona Bank's vice-president, Gordon Sawyer, who proved to be master of the situation. He remained "planted in his chair," answering "innumerable telephone calls in a voice ringing with confidence." Employees of Tucson's banks took their places daily, never knowing when the institutions might be permitted to reopen. An enterprising restaurateur capitalized on the occasion by advertising "holiday dinners." The state high school basketball tournament went on without a hitch despite the holiday. This was in contrast to many California cities, where schools were forced to close. Many other activities went ahead as scheduled, although some social affairs had to be canceled when it was found that IOU's were plentiful but cash was conspicuous by its absence.[36]

By March 7 the barter system was being used in Tucson on a small scale. What money was available turned over time and time again in a very rapid manner. A customer with a $50 bill would purchase a small amount of goods. The store would give its own check in change. The store check would then shortly find its way to another store, and still another store check for a smaller amount in change would be issued. This process would continue until the $50 was finally used up. The supreme irony was the case of a man with a $500 bill who found himself unable to purchase the necessities of life. No one would give him change for so large a sum.[37]

In Tucson, as in other Arizona cities, the immediate concern was food. Charles Wheeler, a wholesale grocer, estimated there were enough groceries in the city to supply all local needs for sixty days. The Eagle Milling Company reported that it had a supply of grain sufficient to feed the town for six months and that food shipments were continuing. Wholesale grocers had gone on a cash basis immediately after declaration of the holiday, and the fear was that, even if available, food would not be adequately distributed for all.[38]

Eleemosynary groups helped ease the concern. The Organized Charities of Tucson, for example, offered to lend food to anyone who could not obtain it because of cash shortage. Only about twenty Tucsonans took advantage of the offer. With a total population of 35,000, Tucson managed to feed all 15,000 who were on some form of charity at the time. C. Edgar Goyette, president of the Organized Charities, reported that all persons receiving aid were being taken care of and everyone was in a "pleasant mood." Others found the holiday an unpleasant nuisance. Countless commercial travelers were marooned in the city, and some businesses were unusually short of cash, having been forced by recent robberies to keep a high percentage of their liquid funds in banks which were now closed.[39]

A complete moratorium on civil actions was announced by Judge C. V. Budlong in Justice Court. No attachments or garnishments were served by his office while the banks were closed. Budlong declared that the state of Arizona was "certainly larger than Justice Court," and no action would therefore be taken in civil matters. In Superior Court, however, the usual procedure was being followed. Mrs. L. H. Burges, clerk, stated that everything was being done on a cash basis and that civil matters were receiving the same attention they were prior to the governor's proclamation. Regular procedures continued in criminal cases also, with all court employees remaining at their jobs.[40]

On March 5 two hundred local businessmen met at the J. C.

Penney store to discuss the situation. It was decided that nothing could be done locally until national and state policies had been made more definite. Most leading merchants expressed the opinion that the governor's action marked the beginning of the end of business difficulties. Checks became increasingly acceptable as a medium of exchange. S. Matt Mansfield, manager of the Penney store, announced he would accept checks for merchandise and give change in cash as long as the supply held out. When it was exhausted, he would give vouchers for change, payable at either Tucson bank. Most grocers agreed to accept these vouchers in lieu of cash. By March 4 the total amount of checks accepted by stores and hotels downtown was over $2,000.[41]

Business in the city continued to be stable despite the currency shortage. This was partially explained by newspaper advertisements paid for by mercantile establishments suggesting that once the banking situation was cleared up, merchandise would be 15 to 20 per cent higher in price. Added support was given this prediction when several food commodities increased in price during the first week of the holiday. Most merchants handling non-food items did report declines in business, but this was by no means universal. One lumberyard, for example, reported that it was actually doing more business since the banks closed. Both of Tucson's motion picture theaters were showing features, and no reduction in attendance was observed. A sizable number of winter visitors undoubtedly contributed to the relative business stability during the period.[42]

Several enterprising businesses took advantage of the holiday to cement old loyalties and to gain new customers. Albert Steinfeld & Company, a retail merchandiser, announced that scrip would be good at all of its departments, and accepted checks from more than 3,000 customers. It also opened 985 new charge accounts during the twelve-day period. The same company, however, found it difficult to meet its payroll, and was forced to pass its regular pay day, although employees in need of cash were given small advances. Other firms, such as Fox West Coast Theatres, were able to meet their payrolls by accumulating cash receipts. A $65,000 cash payroll by the Southern Pacific Railroad on March 6 helped ease Tucson's currency shortage considerably. The postal savings department of the Post Office remained open until March 6, when lack of funds forced it to suspend payments temporarily. It reopened on March 9, limiting withdrawals to $30. Telegraph companies ran into difficulty securing funds to cash wires, and most limited the amount which could be paid.[43]

The society page told of a millionairess who planned to eat nothing but grapefruit on her way home from an Arizona vacation, because of lack of funds. Other wealthy women planned to do their own hair for the first time in years. The *Arizona Daily Star* commented sardonically that apparently "the average woman of wealth can take misfortune with a smile." Not so fortunate were state of Arizona employees, especially University of Arizona men and women, who were being paid with promissory warrants issued by the state government. Many merchants refused to accept these warrants even when the banks were open, and it was particularly difficult to cash them with the banks closed, a sad commentary on the fiscal state of Arizona at the time.[44]

On March 11 the first step toward reopening Tucson's banks was taken when both the Consolidated and Southern Arizona banks opened their doors to cash federal government checks and make change. While they were open for only two hours, hundreds of government employees and compensation recipients were able to replenish their cash reserves. The amount of $75,000 was cashed. On March 14 the banks reopened again for two hours to cash federal checks, make change, and accept deposits. Bank officials insisted that once the banks were officially opened there would be no percentage limitations on the amount which could be withdrawn, a move which helped restore confidence.[45]

By the end of the first week of the holiday, both bankers and the general public were becoming concerned about when the banks would be permitted to reopen. There also remained some worry that once they were open, severe runs on banks might be forthcoming. Much depended on President Roosevelt's restoring public confidence in banking.

Roosevelt's first "fireside chat" on March 12 was a masterpiece in that direction. After explaining what had been done and announcing that beginning the next day there would be a gradual reopening of the banks, the President added: "It needs no prophet to tell you that when the people find that they can get their money . . . the phantom of fear will soon be laid. . . . I can assure you that it is safer to keep your money in a reopened bank than under the mattress." Roosevelt made it clear that a bank not reopened the first day would probably be opened soon thereafter. And he emphasized that a bank that "opens on one of the subsequent days is in exactly the same status as the bank that opens tomorrow." [46]

Commercial banks in the twelve Federal Reserve cities opened their doors on March 13, those in cities having recognized clearing houses (including Phoenix) on March 14, and banks elsewhere on March 15. By rule of the Secretary of the Treasury, the institutions could limit withdrawals when they deemed such were intended for hoarding. San Francisco on March 13 showed how ill-grounded was the latter fear. As the only city in California whose banks were open that first day, San Francisco's reaction to the reopenings was closely watched throughout the West. The fear of large withdrawals gave way to optimism as huge sums of money, much of which may have been hoarded, began pouring into the city's bank vaults, indicative of a trend which was sweeping the country. Federal Reserve cities reported a lively business upturn almost immediately. Some New York department stores were unable to meet the demand, and Chicago witnessed "something of a Christmas rush." The New York Stock Exchange, which reopened with the banks, reported the largest single day's advance in history.[47]

By March 13 nearly every bank in Arizona had applied for permission to reopen. The Phoenix banks awaited only authorization from the federal government and proper license from the Federal Reserve Bank in San Francisco. Permission to reopen was received in the early morning of March 14, and the Valley Bank and Trust Company, the Phoenix National Bank, the First National Bank of Arizona, and the Phoenix Savings Bank and Trust Company swung their doors open for the first full day's banking business in nearly two weeks. Phoenix proved to be an optimistic bellwether, as had San Francisco the day before. Money sacks, briefcases, almost anything capable of carrying money were seen in the bank lobbies on the morning of March 14, waiting to have their contents exchanged for new bank balances. There was, however, the problem of reopening some of the weaker banks. White asked the Valley Bank's Walter Bimson to aid him in examining these banks and deciding what would have to be done to put them on their feet.[48]

Unusual stories of that first day abound. Take, for instance, the one about an elderly man carrying a glass jar who announced he wanted to open an account at one Phoenix institution. Dressed rather shabbily, he proceeded to shock everyone by pulling out roll after roll of $500 gold certificates. Bank patrons joked with one another while they waited for tellers to record deposits or made minor withdrawals to pay overdue bills. Many Phoenix bankers expressed the belief that the President's address the preceding Sunday had been in large part responsible for the orderly scene. Confidence was truly breeding confidence.[49]

On the first day of citywide banking, the Phoenix Clearing House Association reported that deposits had exceeded withdrawals by more than one million dollars. Twice as much money had been placed in the banks as had been taken out. Indeed, withdrawals were about normal, except for instances where the patron was required to sign an affidavit stating the purpose for which the money was being taken. One woman from Los Angeles, desiring to withdraw her $800, had to settle for $400, as that was all that the list of items she wished to purchase would total.

By March 15 banking business was back to normal in the capital city, although police officers were still being stationed at each bank because of large sums of cash being brought by some depositors. Merchandising was considerably better than normal. As in New York, Chicago, and other large cities, milling crowds of package-carrying men and women thronged downtown Phoenix streets. Theaters reported business volume up 20 per cent. "Our business is better than it has been for eighteen months," one real estate man remarked. "The new public feeling," he said, "is general enough to convince the most skeptical that the psychology of depression is past, and the psychology of better times is here."[51]

Executives of Tucson's banks reiterated the President's words when they were unable to reopen the first day. The Consolidated National Bank announced it expected authorization from the Eleventh Federal Reserve District headquarters in Dallas momentarily. At 3:45 A.M. on March 15, official permission was received by telegraph. Seventeen banks, including six state, two national, and nine branches of the Valley Bank opened that day. Eleven remained unlicensed statewide. That morning the Consolidated National's doors opened to a lobby complete with a $500 floral display and Tony Corsal's orchestra playing "Happy Days Are Here Again." The song was unusually appropriate, as more than 5,000 smiling patrons went to the teller windows the first day. By noon some $100,000 in new deposits had been received. This figure had grown to an astounding $640,000 by the end of the banking day. Withdrawals aggregated a minuscule 5 per cent of deposits. On March 18 the bank placed full-page advertisements in Tucson's newspapers announcing that over one million dollars had been added to accounts in four days—with some depositors actually driving one hundred miles to offer congratulations and turn over their cash.[52]

The story at the Southern Arizona Bank and Trust Company was equally optimistic. More than $580,000 was taken in the first day, some customers having to wait in line until noon to reach a teller. In total, Tucson's two banks took in more than $1.2 million the opening day of banking. Some $25,000 in gold certificates and coin was also received. Significantly, more than five times as much money was deposited as was withdrawn.

These glowing reports of restored confidence were echoed throughout the state. Managers of the nine branches of the Valley Bank, for example, reported that deposits in their institutions during the first day exceeded withdrawals by more than $250,000. The Valley Bank's branch at Safford was typical: "For the first hour or more Wednesday morning the bank was unusually busy accepting deposits and transacting business, but before noon the rush was over and the lobby was practically deserted with the exception of a casual depositor." Some $25,000 more was deposited than was withdrawn. In Douglas, about $107,000 was added to accounts after that city's "abbreviated holiday." Deposits exceeded withdrawals by a three-to-one ratio. Prescott banks added a net balance of an eighth of a million dollars along with a substantial amount of gold. Similar reports flowed in from Yuma, Flagstaff, Kingman, and Nogales.[53]

Some banks were not so fortunate. Nationally, 3,423 institutions still had not opened by March 25. This represented about 18 per cent of all banks in operation before the holiday. In Arizona, all but four reopened, producing a mortality rate about the same as on the national level. By March 16 a compilation of the records of twenty-one Arizona financial institutions which had reopened showed that statewide deposits exceeded withdrawals by 1.5 million dollars—the best vote of confidence Arizona's banking system could be given.[54]

The Farmers State Bank in Scottsdale voluntarily turned its business over to the State Banking Department for liquidation. The bank, according to Superintendent White, was not insolvent but had requested liquidation to protect its depositors. The Round Valley Bank in Springerville, after attempting reorganization, was unable to reopen. When valiant efforts by rival Arizona pioneers Joseph Udall and Gustav Becker to save the Round Valley proved futile, Walter Bimson opened a Valley branch in Springerville so the city would not be bankless. This branch was closed, however, in less than two years. Likewise the First National Bank of Florence, temporarily allowed to reopen under a conservator, soon passed out of existence.[55]

One of the more inspiring stories of the period took place in Willcox. There, in earlier days, the Riggs Bank had been founded by the Riggs brothers, old cattlemen. With the death of the founders, the bank passed out of the hands of the Riggs family. During the bank holiday, however, two ranchers approached Bimson in his Phoenix office, inquiring as to the status of the Riggs Bank in Willcox. They explained that their name was Riggs, and although owning no stock in the bank they felt a family responsibility for it. On learning that the bank required $100,000 in cash, these men pledged their cattle ranches and raised additional funds so as to keep it solvent. On April 3 the Riggs Bank reopened as the Bank of Willcox. Three years later it was merged with the Valley National.[56]

The bank holiday in Arizona compelled men to think. They had a vivid demonstration of what the state and nation would be like without banking facilities—a "giant business machine deprived of the bloodstream supplied by intricate banking machinery." Prompt, vigorous, and decisive action by government in temporarily closing the banks without discrimination prevented further demoralization and provided the base of confidence for a thirty-year economic expansion unparalleled in history. The decade of the 1930's was characterized by a stabilization of the banking system in Arizona. The failures in the depression, culminating with the bank holiday, weeded out many of the weaker institutions and reinforced the statewide trend toward multibranch bank operations. This trend, coupled with the federal government's activities in agriculture, gold and silver legislation, mortgage credit, and bank deposit insurance would profoundly influence the nature of Arizona banking in the years ahead.[57]

A clairvoyant was not needed to read the future of Arizona in early 1933. In January of that year, some of her banks were already moving up and out of the depression, while other states were pessimistically preparing for a further debacle. Had it not been for her neighbor's action, Arizona might never have had to close her banks. As it was, the difficulties encountered during those twelve bankless days were probably fewer and less severe than in most other states. In retrospect, Arizona suffered little more than a temporary interruption of business between March 2 and March 14, 1933. By the time Arizona's banks were forced to close, the depression was already giving way to the dawn of a better day.

NOTES

This is an abridged version of a paper entitled "The Commercial Bank 'Holiday' in Arizona," prepared in 1967 under the auspices of the Arizona Bankers Association.

1. Ernest J. Hopkins, *Financing the Frontier* (Phoenix: Valley National Bank, 1950), pp. 222–225.

2. Paul Studenski and Herman E. Krooss, *Financial History of the United States* (New York: McGraw-Hill, 1952), pp. 379–80; "When Banks Were Closed," *Review of Reviews and World's Week,* LXXXVII (April 1933), 53; Major B. Foster *et al., Money and Banking,* 4th ed. (New York: Prentice-Hall, 1960). See also Edwin Lamke and Cyril B. Upham, *Closed and Distressed Banks* (Washington: Brookings Institution, 1934); "The Michigan Moratorium," *New Republic,* LXXIV (March 8, 1933), 90–91.

3. Total state population in 1930 was 435,573; in 1920 it had been 334,162. Phoenix grew from 29,053 in 1920 to 48,118 in 1930 (65.6 per cent). Tucson ex-

panded from 20,292 in 1920 to 32,506 in 1930 (60.1 per cent). *Abstract of the Fifteenth Census of the United States* (Washington, 1933), p. 26.

4. Don C. Bridenstine, "Commercial Banking in Arizona" (Ph.D. dissertation, University of Southern California, 1958), pp. 193–94. The total number of banks in the United States declined by 39.7 per cent during the period.

5. *Ibid.*, p. 131; John M. Chapman, *Concentration of Banking: The Changing Structure and Control of Banking in the United States* (New York: Columbia University Press, 1934), pp. 81–82.

6. Bridenstine, "Commercial Banking in Arizona," pp. 165–79. See also Senate Bill 26, entitled "An Act to Create a State Banking Department, to Provide for the Appointment of a Superintendent of Banks . . . ," *Acts, Resolutions, and Memorials . . . Special Session of the Fifth Legislature . . .* (Phoenix: Manufacturing Stationers, 1922), Chap. 92, pp. 123–58; House Bill 166, entitled "An Act to Provide for the Sale or Collection of Notes, Mortgages, Bonds, or Other Securities That Have Been Pledged to the State of Arizona to Secure Deposits of State Moneys and Funds in Various Banks of the State That Have Become Insolvent, and Declaring an Emergency," *Acts, Resolutions . . . Regular Session of the Seventh Legislature* (Phoenix: Manufacturing Stationers, 1925), Chap. 71, pp. 169–72. Progressivism was not universal. In 1923, Senator Fred T. Colter of Apache County spoke out against charging interest for the use of money. In his Aristotelian thinking, it was "a sin to either pay or receive interest on money." *Coast Banker and Pacific Banker* [CBPB], XLI (March 1923), 342.

7. Hopkins, *Financing the Frontier,* pp. 193, 203; Annie M. Cox, "History of Bisbee, 1872–1937" (M.A. thesis, University of Arizona, 1938), p. 194; *Graham County Guardian* (Safford, Arizona), February 2, 1933; T. N. McCauley, "Co-operation Necessary," *CBPB,* L (April 1933), 160.

8. Bridenstine, "Commercial Banking in Arizona," pp. 196–97.

9. *Record of Banks and Building and Loan Associations of Arizona, July 1, 1929, to June 30, 1932* (Phoenix: Arizona State Banking Department, 1932); *Winslow Mail* (Arizona), January 13 and 27, 1933.

10. Hopkins, *Financing the Frontier,* p. 194. See also Joseph Stocker, "Financing America's Most Flourishing Frontier," *Arizona Highways,* XXXII (November 1956), 5.

11. To bolster the sagging fortunes of the Valley Bank, President Louis D. Ricketts had sold personal securities to raise $330,000 for the bank. Walter R. Bimson was born in Berthoud, Colorado, on April 25, 1892, attended the University of Colorado briefly, worked in the Berthoud National Bank (1912–1916), and served in the United States Navy in World War I. In 1920 he went to work at the Harris Trust and Savings Bank in Chicago, where he became an expert in handling "banker's acceptances" and cotton shipment financing. He was heading the state relief program in Illinois when tapped to assume the presidency of the Valley Bank and Trust Company on January 1, 1933. Bimson became chairman of the board in 1953. *Who's Who in America* (Chicago: A. N. Marquis, 1966), XXXIV, 182.

12. Hopkins, *Financing the Frontier;* speech at Phoenix on March 20, 1962, by Carl A. Bimson (brother of Walter R.) before the Newcomen Society in North America, entitled "Transformation in the Desert—The Story of Arizona's Valley National Bank." See also "The Brash Banker of Arizona," *Saturday Evening Post,* CCXXVI (April 10, 1954), 23; and Keith Monroe, "Bank Knight in Arizona," *American Magazine,* CXL (November 1945), 24–25, 116–22. For 1933 total deposits jumped by $2.4 million, a substantial 35 per cent.

13. *CBPB,* XXXIX (May 1921), 611; *ibid.,* XL (April 1922), 459; *ibid.,* XLIV (March 1927), 292.

14. Dr. Benjamin Baker Moeur of Tempe, a Democrat, served two terms in the governorship, 1933–1937. He had been elected by an overwhelming vote in 1932 and was highly thought of throughout the state.

15. *Arizona Daily Star* (Tucson), March 4, 1933. Although building and loan associations were not directly affected by the proclamation, they were notified of the holiday. Finance companies and other lending organizations were advised to use their own discretion in dealing with the matter. *Graham County Guardian,* March 3, 1933.

16. *Arizona Republic* (Phoenix), March 3, 1933.

17. House Bill 247, entitled "An Act Relating to the Suspension of Business by Institutions Doing a Banking Business, and Authorizing the Regulation and Limitation of Withdrawals of Deposits, and Declaring an Emergency," *Acts, Resolutions . . . Regular Session, Eleventh Legislature . . .* (Phoenix: Sims Printing Company, 1933), pp. 51–52. *Phoenix Republic,* March 3, 1933.

18. *Tucson Daily Citizen,* March 2, 1933.

19. Lamke and Upham, *Closed and Distressed Banks,* p. 11; *Tucson Citizen,* March 3, 1933. On March 3 San Francisco's giant Wells Fargo Bank and the Crocker First National Bank were still open for business. *Bisbee Daily Review* (Arizona), March 4, 1933.

20. James S. Douglas was a prominent Arizonan and father of Lewis W. Douglas, newly appointed U.S. Director of the Budget. See *Tucson Star,* March 4, 1933, and *Bisbee Daily Review,* March 3, 1933.

21. *Tucson Citizen,* March 4, 1933; *Bisbee Daily Review,* March 5, 1933. Nationally, only one bank was closed by force. This was in Enid, Oklahoma, where National Guardsmen enforced Governor William H. Murray's mandatory closing proclamation. Frank Cullen Brophy, *The Bank of Douglas* (privately printed, 1954), p. 21.

22. *Tucson Citizen,* March 3, 1933.

23. *Ibid.,* March 4, 1933.

24. House Bill 258, entitled "An Act, Relating to the Suspension of Business by Institutions Doing a Banking Business, and Authorizing the Regulation and Limitation of Withdrawals of Deposits, and Providing for the Issuance of Scrip . . . and Declaring an Emergency," *Acts, Resolutions . . . Eleventh Legislature,* pp. 60–62.

25. See Bridenstine, "Commercial Banking in Arizona," p. 208.

26. Hopkins, *Financing the Frontier,* p. 227.

27. *Tucson Citizen,* March 6, 1933. The presidential proclamation forced the First National Bank of Nogales and the two institutions still open at Bisbee and Douglas to close. Governor Moeur and Y. C. White on March 7 told bank officials that they would declare the Arizona holiday ended whenever Treasury officials at Washington gave their consent. *Tucson Star,* March 8, 1933.

28. Bridenstine, "Commercial Banking in Arizona," pp. 43–47.

29. *Tucson Citizen,* March 7, 1933; *Tucson Star,* March 8, 1933. Legislation authorizing the use of scrip remained on the books until January 11, 1935.

30. *Phoenix Republic,* March 9, 1933.

31. *Tucson Star,* March 4 and 9, 1933; *Tucson Citizen,* March 3, 6, and 11, 1933; *Phoenix Republic,* March 7, 1933. The *Star* payroll, the second largest in the city, was of significant import, with at least forty merchants accepting its scrip for purchases.

32. *Tucson Star,* March 8 and 9, 1933; *Tucson Citizen,* March 2 and 18, 1933; *Graham County Guardian,* March 10, 1933. House Bill 167, entitled "An Act Declaring the Existence of an Emergency and Providing Procedure in Actions and Foreclosure of Real Estate Mortgages," *Acts, Resolutions . . . Eleventh Legislature,* pp. 57–59. After much controversy, Judge Fred W. Fickett in Superior Court held the mortgage moratorium law unconstitutional. Some suggestions during the period were rather extreme. Senator Frank Pomeroy of Maricopa, for example, introduced a bill suggesting that the governor declare martial law.

33. *Phoenix Republic,* March 5, 1933. Some well-established customers were permitted to cash checks exceeding the amount of purchase.

34. "Making Merry over the Bank Holiday," *New York Herald-Tribune,* March 25, 1933.

35. *Phoenix Republic,* March 4 and 5, 1933.

36. *Fifty Years of Growth in Tucson, 1903–1953* (Tucson: Southern Arizona Bank and Trust Company, 1953), p. 20.

37. *Tucson Star,* March 4 and 7, 1933.

38. *Ibid.,* March 4 and 8, 1933.

39. *Ibid.,* March 8, 1933; *Tucson Citizen,* March 7, 1933.

40. *Tucson Citizen,* March 2, 1933.

41. *Ibid.,* and *Tucson Star,* March 6, 1933. Both the Tucson Gas, Electric Light and Power Company and the Mountain States Telephone and Telegraph Company accepted checks.

42. *Tucson Star,* March 11, 1933. There is, however, no indication that prices increased in this manner at the end of the holiday.

43. *Tucson Citizen,* March 7, 9, and 15, 1933; *Tucson Star,* March 7, 1933.

44. This difficulty was not limited to Tucson. In Yuma, school district warrants were virtually unacceptable by financial institutions. See *Tucson Star,* March 4, 1933; *Yuma Morning Sun,* March 22, 1933.

45. *Tucson Citizen,* March 13, 1933.

46. Studenski and Krooss, *Financial History,* p. 384; *Tucson Citizen,* March 13, 1933.

47. *Tucson Citizen,* March 14, 1933; *Phoenix Republic,* March 15, 1933; *Wall Street Journal,* March 16, 1933.

48. Hopkins, *Financing the Frontier,* p. 228.

49. *Phoenix Republic,* March 13 and 15, 1933.

50. *Ibid.; Tucson Star,* March 15, 1933.

51. *Phoenix Republic,* March 19, 1933.

52. Phoenix was in the Twelfth Federal Reserve District, headquartered in San Francisco, while Tucson and much of southern Arizona were in the Eleventh; this split the state and caused controversy at the time. The Consolidated National Bank, established in 1889, was merged into the Valley Bank and Trust Company in 1934 to form the Valley National Bank, currently the largest in the Rocky Mountain states. *Tucson Citizen,* March 15, 16, and 18, 1933; *Tucson Star,* March 16, 1933.

53. *Graham County Guardian,* March 17, 1933; *Tucson Citizen,* March 15 and 17, 1933; *Phoenix Republic,* March 17, 1933; *Yuma Sun,* March 16, 1933.

54. Bridenstine, "Commercial Banking in Arizona," p. 211; *Phoenix Republic,* March 28, 1933.

55. *Phoenix Republic,* March 16, 1933; Bridenstine, "Commercial Banking in Arizona," p. 211.

56. Hopkins, *Financing the Frontier,* pp. 227–29. See also *Arizona Range News* (Willcox), March 17, April 7, 1933.

57. Jerry F. Sullivan, "The Year in California," *CBPB,* L (June 1933), 252. By the end of 1939, there would be only thirty-six banking offices in the state, in contrast to sixty-eight on the eve of the depression—a loss of 47 per cent for the decade. *Condensed Statement of Reports of State and National Banks of Arizona, December 30, 1939* (Phoenix: State Banking Department, 1940 [?]).

Orange County During the Depressed Thirties: A Study in Twentieth-Century California Local History

Robert L. Pritchard

This selection illustrates the temporary impact of the Great Depression in certain localities on attitudes toward positive government. It points out how the "faith" was shaken for a time but not fundamentally altered, "coming back stronger than ever before." A little more than a year before this article was published, a Newsweek *story ("A Little Piece of America," November 14, 1966, pp. 32, 37) indicated the strength of the faith in Orange County today. In outward ways—the population, now 1.2 million, has doubled three times in twenty years—the county is the "fastest changing . . . in the U.S." Beneath the surface upheaval, it is also "the fastest to resist change." Congressman James Utt, Orange County's "Mr. Conservative," who, as this selection notes, suffered the only defeat of his career in 1934, is quoted in 1966 as stating, "Government is like a child molester who offers candy before his evil act."*

As one might expect, the leaders of the dominant party and the county newspapers are quite conservative. What is striking is that their lead has been followed by the newcomers. "Almost nobody presses the powers in Orange County. Almost nobody cares to. . . . And in Orange County those who care give those who don't just about what they want." This situation cannot be explained away as some sort of aberration, as Easterners and Northern Californians are prone to do. It calls for serious historical and sociological anal-

[Reprinted from *Southern California Quarterly,* L (January 1968), 191–205.]

ysis such as James Q. Wilson provides in "A Guide to Reagan Country: The Political Culture of Southern California," in Commentary, *XLIII (May 1967), 37–45, and Michael P. Rogin and John L. Shover offer in* Political Change in California: Critical Elections and Social Movements, 1896–1968 *(Westport, Conn.: Greenwood, 1970). That Orange County will continue indefinitely to be an area hospitable to the "faith" is doubtful in view of the generation gap described by Tom Goodhue, a resident of the county and now a student at Stanford University, in "A Report on Two Cultures: Orange County, California,"* New Republic, *CLXII (June 20, 1970), 12–13.*

Mr. Pritchard's conclusion that "it was natural that traditionally conservative groups would return to the more comfortable beliefs of an earlier and happier time" will not be disputed. However, his reference to "the so-called First New Deal" and his characterization of it as following "a fairly conservative approach" raise historiographical questions on which there is some disagreement. There has been a growing tendency on the part of New Deal historians to dismiss or to impose considerable qualifications on the "two New Deals" analysis (see William H. Wilson, "The Two New Deals: Valid Concept?," Historian, *XXVIII [February 1966], 268–288, and Carl N. Degler, ed.,* The New Deal *[Chicago: Quadrangle Books, 1970], pp. 17–18). To the extent that historians still accept this analysis they frequently call the early New Deal—particularly with regard to the NRA, as it operated and in terms of its implications—"radical." In this view the anti-business and anti-trust rhetoric of Roosevelt's second term, although it may have represented a "leftward turn" (to use Pritchard's phrase) in appealing to the electorate, was in accord with orthodox progressivism. (An excellent relevant article about a traditionally conservative area is James C. Duram, "Supreme Court Packing and the New Deal: The View from Southwestern Michigan,"* Michigan History, *LII [Spring 1968], 12–27.)*

The first three decades of the twentieth century were times of growth and prosperity for Orange County. From a population slightly in excess of 25,000 in 1900, the county had more than

188,000 people by 1930. The growth rate increased throughout this period, advancing by 80 per cent between 1910 and 1920 and by 90 per cent during the 1920's.[1] The resultant influx of new citizens changed somewhat the traditionally rural and agricultural mode of existence, although the county still derived its primary income from agriculture.

In 1930 the county had more than 200,000 acres of farmland under cultivation. It led the nation in the production of oranges but, in addition, produced a great diversity of other crops, including lemons, avocados, sugar beets, and truck produce. Livestock and poultry production also contributed to the county's agricultural income. Most of its manufacturing was related to agriculture, with food canning and processing contributing most significantly to the total economy.[2]

There were more small than large farmers in the county, but the latter dominated in property ownership, distribution of products, and in shaping the local political viewpoint. The degree of concentration in land ownership is difficult to estimate, but it was a significant factor in the county's economic organization. One California historian contends that in 1930 "3.4 per cent of the total number of growers received 27.7 per cent of the $20 million income from citrus farms in Orange County." [3] The dominant influence in the county's agriculture was the powerful Irvine Company, owner of the huge Irvine Ranch and the leading force in the various and interlocking agricultural associations that shaped the area's economic life.[4]

Oil provided another major stimulant to the county's economic growth in the twenties. The first major discoveries had been made in the 1890's by the Union Oil Company in the vicinity of the present city of Brea. Union started development in 1895 and by 1900 was producing more than 500,000 barrels annually. Other oil companies, including one directed by Edward Doheny, followed Union into the area and developed the highly productive Olinda fields.[5] The county's second great oil boom began in 1919–1920 with the discovery by Union of reservoirs in the Placentia area and the development of the Huntington Beach area by Standard Oil. The latter community virtually overnight became an oil-boom town.

Agriculture and oil were the twin pillars supporting the county's economic growth in the 1920's, but local service businesses also experienced increased prosperity as part of the general economic expansion. The county's growth mirrored the widespread prosperity of the rest of the state and the nation. Its mood reflected the infectious aura of optimism that pervaded the national business community, a mood expressed through feverish stock and real estate speculation. The big real estate boom in Los Angeles had its counterpart in Orange County, much smaller than that of its larger neighbor but no less significant to the county's economic life. The *Orange County Review* noted in April 1922 that "no matter where one journeys in the county these days, he cannot help but notice the remarkable development . . . new structures are rising everywhere. Homes, business blocks, public buildings are being constructed by the hundreds." [6] The beach areas particularly enjoyed a land boom; the modern development of Newport Beach and Balboa began during this period, with waterfront lots ranging from eight hundred to four thousand dollars an acre.[7] The county's inland areas were equally caught up in real estate development, with a steady rise in property values throughout the decade; for example, Santa Ana's assessed valuation showed nearly a threefold increase between 1920 and 1930, from almost $7.5 million to more than $21 million.[8] Real estate development tapered off considerably after 1925, but there seemed to be little in the economic atmosphere of the late 1920's to raise doubt about the future. The danger signals that existed were largely ignored. Then the depression struck.

The great depression of the 1930's was a traumatic experience for many Americans, not only for the severity of its economic impact but because it threatened to destroy the fundamental assumptions that underlay so many views of American life. The material advances of the 1920's, that had achieved for so many a standard of living never dreamed of by their parents, were tangible proof of the "superiority" of the American way. Most Americans needed no reminding of their good fortune—the evidence was there for all to see plainly. Yet their premises about the American system were unceasingly reinforced by the persistent propagandists of the twenties. Sinclair Lewis notwithstanding, most Americans accepted without a moment's hesitation the "booster" philosophy. For people so inclined, who could look around at their own favored condition, it was easy to believe in the promise of a "golden age of prosperity."

Orange County was no exception to this view of the American way of life. If anything, the leading citizens of the county embraced more strongly than most Americans the belief in progress that for so long had been characteristic of the nation's development. This belief manifested itself in a simplistic and fundamentalistic, but completely sincere, kind of patriotism. Reminiscing about his high school days in 1910, the noted Santa Ana attorney, Charles Swanner, stated:

> I recall hearing . . . a stirring patriotic address to the high school assembly on the day before Memorial Day. Those were the days when national patriotism was something everyone was proud of and before the day of those advocating a one world government and making little of the patriots who still carry the torch for Old Glory![9]

A variation of this theme is repeated again and again by those who have recorded Orange County's history. Yet this patriotism did not include a high regard for the government in Washington. The county's leadership might on occasion seek the national government's assistance, as it often did in trying to solve local water problems, but always somewhat reluctantly and never without some sense of guilt.[10] For most Orange County residents the principal tenets of the American way were self-reliance and individualism, which meant, as far as government was concerned, to put one's faith in local government, go to the state if necessary, but never as the initial approach to a problem; and to call on the federal government only as a last resort. As for guidelines in dealing with Washington, the point was clear: never relent on the basic question of local control, for federal regulation was the very antithesis of the traditional American spirit of individualism.

One could point to dozens of illustrations prior to the 1930's when Orange County availed itself of state and federal aid long before it became a matter of last resort, but if the county's conceptions of itself did not always square with the reality of its actions, that did not negate in the least the fervor with which such beliefs were held. The depression severely tested those beliefs. How Orange County residents responded to the test, and the self-conceptions or self-deceptions that they had at the close of the depression decade, can only be determined by examining the degree to which the county was affected economically by the crisis of the thirties.

Compared to some other regions of the country, Orange County was not one of the depression's major disaster areas. Nevertheless, it suffered economic disruption and unemployment on a scale heretofore unknown. At first, it attempted to cope with these problems in much the same way as many other communities—by relying on local private and public relief agencies. By 1932–1933, however, the economic dislocation had taxed local resources beyond the breaking point: the county was forced to accept state and federal assistance.

Between July 1933 and September 1935 Orange County's unemployment relief rolls contained at their highest point more than 17,000 persons, nearly 15 per cent of the total working force. Unemployment did not remain steady at this figure, showing considerable fluctuation because of the high rate of seasonal work; but during this period it never dropped below 9 per cent of the county's labor force.[11] The number of persons out of work generally declined after the fall of 1935, but unemployment remained a persistent problem in the county throughout the thirties, just as it did in the rest of the nation.

Another indicator of the depression's severity in Orange County was a general decline in municipal revenues and a substantial increase in delinquent taxes. Every incorporated city in the county showed large reductions in total revenue collected, and all but one city experienced a drastic increase of taxpayers in arrears on their payments. Santa Ana, then the county's largest city, provided a fairly typical example of this. Between 1931 and 1934 it suffered a 30 per cent decline in revenue and an 80 per cent increase in delinquent taxes.[12] These problems reflected a general decline in municipal expenditures and a substantial inability to deal with the serious problems caused by the depression. The effects of these reduced expenditures would have been even more serious had not the county's rapid population increase of previous decades stopped rather abruptly in the thirties; population increased less than 1 per cent annually between 1930 and 1940.[13]

In the latter stages of the administration of President Herbert

Hoover, the Reconstruction Finance Corporation provided assistance to California counties and helped ease the pressure on overburdened municipalities. Following Franklin Roosevelt's inauguration, Congress established the Federal Emergency Relief Administration, which provided direct relief in California at the state and local level. The state legislature created the California Emergency Relief Administration to administer and distribute both state and federal relief. Under federal mandates that the states provide matching funds, the state legislature passed the Unemployment Relief Bond Act to assist counties and cities in financing emergency relief programs.[14] In addition the federal Civil Works Administration provided funds to finance emergency public works programs. By 1935 total unemployment relief expenditures in California from all these agencies amounted to over $285 million.[15]

Orange County received its share of these infusions of state and federal money, since it was designated by the state as one of the nine counties in California where relief was most urgently required. During 1934 and 1935 the county received more than two million dollars in relief funds, which affected an average of 11 per cent of the local population.[16] Over two-thirds of this money was provided by the federal government, with the remainder contributed by the state and county. In addition to direct relief the county established twenty-two self-help cooperatives under federal grants, an endeavor that employed some six thousand persons.[17] Other federal programs during this period included three Civilian Conservation Corps camps, two federal transient camps, and aid to needy students at local junior colleges.[18]

The federal relief program entered a different phase in 1935 with the establishment of the Works Progress Administration. It superseded all existing programs and concentrated on public works on a vast scale. During the remainder of the depression decade WPA continued to provide substantial federal assistance to the county. In its first two years of operation it expended more than three million dollars in various public works projects, including the construction of schools, libraries, city halls, police stations, and street improvements.[19] Practically every public building constructed in the county during the late thirties included the use of WPA funds. Also, WPA involved itself in a wide range of other activities, including school recreation programs, various types of service schools, and Project No. 3105, which conducted studies of local governmental problems.[20] In addition to the aforementioned programs, considerable federal money came into Orange County through the Public Works Administration, which provided up to 45 per cent financing for worthwhile municipal projects. The most significant of PWA's projects was the assistance it provided for the development of Newport Harbor.[21]

There were many other ways in which federal programs helped combat the depression in Orange County. Local farmers received assistance from government allotment programs under the Agricultural Adjustment Acts. Bankers benefited from Roosevelt's banking holiday in 1933 and the subsequent Treasury Department supervision of bank reopenings. Homeowners gained greater security through the efforts of the Home Owners Loan Corporation and the Federal Housing Administration. Investigation into each of these and other programs could provide material for another lengthy article. However, the conclusion is clear. During the depression Orange County had an unprecedented and unparalleled involvement with the federal government. The county's citizens, whose generally conservative past and orientation had not prepared them for this new development, reacted in a variety of ways that merit further examination.

Orange Countians responded to the depression in much the same way as people did in other parts of the country—with shock and bewilderment. The foundations of their lives and even the very fundamentals on which they based their beliefs were disrupted by severe economic stress. Frightened people sought release from their frustrations in a variety of ways: by pounding the pavement in search of jobs that never materialized and by baring their souls through sometimes angry, sometimes despondent letters to editors of local papers. The county unemployed pleaded to, and demonstrated before, the board of supervisors and various city councils demanding assistance. Local government did what it could with the resources at its disposal. The conservative belief in "rugged individualism" waned, and demands increased for government help. The popular conceptions of the twenties, extolling the great leaders of business, finance, and industry, which had pervaded the thinking of Orange County as well as the rest of the nation, underwent considerable revision.

The most immediate and easily discernible reaction to the depression in Orange County was the effect that it had on local voting patterns. The county's voting record had been consistently Republican. Not a single Democrat had carried the county in presidential or gubernatorial elections in the first thirty years of the twentieth century and, in addition, Republicans had won the vast majority of Congressional and state legislative races. In the presidential election of 1928, Herbert Hoover won in Orange County by better than a four-to-one margin.[22] Precisely why Orange Countians were such reflexive Republicans is difficult to determine. Both major parties contained strongly conservative wings to which local citizens could have been attracted; yet perhaps because the Republican party was more consistently conservative, or perhaps just because it had a stronger base of power in California than did the Democrats, it dominated the political life of the county.

The depression did not completely change the past voting habits of the county's citizens. As with the rest of the country, Orange County appeared to hold Hoover personally responsible for the economic crisis, or at least felt that he had not done enough to combat it. This fact, plus certain ambiguities in Roosevelt's campaign about governmental economy and balanced budgets, caused a local shift to the Democrats. The county joined the statewide and national desire for change by supporting Roosevelt, but only with a 1,200-vote plurality out of close to 50,000 votes cast.[23] This was as far as the local citizenry would go. The county elected Republicans to the state senate and to both state assembly seats and resisted the statewide trend by going two-to-one Republican for the United States Senate.

In the election of 1936 Orange County's response was more consistent. The impact of federal relief programs and the degree to which the New Deal had been able to mitigate the effects of the depression clearly played a part in the county's vote. For the first time in local history the Democrats had gained an edge in registration, with 35,000 Democrats as opposed to 28,000 Republicans. In the presidential election the county joined the national sweep for Roosevelt, although by a margin much smaller than at the national or state level. FDR's plurality in the county exceeded six thousand votes. In addition the vote went Democratic for Congress, the state senate, and for one of the two state assembly districts. The reaction against conservatism is illustrated by the defeat for the state assembly of James Utt, Orange County's "Mr. Conservative" and later multiterm Congressman. It was the only defeat of his long political career. A Republican candidate who later attained national stature as a Republican "moderate," Thomas Kuchel of Anaheim, salvaged the lone G.O.P. assembly seat.[24]

In the gubernatorial races of the depression years Orange County remained more conservative in its voting patterns. However, this response seems to be the result of particular facets of each election, rather than representing a true measure of local views during the worst years of the depression. In 1934 Upton Sinclair received the Democratic nomination for governor against the Republican incumbent, Frank Merriam. Orange Countians viewed Sinclair as a socialist, and even the upheavals of the depression had not brought them to the point where they could support such radicalism. The issue was not liberalism against conservatism, or two differing but acceptable responses to the economic crisis. Rather the issue was preservation of the capitalistic system against "leftist extremism." Sinclair's socialism was a more decisive factor in Orange County than the controversial Townsend Plan, although this too had some bearing on the election. Merriam carried the county by a substantial margin, much larger than his plurality throughout the state. In 1938, when Democrat Culbert Olson carried the state, Orange County went Republican by a plurality of five thousand votes. This vote reflected several factors: Olson's liberalism and association with the leftward turn of the New Deal since 1935; his endorsement of the controversial "Ham and Eggs" plan; and finally, the restoration of considerable prosperity in the county, which brought once more to the surface the traditional deeply ingrained local conservatism. By 1940 Orange County had become securely Republican again, selecting Willkie over Roosevelt for president and electing Republicans to the Senate, House of Representatives, and state legislature.[25]

The general reaction to the depression in the county modified somewhat the local conservatism, but more from confusion about how to combat the depression than out of a fundamental reorientation of belief. Consequently, the strongest liberal trend developed during the first half of the depression, when local economic conditions were at their worst, and declined after 1936 as the county recovered. As the depression waned, conservatism returned as strongly as, or perhaps even stronger than, it had been before 1929. Orange Countians, in other words, attempted to understand the depression within their traditionally conservative frame of reference. They did not regard the social and economic changes wrought by the depression as requiring a permanent expansion in the federal government's role.

In 1932, for example, as the severity of the economic crisis deepened, the well-known county editor R. K. Maxwell summarized the election issues by stating:

> Though individuals, organizations, and political parties continue to disagree on many phases of government, there is one subject upon which individuals and leaders of the greatest political divisions agree; there is . . . unity of purpose in the national drive to reduce government expenses; servitude will come if the tax burden continues at the present rate.[26]

Local citizens, in their letters to the newspapers, in their political advertising, reiterated this theme throughout the campaign of 1932. They contended that government expenditures were too great, taxes were too high, and retrenchment and budget balancing would cure the nation's economic ills. The expanded role of government represented an unhealthy sign for the country. Conservatives and moderates, who encompassed the largest area of the county's political spectrum, generally agreed that retrenchment was the only way to resolve the dangerous problem of governmental deficits. Frank Burk of the *Santa Ana Register,* for many years a moderately progressive Republican, called for drastic action to meet the "emergency" of "mounting deficits" in government.[27] Ultraconservative Ralph Taylor of the California Agriculture Legislative Committee, writing in the *Balboa Times,* called for rigid retrenchment in order to force the government off the "luxury standard" that placed such a burden on the nation's farmers.[28] This might appear to be an unusual response in view of the economic conditions of 1932, but it was in keeping with the county's conservative tradition.

Despite these criticisms of government expenditure and growth, Orange Countians called on both the state and national governments for assistance in combating economic problems and in correcting the evils that had caused the depression. For example, local citizens shared the national reaction against bankers and were willing to see the federal government control their excesses. Two county newspapers favored complete governmental takeover of the Federal Reserve System to solve the country's financial disorders, and one even favored government ownership and control of banking in general.[29] This was a strange view indeed when one considers the glorification of the businessman in the 1920's.

In addition to regulation of banking, local opinion literally demanded increased federal and state aid to combat the mounting problem of unemployment. The *Santa Ana Register* reflected the dichotomy in local thinking when, in the same issue, it called for federal relief of the unemployed, through public works or unemployment insurance, and yet strongly recommended substantial reductions in government expenditures at all levels and an easing of the tax burden.[30] The county clearly faced a crisis of confidence. Its response was not just a matter of Orange Countians' wanting both to have and to eat their cake. Rather it reflected the confusion in the minds of basically conservative people about the events for which their own fundamental philosophy provided no answers. Consequently, they awaited the inauguration of the new President with both hope and apprehension.

The Roosevelt administration, in its first two years, received a surprisingly favorable reaction in Orange County, although the local press exhibited considerable difference of opinion about the New Deal. Near the midway point of his first term, FDR received vigorous support in the county against charges made by former President Hoover that the New Deal violated the American tradition by making individuals pawns of the state. The *Fullerton Tribune* ripped Hoover and defended the New Deal on the premise that old remedies and old theories had had their way for many years, but had failed. If the old ways proved insufficient, the only recourse was to try something new, which Roosevelt had attempted to do.[31]

Samuel Meyer of the *Newport News* lauded Roosevelt for restoring the confidence of business and dismissed as "specious conjecture" all the earlier fears that FDR's election would lead to "regimentation" and to "government interference with business." [32] Meyer's reference to the President as a "sound businessman" was a view widely shared in Orange County, especially among community leaders who made their ideas known.[33] How the large but silent mass of unemployed felt about him was not as readily apparent.

Roosevelt's reaction to Upton Sinclair's bid for the governorship in 1934 elicited a favorable response from the county. FDR did not endorse Sinclair, following, rather, a policy of studied indifference of which the President was a master. Roosevelt's noncommittal stance was taken, probably accurately, in Orange County as a rejection of Sinclair. Since Orange Countians generally viewed Sinclair's election as inviting revolution in the streets and a Communist seizure of power through the ballot box, the President's policy won him many friends. Frank Burk of the *Register* lauded Roosevelt for his nonendorsement and, although defending Sinclair against charges that he was a Communist, attacked him for his opposition to the "profits system." [34] This point was essential to the county's support for the President. The *Anaheim Bulletin* praised him for his devotion to capitalism and for recognizing the interests of business in attempting to cope with the depression.[35] These views make vivid contrast to later assessments of Roosevelt by Orange County's leaders.

Roosevelt's first two years, the so-called First New Deal, involved vigorous action and experimentation to alleviate the depression, but still followed a fairly conservative approach. The administration included many moderate liberals and conservatives, not the type of men to excite fear of revolution. Roosevelt's method of achieving industrial recovery through the NRA was decidedly cooperative toward business. His agricultural programs, providing substantial aid to larger, more prosperous farmers, hardly indicated a desire to do much social leveling. True, the New Deal spent huge sums of money, involved itself in many "make work" programs, and did not appear overly concerned about mounting deficits, but the relief projects were necessary to fight unemployment, and Roosevelt himself, on occasion, made reference to balanced budgets. In sum the First New Deal, aside from such programs as the TVA, was reasonably reassuring to the conservative faith.

In 1935, however, the Roosevelt administration took a decided left turn. It still accepted capitalism, but now it had the new objective of achieving basic reforms within the American system in order to decrease the possibility of another economic disaster. That the system had ingrained weaknesses could hardly be denied; but to conservatives, now that a degree of recovery had been attained, the weaknesses were preferable to any "radical" experiments that might be needed to correct them. Before 1935 both left and right had severely criticized Roosevelt and would continue to do so during the Second New Deal, but increasingly the most vehement attacks came from the right. The conservative reaction against Roosevelt nationally manifested itself in a definite shift of opinion against him in Orange County.

The *Fullerton Tribune,* which had often praised Roosevelt in the past, reflected the new tone of the local press toward the New Deal in 1936:

> It is apparent that a basic issue in the coming national election will be that of concentration of powers in the national government. The New Deal . . . is now demanding that things be so changed . . . as to permit the unlimited functioning of the federal government in its numerous programs on behalf of a "new social order." Such a change would mean an entire overturning of . . . the American system of government. It would bring about the very thing which the builders of the Constitution sought to avoid in the specific reservation to "the states and the people" of powers not definitely assigned to the general government. Concentrated government cannot operate except as a bureaucracy—a bureaucracy working under a dictatorship. It means inevitably a government of men and not of laws. It can function only through complete socialism or complete despotism.[36]

The *Santa Ana Register,* no longer under the direction of the moderate Republican Frank Burk, but now published by the conservative R. C. Hoiles, joined the *Tribune's* denunciation of the New Deal. Hoiles endorsed Landon, but, despite the assurances of the *Literary Digest,* doubted that he could be elected: "The vote will go against those who are really adding to the national wealth and will make it impossible for private initiative to go forward—it will go for regulation, control, and confiscation." [37]

Despite the opposition of the local press, Roosevelt, as previously noted, carried the county in the biggest Democratic victory in its history. Federal assistance proved to be stronger than the newspapers as a factor in determining how the citizens would vote, both nationally and in Orange County. Samuel Meyer of the *Newport News,* in his election postmortem, somewhat reluctantly but succinctly summed up the reasons for Roosevelt's triumph. "FDR has made mistakes, he's wasteful and extravagant, but some of the money filters down to the masses and control does not rest in the hands of the wealthy few. . . . FDR's sympathies have been for the 'little man' and Landon has lined up with the 'same old Big Business forces.'" [38]

The 1936 election demonstrated that, even in conservative Orange County, the people wanted unemployment relief, social security, and a government with a sense of social responsibility. They voted for these things in the face of a steady propaganda barrage of conservative shibboleths about balanced budgets, private initiative, limited government, and preservation of the "profits system." If the people of the county felt their freedom threatened by the New Deal, they did not indicate this in the voting booth. Yet this election, in Orange County and elsewhere, departed considerably from the political responses of the past, and it was perhaps inevitable that the great Roosevelt mandate would be dissipated in the second term. Beginning with the Supreme Court controversy, the Roosevelt consensus steadily deteriorated and conservatism demonstrated a remarkable resilience. The Republican party, prematurely pronounced dead in 1936, staged a stunning comeback, and the Southern Democrat–Conservative Republican coalition substantially brought the New Deal to a halt. As these things took place, it was natural that traditionally conservative groups would return to the more comfortable beliefs of an earlier and happier time. This happened in Orange County, and the election of 1936 simply became the exception that proved the rule of the county's consistent conservatism.

Orange County's conservative resurgence was due not only to

the leftward turn of the New Deal during FDR's second term, but also to an increasingly hostile attitude toward organized labor. California had its share of labor difficulties in the thirties and Orange County itself was plagued by farm-labor strikes in 1935, 1936, and 1938. Labor became more militant and more successful on a national scale than at any previous time in American history. Hardly a day passed without newspaper coverage of some major strike. Orange County, although not industrialized enough to feel the full impact of labor problems, still responded strongly to this major national issue. Since labor challenged strongly held beliefs about contract rights and individualism, the county's reaction was basically antagonistic. Local citizens identified labor with the militance of the C.I.O., and the C.I.O. increasingly with Communism, an attitude not entirely without a basis in fact. As the New Deal increasingly aligned itself with labor, it lost more and more support in Orange County.

The local press led the assault on New Deal labor policies. Even the *Anaheim Bulletin,* which stuck with Roosevelt through the 1936 campaign, criticized certain facets of the administration's program for labor, especially toward laws regulating child labor. A child labor amendment would "strike a cruel blow against the only known method we have for developing a sturdy, able citizenry." [39] However, the *Bulletin* was less inclined than most local papers just to dismiss labor demands as "socialistic" and "communistic," and even took a balanced view of the county's agricultural strikes in 1935, despite siding with the growers.[40] The response of the *Fullerton Tribune* to local labor problems in 1936 typified the general reaction of the county's newspapers. It opposed demands for the union shop and implied that the motivating force behind the strikes was a sinister Communist plot to overthrow capitalism.[41] Editorials raised the issue of communism with increasing frequency in the late thirties and consistently identified it with labor.

That there were Communists in the labor movement in the 1930's can hardly be denied, but to suggest that they controlled labor or that there would be no labor strife without them, as Orange Countians were prone to do, represented either a serious misunderstanding of the problem or a willingness to believe what they wanted to believe. The increased hostility to labor and the New Deal, and the increased connecting of both with socialism, communism, and un-Americanism, expedited the conservative resurgence in the county and prepared the way for its growth in the postwar era. It also prepared the way for the emotional reaction to communism in the late 1940's and early 1950's, a reaction that is still very much a part of the county's attitude. Even the tremendous population growth since World War II, which has wrought such fundamental changes in Orange County's economic life, has not significantly altered its fundamentally conservative political orientation. This basic conservatism, which has endured in the face of change and transition, seems to be an intrinsic facet of the Orange County character, a faith that even outsiders adopt once they set foot in the area. The Great Depression, with its consequent expansion of the governmental role, shook the faith for a time but did not fundamentally alter it. When it recovered from the ordeal of the thirties, it came back stronger than ever before.

NOTES

1. Security First National Bank Research Department, *The Growth and Economic Structure of Orange County* (Los Angeles, 1961), p. 1.
2. *Ibid.*, p. 21.
3. Carey McWilliams, *Southern California: An Island on the Land* (New York, 1946), p. 212.
4. Robert Glass Cleland, *The Irvine Ranch of Orange County* (San Marino, Calif., 1952), pp. 125–133.
5. Purl Harding, *History of Brea* (Brea, Calif., 1950), pp. 1–2.
6. Leo J. Friis, *Orange County Through Four Centuries* (Santa Ana, Calif., 1965), p. 132.
7. Samuel A. Meyer, *Fifty Golden Years: A History of Newport Beach, 1906–1956* (Newport Beach, Calif., 1957), p. 50.
8. Thomas B. Talbert, ed., *The Orange County History Volumes and Reference Work,* 3 vols. (Whittier, Calif., 1963), I, 273.
9. Charles D. Swanner, *Fifty Years a Barrister in Orange County, 1915–1965* (Claremont, Calif., 1965), p. 26.
10. Samuel Armor, "Flood Control and Water Conservation," *Papers of the Orange County Historical Society* (Santa Ana, Calif., 1936), II, 102–103.
11. State Relief Administration of California, *Review of Activities, 1933–1935* (Sacramento, 1936), pp. 281–282.
12. California Emergency Relief Administration Municipal League Project, *Report of Survey of Orange County Cities* (Orange County, Calif., 1935).
13. Security First National, *Growth of Orange County,* p. 1.

14. California Emergency Relief Administration, *Monthly Bulletin,* I (August 1934), p. 4.

15. State Relief Administration, *Review,* p. 25.

16. *Ibid.,* p. 312.

17. State Relief Administration of California, *Summary Report, 1933–1934,* p. 36.

18. State Relief Administration, *Review,* pp. 166, 271.

19. *Santa Ana Register,* October 26, 1937, p. 5, col. 5.

20. *Ibid.,* October 12, 1937, p. 3, col. 3; October 26, 1937, p. 5, col. 4; September 23, 1937, p. 1, col. 2; and October 27, 1937, p. 3, col. 3.

21. Meyer, *Fifty Golden Years,* p. 135. Also *Newport News,* June 20, 1935, p. 1, cols. 2–3; October 8, 1936, p. 1, cols. 7–8.

22. California Secretary of State, *Statement of Vote, 1928,* pp. 4–7.

23. California Secretary of State, *Statement of Vote, 1932,* pp. 4–9.

24. California Secretary of State, *Statement of Vote, 1936,* p. 36.

25. California Secretary of State, *Statement of Vote, 1940,* pp. 5–19.

26. *Fullerton Daily News Tribune,* October 31, 1932, p. 2, col. 1.

27. *Santa Ana Register,* October 27, 1932, p. 16, col. 1.

28. *Balboa Times,* November 10, 1932, p. 7, col. 5.

29. *Ibid.,* October 13, 1932, p. 2, col. 1. Also, the *La Habra Star,* as quoted in the *Fullerton Daily News Tribune,* October 25, 1932, p. 2, cols. 2–4.

30. *Santa Ana Register,* October 13, 1932, p. 16, col. 1.

31. *Fullerton Daily News Tribune,* September 5, 1934, p. 2, col. 1.

32. *Newport News,* January 3, 1935, p. 6, cols. 1–2.

33. *Ibid.,* January 10, 1935, p. 6, col. 1.

34. *Santa Ana Register,* November 2, 1934, p. 28, cols. 1–2.

35. *Anaheim Bulletin,* January 5, 1935, p. 4, col. 1.

36. *Fullerton Daily News Tribune,* July 1, 1936, p. 2, col. 1.

37. *Santa Ana Register,* November 4, 1936, p. 16, col. 1.

38. *Newport News,* November 5, 1936, p. 2, col. 1.

39. *Anaheim Bulletin,* January 11, 1935, p. 4, col. 1.

40. *Ibid.,* February 19, 1935, p. 4, col. 1.

41. *Fullerton Daily News Tribune,* July 15, 1936, p. 2, col. 1.

National Generalization, Local Test IV

Victims of the Great Depression: The Question of Blame and First-Person History

William R. Phillips and Bernard Sternsher

Textbooks often include the assertion that most victims of the Great Depression, in accordance with the traditional American belief in self-reliance, blamed themselves for their plight. As noted in the preface, this judgment was considered in a 1977 article which cited relevant research in the 1930s. The following selection presents further inquiry which tests the conclusions reached in 1977. It includes analysis of collections of letters from the "down and out" and the working poor to President Roosevelt, Mrs. Roosevelt, Relief Administrator Harry Hopkins, and Secretary of Labor Frances Perkins, and a Works Progress Administration Research Division report containing interviews with a systematically selected sample of forty-five families in Dubuque, Iowa. The WPA publication is especially relevant to this volume because it affords a basis for assessing the national generalization with respect to the attitudes of respondents in a specific locality.

Reading about the Great Depression, one frequently encounters a view that has achieved the status of an axiom: that the average American worker blamed his economic hardship on himself, not on the capitalist system, and that socialism and communism thus failed to develop a mass base in the United States during the 1930s. This self-blame was presumably in accord with Americans' widespread belief in individualism or self-reliance and in the traditional view of poverty: if you are poor, it is your own

[William R. Phillips teaches at Port Clinton (Ohio) Junior High School and Tiffin (Ohio) University.]

fault. Self-blame also helped to explain the reluctance to accept relief and, if one had to receive relief, a preference for work relief over direct (or dole or home or market-basket) relief.

Touring America in 1935, the writer Sherwood Anderson observed, "There is in the average American a profound humbleness. People seem to blame themselves."[1] In *The Grapes of Wrath*, published in 1939, John Steinbeck portrayed the wretched as blaming themselves rather than the system. In 1940, E. Wight Bakke concluded that despite the depression nearly all the unemployed in New Haven still accepted the capitalist system.[2] Three decades later, in "The Poor in the Great Depression," David J. Rothman alluded to the time-honored idea that the poor were "essentially responsible for their difficulties" and stated that "Despite the magnitude of the problem and the unprecedented government response, a very traditional attitude toward poverty persisted through the Depression." The unemployed thus "insisted on blaming themselves for their misery, defining their problems as internal, not external.... They passionately and honestly told the interviewers that before taking relief they would 'rather be dead and buried.'"[3] In 1974, in *The American Dream of Success*, Lawrence Chenoweth concluded that during the thirties Americans clung tenaciously to their individualistic faith, a faith producing "embarrassment when we fail, discomfiture in accepting assistance from others.... Even with one out of four citizens out of work, the unemployed often blame themselves for their economic problems."[4] Meanwhile, the assumption or assertion of widespread self-blame often appeared in textbooks (a matter to which we shall return). Thomas C. Cochran, for example, wrote in a textbook published in 1968:

> But never in this time of material, social, and moral prostration was there any threat of revolution, or even any important rise of radicalism in American politics. The American cultural traditions of self-help and individual responsibility seemed, for the most part, to make sufferers feel guilty and perhaps sullen and resentful, but not ready to rebel or fight for a new order.[5]

In an article in *Social Science History* in 1977, Bernard Sternsher posed several questions about this maxim that the average worker in the 1930s blamed himself for his plight.[6] The first three were: Did most or many victims of the Great Depression blame themselves for their plight? If they did not, did their attitude lead to radical—that is, fundamentally anticapitalistic—thought? And did radical thought lead to radical behavior? (In other words, excluding those who were fatalistic about hard times, blaming fate or God, for example, might one expect to find potential radical thinkers and activists among depression victims who blamed something other than themselves—the capitalist system, Hoover, businessmen—for their plight?)

Sternsher's search for answers to these questions began with an examination of relevant literature, especially contemporary writings in journals devoted to social service, sociology, psychology, social psychology, and psychiatry. Historians had done very little with this literature, which displayed considerable variety.[7] Diversity marked the size and composition of research samples, the questions asked, and the techniques of inquiry: interviews, questionnaires, analysis of records, and participation (living among one's subjects) were employed singly or in different combinations. There was also dissimilarity in the dates and duration of the investigations. Some studies offered only occasional comments on attitudes toward self and situation while others attempted to classify psychological and attitudinal responses to the depression with varying degrees of comprehensiveness. Still, despite its limitations, this literature provided the best available information for testing impressions about depression victims' views on responsibility for their condition.

Among the inquiries considered (with dates of publication) were studies of relief recipients in Seattle (1935), St. Louis (1934), Los Angeles (1935), Chicago (1934), and Scranton (1932); lodgers in shelters for transient men in Palo Alto (1932) and Chicago (1935); unemployed workers in Philadelphia (1931) and in a location unspecified by two University of Nebraska investigators (1935); employed and unemployed engineers in New York City (1934); and residents in various categories in Akron (1941), Minneapolis (1936), Chicago (1938), and New Haven (1940). In sum, the data did not support the assertion that in the 1930s the average American worker blamed himself for his plight. In the Seattle study, for example, 72 of 147 subjects (49 percent) could be classified as not blaming themselves. The same could be said of 60 of 136 respondents (38.2 percent) in the Palo Alto inquiry, 80 of 100 men from relief families (80 percent) in the St. Louis investigation, and 25 of 49 unemployed men (51 percent) in the University of Nebraska survey.

The data also indicated a minimum of critical thinking (in the form of objective explanations for the crisis rather than proposals of utopian schemes, war, and revolution unconnected with doctrine) which led to left-radical, anticapitalist doctrine. Those relatively few folk who espoused radical thought usually did not engage in radical behavior: it was a long leap from radical thought to radical action. Comparatively few victims of the depression moved through a sequence of self-blame, non-self-blame, critical thinking, radical thought, and radical action. Finally, while focusing on the matter of blame, Sternsher cited nine studies of relief recipients' attitudes which indicated overwhelming approval of work relief.[8]

Sternsher's article raises the question whether various kinds of first-person history—letters, reminiscences, interviews (contemporary and later), diaries, autobiographies, and Federal Emergency Relief Administration and Works Progress Administration field investigators' reports—might shed further light on the question of self-blame. A careful reading would be required, because first-person history does not contain questionnaires on blame for the Great Depression.

A list of books and articles of first-person history (not counting autobiographies) about the depression contains more than ninety items. This literature includes at least six article-length collections of letters written by victims of the depression[9] and two book-length compilations: Robert S. McElvaine's *Down and Out* (1983) and Gerald Markowitz and David Rosner's *"Slaves of the Great Depression"* (1987).[10] In *Down and Out*, containing letters most of which were directed to President Roosevelt, Mrs. Roosevelt, or Harry Hopkins, McElvaine, in his introduction, addresses the matter of self-blame, but he does not carry the discussion much beyond that of Sternsher's 1977 article.[11] In his headnotes to the various sections of *Down and Out*, McElvaine continually refers, explicitly or implicitly, to the matter of self-blame and related attitudes: the unscathed take the traditional view of poverty; middle-class victims are embarrassed by their plight; even the poor are ashamed to ask for help; rural and small-town people continue to believe in individualism, self-reliance, hard work, and thrift; poor blacks share middle-class values, especially the work ethic; children are free from the self-blame so common among their parents; poor people share the view that many relief recipients are lazy and intemperate; the unemployed prefer work relief to the dole; conservatives believe the down-and-out are there because they deserve to be.[12] On the other hand, some see relief as a right, and most "desperate" and "cynical" folk do not blame themselves for their plight.[13] (McElvaine's treatment of self-blame in his book *The Great Depression* [1984] is similarly impressionistic.[14])

Introducing *Down and Out*, McElvaine comments on a point Sternsher noted in his 1977 article—differences between the "old poor," who experienced poverty well before the Great Depression struck, and the "new poor," who suffered only after the Great Crash of 1929. McElvaine finds this distinction "important but perhaps not as helpful in understanding attitudes as it might at first appear. The central fact about the depression, after all, was that most victims were newly poor."[15] McElvaine then emphasizes a factor which Sternsher treated somewhat cursorily: as time passed, the new poor became the old poor and moved from blaming themselves to blaming others. The "majority of Americans seem, in the early depression years, to have blamed themselves for their problems."[16] "By 1932, however, attitudes toward the unemployment crisis were beginning to change, mainly because suffering had become so widespread that it was now more difficult to contend that the problem was the fault of the victim."[17] McElvaine continues: "Almost all of the studies that connect self-blame and newness to suffering were made in 1934 or before. This may have been too early to see any significant trend away from self-blame as the newness of a Depression victim's poverty faded."[18] Also as a reflection of the passage of time, McElvaine refers to declining faith in the work ethic: "By 1937 a plurality among the poor questioned in a nationwide poll said they did *not* think that today any young man with thrift, ability, and ambition has the opportunity to rise in the world, own his own home, and earn $5,000 a year."[19]

Still, the Seattle and University of Nebraska studies of 1935 found substantial percentages of people who blamed themselves for their troubles—51 and 49 percent, respectively. These investigations indicate significant representation in *both* categories. At the same time, they by no means preclude the possibility that self-blame declined over time. (Ideally, we would have percentages for attitudes in the years before and after these studies.)

In *"Slaves of the Great Depression,"* Markowitz and Rosner present letters written by employed workers, most of them to President Roosevelt, Mrs. Roosevelt, or Secretary of Labor Frances Perkins. "Much has been written about the unemployed; here we see that the inadequacy of wages and conditions of work itself could lead to the same results for the employed."[20] The letters in this volume vividly demonstrate that employed workers, "shackled to their jobs and whipped into submission,"[21] often suffered brutal exploitation. Submission, however, was not accompanied by self-blame. Admission of personal shortcomings was evident in only two of 141 letters. A foreman in a furniture factory in Paris, Texas, wrote, "I am not smart or I would be in a different line of work & better up in ever [sic] way." An employee of the Briggs Manufacturing Company in Detroit informed the President, "I am not educated enough to have an easy life, but all I want, and everybody else is to make an honest living."[22]

Besides examining letters, we also can turn to interviews. Seven publications contain federal-agency interviews, including six volumes of Federal Writers' Project materials[23] and Jesse A. Bloodworth and Elizabeth H. Greenwood's *The Personal Side*, a compilation of interviews conducted in 1937 and 1938 by the Works Progress Administration (WPA) Research Division with forty-five "wage-earning" families—some on relief, others not—in Dubuque, Iowa.[24] Among these collections, only *The Personal Side* presents a systematically selected and categorized sample, from a given locality, whose attitudes speak to the question of self-blame.

Bloodworth and Greenwood considered Dubuque an ideal locale for their inquiry: its population was between 35,000 and 50,000; it was not a "satellite to a larger city"; it had a high proportion of white citizens; and "it had felt the full impact of the Depression." The authors sought to examine "the human side of economic distress" and to demonstrate that the "real problem of unemployment lies with the great majority of those who are just ordinary people in trouble."[25]

After ensuring the randomness of their sample and verifying

the "wage-earning" (as distinguished from professional, proprietary, and managerial) status of the families chosen for interviewing, the authors undertook their investigation. Their technique, as they described it, "was less an interview than a friendly talk about things in general and the depression in particular."[26] The forty-five case histories thus gathered were divided into three main groups:

> Those who had been on relief and have now returned to private employment are included in the first section, "From Relief to Private Employment." Those who received no relief while unemployed and are now working in private industry are included in the section, "By Their Own Boot-Straps." In the last section, "Still Without Jobs," are the stories of families, relief and non-relief, which have failed to get back in private industry.[27]

In regard to the category "Still Without Jobs," the authors considered WPA work as relief rather than employment—an ironic definition since the study itself was conducted under WPA sponsorship. But it accorded with the practice of the Bureau of Labor Statistics which counted employees of the Civilian Conservation Corps and the WPA as unemployed. If this definition had not been used, unemployment levels for 1933–1941 would have been reported at 2.0 to 3.5 million fewer people and 4 to 7 percentage points lower.[28]

A few general observations on the interviews may be in order, even if they confirm the obvious. The families interviewed suffered, and endured, considerable material and psychological hardship. Meager diets, inadequate shelter, poor clothing, and the utter absence of recreation were the rule, not the exception. In some instances hardship took on tragic proportions, as in the case of the Kroll family, who had the mortgage on their home foreclosed even though they had paid $5,800 of the $6,400 principal. For some reason they had been declared ineligible for a Home Owners Loan Corporation loan. Mrs. Kroll, a devoted housekeeper whose home was the be-all and end-all of her existence, was inconsolable and died from depression three months after the foreclosure.[29]

In several instances businesses exploited laborers, who, of course, were in abundant supply and desperate for any type of work. One man, Mr. Whitney, once unloaded thirty-six tons of coal in eight hours for a wage of ten cents an hour! He also worked eighty-four hours during one week in an insulating factory and was paid twenty-eight dollars for his efforts.[30] Another family, the Stetsons, paid premiums to an insurance company which had been bankrupt for more than two years.[31] One individual commented that after the onset of the depression factories worked employees harder and for less pay.[32]

The administration of relief was often inconsistent, degrading to the recipients, and in some cases patently unjust. While some families received food orders the same day they applied, others waited weeks, sometimes months. In one case the welfare office insisted that a family have its telephone disconnected even though the wife's meager income from sewing depended on her keeping in touch with her customers.[33] One man was berated by a relief worker for applying for financial assistance.[34] Another worker waited seven months, during which time he had no income, before applying for relief, only to have his request denied. More than a year later his application was approved when a caseworker verified his need.[35]

In order to examine the expressed attitudes from Dubuque in a more systematic fashion, we have compiled two tables from the interview information. Table 1 indicates feelings about accepting relief; Table 2 indicates feelings about the causes of widespread unemployment and general economic stagnation.

Although one might have hoped for a more precise methodological instrument, a few generalizations can safely be made. An overwhelming majority of men[36]—twenty-five of thirty expressing an opinion—indicated their reluctance either to apply for or to accept any type of financial or other assistance. Several men claimed they stood outside the relief office for days before finally "swallowing their pride" and going in. Among those who actually accepted some type of relief, many felt "embarrassed," "sick," "humiliated," or "disgraced." One man said that applying for relief was the hardest thing he ever had to do in his life.[37] Of those who expressed an opinion, more than 80 percent (thirty-five of forty-two) expressed feelings very similar to those just mentioned.

Second, a preference for work relief over direct relief was indicated by all thirty-one of those who expressed an opinion.

TABLE 1: REACTIONS TO ACCEPTING RELIEF

Respondent Status	Reluctant*	Accepting+	No Opinion	Preferred Work Relief to Direct Relief		
				Yes	No	No Opinion
From relief to private employment	14	4	0	17	0	1
Young (under 21)	6	2	0	8	0	0
Old (over 50)	3	1	0	4	0	0
Mid Years (22-49)	5	1	0	5	0	1
By their own bootstraps#	10	1	0	NA	NA	NA
Still without jobs	11	1	3	14	0	2
White collar	2	0	0	2	0	0
Construction workers	2	1	0	2	0	1
Young workers	1	0	2	3	0	0
Industrial discards**	4	0	1	5	0	1
Farmers in town	2	0	0	2	0	0
Totals	35	6	3	31	0	3

*Very reluctant and/or ashamed.
+Accepting with relative equanimity or as needed.
#Although those in this category never received relief, their feelings toward having to accept it may be inferred from their general remarks. Those who expressed strong opposition to direct relief or who were proud they did not have to accept it were counted in the "Reluctant" column.
NA Not applicable.
**Handicapped physically or by age.

TABLE 2: RESPONSIBILITY OR ASSIGNED BLAME FOR THE DEPRESSION

Respondent Status	Economic Factors					Personal Factors		Other	
	Labor-Saving Machinery	Mal-distribution of Wealth	Overproduction	Excess Labor Supply	Stock Market Speculation*	Businessmen	Dubuque Chamber of Commerce	Don't Know	No Opinion
From relief to private employment	5	5	1	0	1	3	1	2	7
Young (under 21)	3	3	1	0	0	1	1	1	2
Old (over 50)	1	1	0	0	1	1	0	0	2
Mid years (22-49)	1	1	0	0	0	1	0	1	3
By their own bootstraps	4	1	1	0	2	1	1	0	3
Still without jobs	6	4	0	2	1	1	5	1	4
White collar	1	0	0	1	1	1	1	0	0
Construction workers	1	1	0	0	0	0	2	1	1
Young workers	1	1	0	1	0	0	1	0	1
Industrial discards	2	1	0	0	0	0	1	0	2
Farmers in town	1	1	0	0	0	0	0	0	0
Totals+	15	10	2	2	4	5	7	3	14

*If this category were labeled "Speculators" it would be a personal factor.
+These figures exceed 45, the number of families interviewed, because often a family mentioned more than one factor.

The interviewees' profound sense of contrition, however, should not be confused with self-blame. A significant number (fourteen) expressed no opinion on the matter of responsibility, reflecting perhaps a certain apathy or passive resignation, while only two men advocated "radical" alternatives.[38] Although an individualistic spirit prevailed among almost all of those queried—as can be inferred from the reluctance and shame over accepting relief—such feelings should not be equated or confused with self-blame for one's economic predicament. *In no case did anyone blame himself.*

These comments on the depression by Dubuque residents did not amount to systematic or comprehensive critical thinking, but they did include components of a fairly sophisticated causal analysis. They also vitiated Chenoweth's observation that "our love of individualism helps account for . . . our inability to perceive external sources of our stress."[39] A common analysis of the coming of the depression emphasizes an increase in productivity through technological advance or the development of labor-saving machinery; the failure to pass on the resultant production cost savings to workers in the form of higher wages or to consumers in the form of lower prices; the increase in profits and in concentration of income so long as the product was being sold; and the eventual production of more than consumers could buy, leading to a downward spiral in economic activity and mounting unemployment. Meanwhile, substantial portions of concentrated profits were invested in capital plant (to produce more goods even though, beginning in 1926, there was difficulty in disposing of the product of existing plant) or were devoted to speculation in real estate and stocks.[40]

Table 2 indicates that five of these factors were cited by those who were interviewed: labor-saving machinery (cited by 15 persons), maldistribution of wealth (10), overproduction (2), excess labor supply (2), and stock market speculation (4). If systematic or critical thinking were involved, however, one would expect roughly equal numbers of citations for all five factors.

The citations of businessmen (5) and the Dubuque Chamber of Commerce (7) are personal rather than abstract. What is striking about the personal category is the absence of blame for politicians. We know that nationally the Democratic party became the majority party at the presidential level in the 1930s, and that the

Republican party suffered from its association with the coming of the depression. That declining Republican appeal went hand in hand with the coming of hard times is evident in the presidential vote in Dubuque County:[41]

	Democratic	Republican	Other
1920	7,636 (38.0)*	12,436 (62.0)	928
1924	5,718 (40.8)	8,280 (59.2)	10,568
1928	19,437 (66.6)	9,744 (33.4)	—
1932	19,210 (74.0)	6,747 (26.0)	1,042
1936	16,291 (66.3)	8,275 (33.7)	—
1940	13,805 (48.6)	14,590 (51.4)	46
1944	12,867 (50.7)	12,502 (49.3)	—

*percentage of two-party vote

Without discussing the vast literature on voter behavior and party systems,[42] one may note that Dubuque County showed the same degree of Republican dominance enjoyed by the GOP in the Harding landslide of 1920; experienced the complications of a three-way contest in 1924; and departed from the overall national pattern in 1928 when, owing to a substantial Catholic population, it was one of only six Iowa counties out of ninety-nine that gave a majority to Al Smith. (In three of these instances, Smith's margin was less than two percentage points, while his greatest margin was in Dubuque County.) In 1932 Roosevelt received an even higher percentage of the vote than Smith had won, political scientists attributing this to anti-Hoover rather than pro-Roosevelt sentiment. Roosevelt, after four years in office, enjoyed continuing, though less, dominance in the landslide of 1936, and lost to Wilkie narrowly in 1940.

The interviews in *The Personal Side* were conducted from December 1937 to April 1938, or during the period of decline in Roosevelt's strength from its peak of 1936 to just before the Republicans' sensational national comeback in the elections of 1938 when they picked up eighty-one seats in the House and eight in the Senate. It may be that anti-Hoover sentiment waned along with pro-Roosevelt sentiment, the decline in FDR's popularity being understandable in terms of the severe recession of 1937–1938 which encompassed the interviewing period, among other factors.[43] In any event, expressing an opinion in the ballot box and stating one to an interviewer are two different things, and one cannot explain why residents of Dubuque failed to mention politicians when assigning blame for the Great Depression.

Nor, for that matter, can one easily explain why the interviewees did not blame themselves for their plight. The assumption that individualism and the work ethic produced self-blame is obviously ill-founded. What distressed most workers, it would seem, was their inability to extricate themselves from their plight regardless of how hard they worked. A sense of confusion may have resulted from this perceived unreliability of the work ethic. If one worked hard, one got ahead; if one did not get ahead, it was because one did not work hard. But what of the man who unloads thirty-six tons of coal in eight hours for eighty cents, or who diligently but vainly seeks employment? Why would we expect him readily to accept culpability for his desperate circumstances? The data indicate that, at least among the Dubuque interviewees, he did not.

In considering this question of self-blame, are we reinventing the wheel? Is this trip necessary? We think it is, for at least three reasons: (1) analysis of the Dubuque interviews is in the scientific tradition of replication; (2) it is in the historical tradition of testing of national-level generalizations by local specific; and (3) more research is needed to eliminate unexamined assumptions from college textbooks in American history. Examination of twenty survey texts published in the 1980s reveals ten that had nothing to say directly or indirectly on the question of blame.[44] Six stressed self-blame:

> Americans simply did not interpret the Great Depression as evidence that capitalism had failed. During prosperous times, Americans had believed that individual success was primarily due to individual initiative, and not to general social conditions. So their initial response to the depression was to blame themselves for the hardships that beset them.[45]

> To the men and women suddenly without incomes, the situation was frightening and bewildering. Most had grown up believing that every individual was responsible for his or her own fate, that unemployment and poverty were signs of personal failure; and even in the face of national distress, many continued to believe it.[46]

> These formerly solid working-class and middle-class families strongly believed in the work ethic and the American dream and suddenly found themselves floundering in a society that no longer had a place for them. They were proud people who felt humiliated by their plight.[47]

> "I'm beginning to wonder what's wrong with me," ran a typical observation from a man out of work for a month. "Even my family is beginning to think I'm not trying."[48]

> In fact, large numbers of men who were unable to fulfill their roles as breadwinners lost their self-respect, became immobilized, and stopped looking for work, while others took their frustrations out in drink and became self-destructive or abusive to their families.[49]

> Not everyone went hungry during the Depression or stood in breadlines or lost jobs, but almost everyone was affected in one way or another, and many of the victims tended to blame themselves.[50]

One survey text offered a statement indirectly related to the question of blame:

> Meanwhile, remarkably few people seemed to lose confidence in the capitalistic system.[51]

Another emphasized self-blame with respect to a particular sector of the labor force:

> Later studies argued that the most severe anxieties struck white-collar males, whose sense of personal worth depended entirely on their jobs and earnings.[52]

One text presented a combination of attitudes:

> Most Americans—black or white—met the new crisis not with violence, protest, or political extremism, but with bewilderment and an inability to fix blame. They scorned business people, of course, but often they blamed themselves as well, as the traditional ideology of the self-made man had taught them to do.[53]

Finally, only one text stressed that blame was placed elsewhere:

> ...but by 1932 businessmen who had in the 1920's taken credit for prosperity now found themselves saddled with the blame for hard times.[54]

These textbooks are neither all right nor all wrong. Statements about the question of blame, however, ought to be comprehensive. Many years ago the *New Yorker* announced that it was not being published for the little old lady in Dubuque, Iowa. Nor do sweeping statements about self-blame apply to many residents of her community or, in all probability, many residents of other communities across the United States. Many Americans blamed themselves for their plight, but many others did not.

NOTES

1. Sherwood Anderson, *Puzzled America* (New York: Scribner's, 1935), 46, cited in John A. Garraty, *Unemployment in History: Economic Thought and Public Policy* (New York: Harper Colophon Books, 1979), 181 n. 24.

2. E. Wight Bakke, *Citizens Without Work: A Study of the Effects of Unemployment upon the Workers' Social Relations and Practices* (New Haven: Yale University Press, 1940), 46–70, cited in Garraty, *Unemployment in History*, 184 n. 29.

3. David J. Rothman, "The Poor in the Great Depression," in John A. Garraty, ed., *Historical Viewpoints: Notable Articles from American Heritage*, 5th ed. (New York: Harper and Row, 1987), II, 315, 317.

4. Lawrence Chenoweth, *The American Dream of Success: The Search for Self in the Twentieth Century* (Belmont, Calif.: Wadsworth, 1974), 63–64.

5. Thomas C. Cochran, *The Great Depression and World War II, 1929–1945* (Glenview: Scott, Foresman, 1968), 14.

6. Bernard Sternsher, "Victims of the Great Depression: Self-Blame/Non-Self-Blame, Radicalism, and Pre-1929 Experiences," *Social Science History*, 1 (Winter 1977), 137–77.

7. Garraty, *Unemployment in History*, 177–84, cites five sources drawn on by Sternsher in his 1977 article: E. H. Sutherland and H. J. Locke, *Twenty Thousand Homeless Men: A Study of Unemployed Men in Chicago Shelters* (Philadelphia: Lippincott, 1936); Mirra Komarovsky, *The Unemployed Man and His Family—The Effects of Unemployment upon the Status of the Man in Fifty-nine Families* (New York: Dryden Press, 1940); Abram Kardiner, "The Role of Economic Security in the Adaptation of the Individual," *The Family*, 17 (October 1936), 187–97; A. C. Tucker, "Some Correlates of Certain Attitudes of the Unemployed," *Archives of Psychology*, No. 245 (February 1940); and Bakke, *Citizens Without Work*. Sternsher noted that the only place he had seen a citation by a historian of Gabriel Almond and Harold D. Lasswell, "Aggressive Behavior by Clients Towards Public Relief Administrators: A Configurative Analysis," *American Political Science Review*, 28 (August 1934), 643–55, was in Garraty, "Unemployment During the Great Depression," *Labor History*, 17 (Spring 1976), 156.

8. Sternsher, "Victims of the Great Depression," 149, 172 n. 37, 172–73 n. 38.

9. John L. Shover, "Depression Letters from American Farmers," *Agricultural History*, 36 (July 1962), 163–68; James A. Beddow, "Depression and New Deal: Letters from the Plains," *Kansas Historical Quarterly*, 43 (Summer 1977), 140–53; William T. Schmidt, ed., "Letters to the President: Mississippians to Franklin D. Roosevelt, 1932–1933," *Journal of Mississippi History*, 40 (August 1978), 231–52;

Julia Kirk Blackwelder, "Letters from the Great Depression: A Tour Through a Collection of Letters to an Atlanta Newspaperwoman," *Southern Exposure*, 6 (Fall 1978), 73–77; R. Douglas Hurt, "Letters from the Dust Bowl," *Panhandle-Plains Review*, 52 (1979), 1–13. David Lamoreaux with Gerson C. Eisenberg, "Baltimore Views the Great Depression, 1929–1933," *Maryland Historical Magazine*, 71 (Fall 1976), 428–42, analyzes letters to the editors of the Sunpapers.

10. Robert S. McElvaine, ed., *Down and Out in the Great Depression: Letters from the Forgotten Man* (Chapel Hill: University of North Carolina Press, 1983): Gerald Markowitz and David Rosner, ed., *"Slaves of the Great Depression": Workers' Letters about Life on the Job* (Ithaca: Cornell University Press, 1987).

11. Near the beginning of his introduction to *Down and Out*, McElvaine refers to studies of the unemployed by psychologists and sociologists and lists in a related note (236 n. 8) twenty-five sources, twenty-two of which had been used by Sternsher. Further along in his introduction (10–11), McElvaine relies on five sources Sternsher had cited (as well as Sternsher's article itself): Ruth Shonle Cavan and Katherine Howard Ranck, *The Family and the Depression: A Study of One Hundred Chicago Families* (Chicago: University of Chicago Press, 1938); Almond and Lasswell, "Aggressive Behavior by Clients Toward Public Relief Administrators"; Philip Eisenberg and Paul F. Lazarsfeld, "The Psychological Effects of Unemployment," *Psychological Bulletin*, 35 (June 1938), 358–90; Melvin J. Vincent, "Relief and Resultant Attitudes," *Sociology and Social Research*, 9 (September–October 1935), 27–33; and Francis Fox Piven and Richard A. Cloward, *Regulating the Poor: The Functions of Public Welfare* (New York: Vintage Books, 1972).

12. McElvaine, *Down and Out*, 37, 53–54, 69, 81, 115, 125, 145.

13. *Ibid.*, 125, 157, 175.

14. McElvaine, *The Great Depression: America, 1929–1941* (New York: Times Books, 1984) 172–81, 185.

15. McElvaine, *Down and Out*, 11.

16. *Ibid.*, 19.

17. *Ibid.*, 23.

18. *Ibid.*, 11.

19. *Ibid.*, 19.

20. Markowitz and Rosner, ed., *"Slaves of the Depression,"* 8.

21. *Ibid.*, 8.

22. *Ibid.*, 21, 25. Thirty-four letters were written by officials to workers or to other officials.

23. W. T. Couch, ed., *These Are Our Lives: As Told by the People and Written by the Members of the Federal Writers' Project of the Works Progress Administration in North Carolina, Tennessee, and Georgia* (Chapel Hill: University of North Carolina Press, 1939; New York: W. W. Norton, 1975, paperback); Tom E. Terrill and Jerrold Hirsch, ed., *Such as Us: Southern Voices of the Thirties* (Chapel Hill: University of North Carolina Press, 1978; New York: W. W. Norton, 1979, paperback); Ann Banks, *First Person America* (New York: Alfred A. Knopf, 1980); John L. Robinson, ed., *Living Hard: Southern Americans in the Great Depression* (Washington, D.C.: University Press of America, 1981, paperback); James Seay Brown, Jr., *Up Before Daylight: Life Histories from the Alabama Writers' Project, 1938–1939* (University: University of Alabama Press, 1982); C. Edward Doty, ed., *The First Franco-Americans: New England Life Histories from the Federal Writers' Project, 1938–1939* (Orono: University of Maine Press, 1985, paperback). See also Jerrold Hirsch and Tom E. Terrill, "Conceptualization and Implementation: Some Thoughts on Reading the Federal Writers' Project Southern Life Histories," *Southern Studies*, 18 (1979), 351–62; Leonard Rapport, "How Valid Are the Federal Writers' Project Life

Stories: An Iconoclast Among the Believers," *Oral History Review* (1979), 6–17; Tom E. Terrill and Jerrold Hirsch, "Replies to Leonard Rapport's 'How Valid Are the Federal Writers' Project Life Stories: An Iconoclast Among the True Believers,'" *Oral History Review* (1980), 81–92.

24. Jesse A. Bloodworth and Elizabeth H. Greenwood, ed., *The Personal Side* (Washington, D.C.: Works Progress Administration, Division of Research, 1939; New York: Arno Press, 1971).

25. *Ibid.*, 106–09.

26. *Ibid.*, 7.

27. *Ibid.*, 11.

28. Michael R. Darby, "Three and a Half Million U.S. Employees Have Been Mislaid: Or, an Explanation of Unemployment, 1934–1941," *Journal of Political Economy*, 84 (February 1976), 2–16.

29. Bloodworth and Greenwood, ed., *The Personal Side*, 106–09.

30. *Ibid.*, 35, 38.

31. *Ibid.*, 83.

32. *Ibid.*, 382.

33. *Ibid.*, 95–96.

34. *Ibid.*, 84.

35. *Ibid.*, 167.

36. Most of the opinions elicited by the interviewers were those of male heads of household; seldom did wives offer their views.

37. *Ibid.*, 95.

38. One man, *ibid.*, 387, found the Townsend Plan appealing; another, *ibid.*, 192, favored extreme centralization for the purpose of avoiding conflict between state and federal legislation, but he was also opposed to unions.

39. Chenoweth, *The American Dream of Success*, 63.

40. Bernard Sternsher, ed., *The New Deal: Laissez Faire to Socialism* (St. Louis: Forum Press, 1979), 28–29, ascribes this view to Rexford G. Tugwell.

41. Richard M. Scammon, compiler and ed., *America at the Polls: A Handbook of Presidential Election Statistics, 1920–1964* (Pittsburgh: University of Pittsburgh Press, 1965).

42. This literature is surveyed in Bernard Sternsher, "The Emergence of the New Deal Party System: A Problem in Historical Analysis of Voter Behavior," *Journal of Inter-disciplinary History*, 6 (Summer 1975), 127–49, and Sternsher, "The New Deal Party System: A Reappraisal," *ibid.*, 15 (Summer 1984), 53–81.

43. Alan Jones, "The New Deal Comes to Iowa," in Lawrence E. Gelfand and Robert J. Neymeyer, ed., *The New Deal Viewed from Fifty Years* (Iowa City: Center for the Study of the Recent History of the United States, 1983), 29–37, delineates the repudiation of the New Deal in Iowa by the end of 1938.

44. Thomas A. Bailey and David M. Kennedy, *The American Pageant*, 8th ed., II (Lexington, Mass: D. C. Heath, 1987); John Morton Blum, Arthur M. Schlesinger, Jr., William S. McFeely, Kenneth M. Stampp, Edmund S. Morgan, and C. Vann Woodard, *The National Experience*, Part 2: *A History of the United States Since 1865*, 7th ed. (San Diego: Harcourt Brace Jovanovich, 1989); Robert A. Divine, T. H. Breen, George M. Fredrickson, R. Hal Williams, *America: Past and Present*, 2nd ed. (Glencoe: Scott, Foresman, 1987); John A. Garraty and Robert A. McCaughey, *The American Nation: A History of the United States*, 6th ed. (New York: Harper and Row, 1987); Rebecca Brooks Gruver, *An American History: A Survey*, 4th ed. (Reading, Mass.: Addison-Wesley, 1985); Winthrop D. Jordan and Leon F. Litwack, *The United States*, 6th ed. (Englewood Cliffs: Prentice-Hall, 1987); Norman K. Risjord, *America: A History of the United States*, 2nd ed., II: *Since 1865* (Englewood

Cliffs: Prentice-Hall, 1985); Stephen Thernstrom, *A History of the American People*, 2nd ed. (San Diego: Harcourt Brace Jovanovich, 1989); George Brown Tindall, *America: A Narrative History*, 2nd ed. (New York: W. W. Norton, 1988); Irwin Unger, *These United States: The Questions of Our Past*, 4th ed., II: *Since 1865* (Boston: Little, Brown, 1989).

45. Joseph R. Conlin, *The American Past: A Survey of American History*, 2nd ed. (San Diego: Harcourt Brace Jovanovich, 1987), 721.

46. Richard N. Current, T. Harry Williams, Frank Freidel, and Alan Brinkley, *American History: A Survey*, 7th ed. (New York: Alfred A. Knopf, 1987), 708.

47. James A. Henretta, W. Elliott Brownlee, David Brody, and Susan Ware, *America's History Since 1865* (Chicago: Dorsey Press, 1987), 768.

48. Robert Kelley, *The Shaping of the American Past*, 4th ed., II: *1865 to Present* (Englewood Cliffs: Prentice-Hall, 1986), 584.

49. James Kirby Martin, Randy Roberts, Steven Mintz, Linda O. McMurry, and James H. Jones, *America and Its People* (Glenview: Scott, Foresman, 1989), 783.

50. Gary B. Nash, Julie Roy Jeffrey, John R. Howe, Peter J. Frederick, Allen F. Davis, and Allen M. Winkler, *The American People: Creating a Nation and a Society* (New York: Harper and Row, 1986), 791.

51. Arthur S. Link, Stanley Coben, Robert V. Remini, Douglas Greenberg, and Robert McMath, Jr., *The American People: A History*, II: *Since 1865* (Arlington Heights, Ill.: AHM, 1987), 676.

52. Bernard Bailyn, Robert Dallek, David Brion Davis, David Herbert Donald, John L. Thomas, and Gordon S. Wood, *The Great Republic: A History of the American People*, 3rd ed., II (Lexington, Mass.: D. C. Heath, 1985), 728.

53. Mary Beth Norton, David M. Katzman, Paul D. Escott, Howard P. Chudacoff, Thomas J. Paterson, and William Tuttle, Jr., *A People and a Nation: A History of the United States*, 2nd ed., II: *Since 1865* (Boston: Houghton Mifflin, 1986), 723.

54. Samuel E. Morison, Henry Steele Commager, and William E. Leuchtenburg, *A Concise History of the American Republic*, 2nd ed. (New York: Oxford University Press, 1983), 595.

FOR FURTHER READING

STATES

Books

John L. Bell, Jr., *Hard Times: Beginnings of the Great Depression in North Carolina, 1929–1933* (Raleigh: North Carolina Department of Cultural Resources, Division of Archives and History, 1982).

George T. Blakey, *Hard Times and New Deal in Kentucky, 1929–1939* (Lexington: University Press of Kentucky, 1986).

James I. Clark, *Wisconsin Meets the Great Depression* (Madison: State Historical Society of Wisconsin, 1956).

Thomas H. Coode and John F. Baumann, *People, Poverty and Politics: Pennsylvanians During the Great Depression* (Lewisburg, Pa.: Bucknell University Press, 1981).

Ronald L. Heinemann, *Depression and New Deal in Virginia: The Enduring Dominion* (Charlottesville: University Press of Virginia, 1983).

Kenneth S. Hendrickson, ed., *Hard Times in Oklahoma: The Depression Years* (Oklahoma City: Oklahoma Historical Society, 1983).

Donald W. Whisenhunt, *The Depression in Texas: The Hoover Years* (New York: Garland, 1983).

James Wickens, *Colorado in the Great Depression* (New York: Garland, 1979).

Articles

Leonard J. Arrington, "Arizona in the Great Depression Years," *Arizona Review*, 17 (December 1968), 11–19; and "Idaho and the Great Depression," *Idaho Yesterdays*, 13 (Summer 1969), 2–8.

Michael S. Holmes, "From Euphoria to Cataclysm: Georgia Confronts the Great Depression," *Georgia Historical Quarterly*, 58 (Fall 1974), 313–30.

Clifford R. Hope, Sr., "Kansas in the 1930's, " *Kansas Historical Quarterly*, 36 (Spring 1970), 1–12.

Clark Johnson, "Burlington Since the 1930's: Change and Continuity in Vermont's Largest City," *Vermont History*, 27 (Winter 1969), 52–62.

Charles M. Kimberly, "The Depression in Maryland: The Failure of Voluntarism," *Maryland Historical Magazine*, 70 (Summer 1970), 189–202.

Gail S. Murray, "Forty Years Ago: The Great Depression Comes to Arkansas," *Arkansas Historical Quarterly*, 29 (Winter 1970), 291–312.

James. S. Olson, "The Depths of the Great Depression: Economic Collapse in West Virginia, 1932–1933," *West Virginia History*, 38 (April 1977), 214–25.

Richard T. Ortquist, "Unemployment and Relief: Michigan's Response to the Depression During the Hoover Years," *Michigan History*, 57 (Fall 1973), 209–36.

Donald W. Whisenhunt, "The Great Depression in Kentucky: The Early Years," *Register of the Kentucky Historical Society*, 67 (January 1969), 55–62.

Dissertations

Charles Michael Kimberly, "The Depression and New Deal in Maryland," American University, 1974.

Peter Joseph Lombardo, Jr., "Connecticut in the Great Depression, 1929–1933," University of Notre Dame, 1979.

Roger D. Tate, Jr., "Easing the Burden: The Era of Depression and New Deal in Mississippi," University of Tennessee, 1978.

GOVERNORS

Books

Bernard Bellush, *Franklin D. Roosevelt as Governor of New York* (New York: Columbia University Press, 1954); and *He Walked Alone: A Biography of John Gilbert Winant* (The Hague: Mouton, 1968) (New Hampshire).

Keith L. Bryant, Jr., *Alfalfa Bill Murray* (Norman: University of Oklahoma Press, 1968) (Oklahoma).

William A. Cosnell, *The Political Career of John S. Fisher, Governor of Pennsylvania, 1927–1931* (Pittsburgh: University of Pittsburgh Press, 1949).

Wilbur Cross, *Connecticut Yankee: An Autobiography* (New Haven: Yale University Press, 1943).

A. Wigfall Green, *The Man Bilbo* (Baton Rouge: Louisiana State University Press, 1963) (Mississippi, brief on governorship).

M. Nelson McGeary, *Gifford Pinchot: Forester-Politician* (Princeton, N.J.: Princeton University Press, 1960) (Pennsylvania).

George H. Mayer, *The Political Career of Floyd B. Olson* (Minneapolis: University of Minnesota Press, 1951) (Minnesota).

Chester M. Morgan, *Redneck Liberal: Theodore G. Bilbo and the New Deal* (Baton Rouge: Louisiana State University Press, 1985).

Joseph L. Morrison, *Governor O. Max Gardner: A Power in North Carolina and New Deal Washington* (Chapel Hill: University of North Carolina Press, 1971).

Allen P. Sindler, *Huey Long's Louisiana: State Politics, 1920–1952* (Baltimore, Md.: Johns Hopkins University Press, 1956).

Harvey Walker, *Constructive Government in Ohio: The Administration of Governor Myers Y. Cooper* (Columbus: Ohio History Press, 1948).

T. Harry Williams, *Huey Long* (New York: Knopf, 1969).

Articles

Loren B. Chan, "California During the Early 1930s: The Administration of Governor James Rolph, Jr., 1931–1934," *Southern California Quarterly*, 63 (Fall 1981), 262–82.

Robert T. Hawkes, Jr., "The Emergence of a Leader: Harry Flood Byrd, Governor of Virginia, 1926–1930," *Virginia Magazine of History and Biography*, 82 (July 1974), 260–81.

John E. Miller, "Governor Philip F. LaFollette's Shifting Priorities from Redistribution to Expansion," *Mid-America*, 58 (April–July 1976), 119–26.

Mary Murray, "Connecticut's Depression Governor: Wilbur L. Cross," *Connecticut History*, 16 (August 1975), 44–64.

James S. Olson, "Gifford Pinchot and the Politics of Hunger, 1932–1933," *Pennsylvania Magazine of History and Biography*, 96 (October 1972), 508–20.

Robert L. Woodbury, "Wilbur Cross: New Deal Ambassador to a Yankee Culture," *New England Quarterly*, 41 (September 1968), 323–40.

CITIES

Books

Roger Biles, *Memphis in the Great Depression* (Knoxville: University of Tennessee Press, 1986).

Sidney Fine, *Frank Murphy: The Detroit Years* (Ann Arbor: University of Michigan Press, 1975).

Charles H. Trout, *Boston, the Great Depression, and the New Deal* (New York: Oxford University Press, 1977).

Articles

Roger Biles, "The Persistence of the Past: Memphis in the Great Depression," *Journal of Southern History*, 52 (May 1986), 183–212.

William H. Chafe, "Flint and the Great Depression," *Michigan History*, 53 (Fall 1969), 225–39.

Roman Heleniak, "Local Reaction to the Great Depression in New Orleans, 1929–1933," *Louisiana History*, 10 (Fall 1969), 289–306.

Iwan Morgan, "Fort Wayne and the Great Depression: The Early Years, 1929–1933," *Indiana Magazine of History*, 80 (June 1984), 122–45.

Richard A. Noble, "Paterson's Response to the Great Depression," *New Jersey History*, 96 (Autumn–Winter 1978), 87–98.

Ronald L. Nye, "The Challenge to Philanthropy: Unemployment Relief in Santa Barbara, 1930–1932, *California Historical Quarterly*, 56 (Winter 1977/78), 310–27.

James S. Olson and Liz Byford, "Oasis in East Texas: Conroe and the Depression, 1929–1933," *Texana*, 12 (No. 2, 1974), 126–41.

Paul L. Shinn, "Eugene in the Depression, 1929–1935," *Oregon Historical Quarterly*, 86 (Spring 1985), 341–69.

Frederick Mercer Van Sickle, "A Special Place: Lake Forest and the Great Depression, 1929–1940," *Illinois Historical Journal*, 79 (Summer 1988), 113–26.

Chapter

Lewis Lansky, "Buffalo and the Great Depression, 1929–1933," in Milton Plesur, ed., *An American Historian: Essays to Honor Selig Adler* (Buffalo: State University of New York at Buffalo, 1980), 204–13.

Dissertations

John F. Bauman, "The City, the Depression, and Relief: The Philadelphia Experience, 1929–1939," Rutgers University, 1969.

Norma Lasalle Daoust, "The Perils of Providence: Rhode Island's Capital City during the Depression and New Deal," University of Connecticut, 1982.

Douglas Lee Fleming, "Atlanta, the Depression, and the New Deal," Emory University, 1964.

Michael John Kotlanger, "Phoenix, Arizona: 1920–1940," Arizona State University, 1983.

Leonard Leader, "Los Angeles and the Great Depression," University of California at Los Angeles, 1972.

Paul Strom Lofton, Jr., "A Social and Economic History of Columbia, South Carolina, During the Great Depression, 1929–1940," University of Texas, 1977.

Glenna Christine Matthews, "A California Middletown: The Social History of San Jose in the Depression," Stanford University, 1977.

Richard J. Meister, "A History of Gary, Indiana, 1930–1940," University of Notre Dame, 1967.

William Henry Mullins, "San Francisco and Seattle During the Hoover Years of the Depression," University of Washington, 1975.

Paul Anthony Stellhorn, "Depression and Decline: Newark, New Jersey: 1929–1941," Rutgers University, 1982.

MAYORS

Books

Richard J. Connors, *A Cycle of Power: The Career of Jersey City Mayor Frank Hague* (Metuchen, N.J.: Scarecrow Press, 1971).

James M. Curley, *I'd Do It Again: A Record of All My Uproarious Years* (Englewood Cliffs, N.J.: Prentice-Hall, 1957) (Boston).

Joseph F. Dineen, *The Purple Shamrock: The Hon. James Michael Curley of Boston* (New York: W. W. Norton, 1949).

Sidney Fine, *Frank Murphy: The Detroit Years* (Ann Arbor: University of Michigan Press, 1975) (also listed above).

Gene Fowler, *Beau James: The Life and Times of Jimmy Walker* (New York: Viking, 1949) (New York).

Alex Gottfried, *Boss Cermak of Chicago: A Study of Political Leadership* (Seattle: University of Washington Press, 1962).

J. Woodford Howard, Jr., *Mr. Justice Murphy: A Political Biography* (Princeton, N.J.: Princeton University Press, 1968) (Detroit).

Richard D. Lunt, *The High Ministry of Government: The Political Career of Frank Murphy* (Detroit: Wayne State University Press, 1965).

Dayton D. McKean, *The Boss: The Hague Machine in Action* (Boston: Houghton Mifflin, 1940).

Chapter

Richard J. Connors, "Politics and Economics in Frank Hague's Jersey City," in William C. Wright, ed., *New Jersey Since 1860: New Findings and Interpretations* (Trenton: New Jersey Historical Commission, 1972), 76–91.

BOSSES

Books

Lyle Dorsett, *The Pendergast Machine* (New York: Oxford University Press, 1968) (Kansas City).

Edward J. Flynn, *You're the Boss* (New York: Viking, 1947) (Bronx, New York).

William D. Miller, *Mr. Crump of Memphis* (Baton Rouge: Louisiana State University Press, 1964).

William H. Reddig, *Tom's Town: Kansas City and the Pendergast Legend* (Columbia: University of Missouri Press, 1986). Originally published in 1947.

Frank S. Robinson, *Machine Politics: A Study of Albany's O'Connells* (New Brunswick, N.J.: Transaction Books, 1977).

Articles

Alan Bussel, "The Fight Against Boss Crump: Editor Neeman's Turn," *Journalism Quarterly*, 44 (Summer 1967), 250–56.

Larry Grothaus, "Kansas City Blacks, Harry Truman, and the Pendergast Machine," *Missouri Historical Review*, 69 (October 1974), 65–82.

COUNTIES

Article

Mary Kay Smith, "Dark Days of the Depression: Lonoke County, Arkansas, 1930–1933," *Red River Valley Historical Review*, 7 (Fall 1982) 14–23.

Dissertation

John Craft Taylor, "Depression and New Deal in Pendleton: A History of a West Virginia County from the Great Crash to Pearl Harbor, 1929–1941," Pennsylvania State University, 1980.

Bernard Sternsher is Professor of History at Bowling Green State University. He attended the public schools of Fall River, Massachusetts, and Mount Hermon School, and earned his B.A. at the University of Alabama and his A.M. and Ph.D. at Boston University. Before joining the faculty of Bowling Green in 1969, he taught at the Rochester Institute of Technology, Fairleigh Dickinson University, and Seton Hall University.

Mr. Sternsher is the author of *Rexford Tugwell and the New Deal* (Rutgers University Press, 1964), for which he received the Phi Alpha Theta Book Prize, and *Consensus, Conflict, and American Historians* (Indiana University Press, 1975). He has also edited *The New Deal: Doctrines and Democracy* (1966; revised and reissued as *The New Deal: Laissez Faire to Socialism*, 1979) and *The Negro in Depression and War* (1969). He has contributed numerous articles and chapters to scholarly publications, most recently "Harry Truman" in *Popular Images of American Presidents* (1988) and "Two Views of Eisenhower" in *Psychohistory Review* (1989).